Table of Contents

Deanne Ritchie

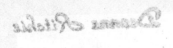

 This book is printed on recycled paper.

Multiage Resource Book. © Copyright 1993 by The Society For Developmental Education.
All rights reserved. Printed in the United States of America.
Published by The Society For Developmental Education, Northgate, P.O. Box 577, Peterborough, New Hampshire 03458, 1-800-462-1478.

FIRST EDITION

First Printing, April 1993
Second Printing, June 1993
Third Printing, March 1994

Executive Director: Jim Grant
Editor: Deborah Sumner
Cover design: Susan Dunholter
Cover photo courtesy of: *Teaching/K-8* (Oct. 1992 edition)
                          40 Richards Avenue
                          Norwalk, CT 06854

                          John Flavell, photographer
                                and
                          Anne Keene, Pikeville Independent School District, Pikeville, KY

SDE Design Director: Susan Dunholter
Production Coordinator: Deborah Fredericks

ISBN 0-9627389-6-4 (paperback)

The Multiage • Continuous Progress Children's Bill of Rights

by Jim Grant,
National Alliance of Multiage Educators

1. *Every child has the right to attend a continuous progress program.*

2. *Every child has the right to the continuity of having a teacher for more than one year.*

3. *Every child has the right to experience continual learning success.*

4. *Every child has the right to take an extra year in a multiage program without the stigma of school failure.*

5. *Every child has the right to freedom from tracking.*

6. *Every child has the right to learn in a developmentally appropriate program.*

7. *Every child has the right to learn in a heterogeneous classroom.*

8. *Every child has the right to learn in a whole language classroom.*

9. *Every child has the right to learn in a cooperative learning classroom.*

10. *Every child has the right to evaluation that uses authentic assessment tools.*

THE SOCIETY FOR DEVELOPMENTAL EDUCATION
Northgate, Route 202, P.O. Box 577, Peterborough, NH 03458
1-800-462-1478 or (603) 924-9621

Ready to Learn: A Seven-Step Strategy

A distinguished educator presents a comprehensive blueprint for achieving the nation's first education goal.

———

Ernest L. Boyer

In Ready to Learn: A Mandate for the Nation, Ernest L. Boyer, president of the Carnegie Foundation for the Advancement of Teaching, examines the challenges posed by the first of the national education goals—that by the year 2000 all children will come to school "ready to learn." The following is a summary of the book's seven-step strategy for achieving this goal.

Step 1. A Healthy Start

Good health and good schooling are inextricably interlocked, and every child, to be ready to learn, must have a healthy birth, be well nourished, and well protected in the early years of life.

• Today's students are tomorrow's parents; every school district in this country should offer all students a new health course called "The Life Cycle," with study units threaded through every grade.

• The federal nutrition program for women, infants, and young children, known as WIC, should be fully funded so that every eligible mother and infant will be served.

• A network of neighborhood-based Ready-to-Learn Clinics should be estab-

Ernest L. Boyer is president of the Carnegie Foundation for the Advancement of Teaching.

Excerpted with permission from *Ready to Learn: A Mandate for the Nation,* published in 1991 by the Carnegie Foundation for the Advancement of Teaching, Princeton, New Jersey. Copyright © 1991, The Carnegie Foundation for the Advancement of Teaching.

lished in every underserved community across the country to ensure access to basic health care for all mothers and preschool children.

• The National Health Service Corps should be expanded to ensure that a well trained health and education team is available to staff the proposed clinics.

———

> *"Every child should live in a language-rich environment in which parents speak frequently to their children..."*

———

• Every state should prepare a county-by-county Maternal and Child Health Master Plan to assure that all regions are covered and that existing resources are well used.

• Funding for two key federal health programs—Community and Migrant Health Centers and Maternal and Child Health Block Grants—should be significantly increased, with awards made to states that have justified the need based on a master plan.

Step 2. Empowered Parents

The home is the first classroom. Parents are the first and most essential teachers; all children, as a readiness requirement, should live in a secure environment where

empowered parents encourage language development.

• Every child should live in a language-rich environment in which parents speak frequently to their children, listen carefully to their responses, answer questions, and read aloud to them every day.

• A new Ready-to-Learn Reading Series, one with recommended books for preschoolers, should be prepared under the leadership of the American Library Association.

• A comprehensive parent education program should be established in every state to guarantee that all mothers and fathers of preschool children have access to such a service.

• A national Parent Education Guide, focusing on all dimensions of school readiness, should be prepared collaboratively by state departments of education and distributed widely to parents.

• Every community should organize a preschool PTA—supported and encouraged by the National Congress of Parents and Teachers—to bring parents of young children together and to build a bridge between home and school.

Step 3. Quality Preschool

Since many young children are cared for outside the home, high quality preschool programs are required that not only provide good care, but also address all dimensions of school readiness.

• Head Start should be designated by Congress as an entitlement program and

be fully funded by 1995 to ensure that every eligible child will be served.

• Every school district in the nation should establish a preschool program as an optional service for all three- and four-year-olds not participating in Head Start.

• The new federal initiative—the Child Care and Development Block Grants—should be used by states to start new programs that expand the quality of care for small children, especially in disadvantaged communities.

• A National Forum on Child-Care Standards should be convened by the National Association for the Education of Young Children. The Forum's recommendations should be adopted by all states, so that by the year 2000 every day care center in the country is licensed to meet these standards.

• Every community college should make it a special priority to establish an associate degree called the Child-Care Professional and also establish a collaborative relationship with local day care and preschool programs, offering inservice programs for teachers and providers.

Step 4. A Responsive Workplace

If each child in America is to come to school ready to learn, we must have workplace policies that are family-friendly, ones that offer child-care services and give parents time to be with their young children.

• All employers should make at least 12 weeks of unpaid leave available to parents of newborn or adopted children, to allow time for the bonding that is so essential to a child's social and emotional well-being.

• Flexible scheduling and job sharing should be available to employees to help them better balance work and family obligations.

• Parents of preschool children should be given at least two parenting days off each year, with pay, to visit with their children in day care and preschool programs, and to consult with teachers.

• All employers should help their workers gain access to high quality child-care and preschool services, either on-site or at local centers. A child-care information and referral service also should be available to workers.

• A national clearinghouse should be established, perhaps by the National Alliance of Business, to help employers promote family-friendly work policies.

Step 5. Television as Teacher

Next to parents, television is the child's most influential teacher. School readiness requires television programming that is both educational and enriching.

• Each of the major commercial networks—CBS, NBC, ABC, and Fox—should offer, at an appropriate time, at least one hour of preschool educational programming every week.

• A Ready-to-Learn television guide should be prepared, listing programs on all channels that have special educational value for young children.

• Companies producing and selling products geared to young children—toys, breakfast cereals, fast foods—should help underwrite quality educational television for preschoolers.

• Every hour of children's programming on commercial networks should include at least one 60-second Ready-to-Learn message that focuses on the physical, social, or educational needs of children.

• Twenty million dollars should now be appropriated to the National Endowment for Children's Educational Television to support the creation of educational programs for preschoolers.

• A Ready-to-Learn cable channel should be established, working collaboratively with public television, to offer programming aimed exclusively at the educational needs and interests of preschool children.

• A National Conference on Children's Television should be convened to bring together broadcast executives, corporate sponsors, educators, and children's advocates to design a decade-long school-readiness television strategy.

Step 6. Neighborhoods for Learning

Since all children need spaces and places for growth and exploration, safe and friendly neighborhoods are needed, ones that contribute richly to a child's readiness to learn.

• A network of well designed outdoor and indoor parks should be created in every community to give preschoolers opportunities for exercise and exploration.

• "Street playgrounds" should be established in every urban area to make open spaces for creative play and learning immediately available to children.

• Every library, museum, and zoo should establish a school readiness program for preschoolers. The funding of such services should be given top priority by each community.

• Every major shopping mall should include in its facility a Ready-to-Learn Center, an inviting, creative space where young children can engage in play and learning.

• A Ready-to-Learn Youth Service Corps should be organized to make it possible for school and college students to serve as volunteers in children's Ready-to-Learn Centers, libraries, and playgrounds in every community.

Step 7. Generation Connections

Connections across the generations will give children a sense of security and continuity, contributing to their school readiness in the fullest sense.

• Schools, day care centers, and retirement villages should redesign their programs to bring young and old together, building bridges across the generations.

• A "Grandteacher Program" should be created in communities across the country, one in which older people participate as mentors in day care centers and preschools.

• Every community should organize a series of intergenerational projects—called "Grand Days" perhaps—in which senior citizens engage in activities and excursions with young children. □

FOR FURTHER INFORMATION

Copies of *Ready to Learn: A Mandate for the Nation*, from which this article is excerpted, are available for $8 each (30% discount for bulk orders) from the Princeton University Press, 3175 Princeton Pike, Lawrenceville, NJ 08648. Telephone 609-896-1344.

A Roll Call of the Unready

According to a survey of kindergarten teachers taken by the Carnegie Foundation in 1991, a nationwide average of 35 percent of their students were not ready to participate successfully in school. The state averages were:

State	% of students not ready	State	% of students not ready
Alabama	36%	Montana	28%
Alaska	34	Nebraska	29
Arizona	35	Nevada	39
Arkansas	42	New Hampshire	29
California	38	New Jersey	27
Colorado	32	New Mexico	40
Connecticut	24	New York	36
Delaware	42	North Carolina	39
Florida	38	North Dakota	23
Georgia	41	Ohio	33
Hawaii	47	Oklahoma	40
Idaho	26	Oregon	32
Illinois	31	Pennsylvania	29
Indiana	32	Rhode Island	40
Iowa	25	South Carolina	40
Kansas	27	South Dakota	29
Kentucky	40	Tennessee	39
Louisiana	39	Texas	37
Maine	30	Utah	26
Maryland	31	Vermont	28
Massachusetts	26	Virginia	34
Michigan	27	Washington	33
Minnesota	24	West Virginia	34
Mississippi	41	Wisconsin	32
Missouri	33	Wyoming	26

On Tracking and Individual Differences: A Conversation with Jeannie Oakes

John O'Neil

The widespread practice of tracking students won't be dismantled until we truly believe that schools can help "make children smart," says Jeannie Oakes.

A former teacher and researcher in John Goodlad's landmark Study of Schooling, Jeannie Oakes burst onto the education scene with the 1985 publication of Keeping Track, *her research-based account of the devastating effects of tracking in public schools. Oakes has since become the country's best-known expert on tracking, one of the most hotly debated issues in education. A UCLA professor and researcher with the RAND Corporation, Oakes most recently co-authored* Making the Best of Schools *with her husband, Martin Lipton.*

Your book **Keeping Track** *really helped to raise awareness of the effects of tracking, particularly on students who are placed in the lower tracks. Is tracking still as widespread as you portrayed it?*

I think that more people are now aware of the uneven distribution of learning experiences and access to resources than when I wrote *Keeping Track*. This increased awareness has led to lots of discussion and, increasingly, efforts to create alternatives to a tracked school. But I think that if we took a sample of American schools today, we would find that probably 80 percent of the secondary schools and maybe 60 percent of the elementary schools still use some form of between-class grouping based on the perceptions educators have about children's ability to learn.

It might help to clarify some terms. What do you mean by "tracking" and "ability grouping"?

Well, those terms are used very sloppily to describe a wide variety of programs, so I don't find it very useful to distinguish between them in that way.

When I talk about harmful effects of tracking and ability grouping, I'm talking about all of those forms of grouping that are characterized by educators making some rather global judgment about how smart students are—either in a subject field or across a number of subject fields. Sometimes, it's defined in terms of IQ, sometimes it's defined in terms of past performance, sometimes the criteria are predictions of how well children are likely to learn. In other words, some grown-ups in the school are making a judgment about how smart the students are.

I also worry that students get placed in these groups in a rather public way. The groups are a very public part of the school's culture that reflects judgments that adults have made about children's current and future abilities. Within that culture, the groups take on a very hierarchical nature: we talk about top groups, bottom groups, middle groups, high groups, low groups. And often in the culture of the schools, the "top group" quickly becomes the "top kids," in a very value-laden way. So the students take their place in the hierarchy and the values associated with it.

Often, in the culture of the schools, the "top group" quickly becomes the "top kids," in a very value-laden way.

And this begins very early in school?

Yes. It can start with two-tiered kindergartens. Some children, probably because they've had a rich preschool experience, are considered ready for a kindergarten experience that, unfortunately, is like the old 1st grade curriculum pushed down into kindergarten. The rest are grouped in "developmental" kindergartens. When you go into schools that have two-track kindergarten programs, even if they're called developmental and academic, there is just no mistaking that everybody knows where the children thought to have the most promise are. As a consequence of all this, kids experience a large portion of their school day and school year very, very differently from one another.

How is school different for students in different tracks?

First of all, I should say that instruction across tracks is probably more alike than it is different—teachers talk, students are passive, and so on.

Having said that, to the extent that we find students engaged in experience-based learning—hands-on and critical thinking activities that apply to the content of what they're learning, challenging problems that are likely to have more than one right answer or more than one way of achieving the answer, deeply contextualized curriculum—we find those things far more often in top-track classes than we do in bottom-track classes. The middle track falls somewhere in between.

What is school like for students in the bottom track?

The bottom track is distinctly different. It's typically dominated by strategies that are passive; students do lots of worksheets, they tend to work alone. We find in science, for example, that the amount of time students sit by themselves reading out of textbooks is far greater than in top-track classes, where students are more involved in doing science, often working in groups doing projects.

Ironically, we're finding out that for children who have difficulty in school, the kinds of experiences that are easiest for them are *not* low-level, abstract worksheets, or the disconnected, fragmented curriculum that is typical of the low track.

What sort of curriculum do they need?

If we pay attention to what cognitive and developmental psychologists have been telling us over the last 20 years, the rich, contextualized, problem-oriented curriculum that we usually think of as appropriate for the highest-achieving students is also the most promising kind of curriculum for children who have difficulty doing traditional school learning. So I think that the curriculum issue needs to be turned on its head: we need to realize that the kind of drill-and-skill curriculum that we've traditionally offered low-track students probably makes knowledge *less* accessible to them than would a richer and more demanding curriculum that better approximates real-life problem solving.

Why is instruction so different for these students in the lower track? I can't imagine that teachers would rather teach watered-down academic content.

Part of the answer is that the teachers who are most likely to be assigned to low-track classes are the least experienced, those without teaching credentials, and, at the secondary level, those with the lowest levels of preparation in their subject fields. We also see differences in teachers' confidence levels: teachers who are the most efficacious are most often assigned to the high track. So students in the low track are more likely to be saddled with teachers who have a smaller repertoire and less confidence. Then there's the limit that all teachers face about how you balance rich educational activity with classroom control.

What do you mean?

In many schools, students who misbehave are placed in the low track. There's a stange belief in the culture of many schools that disruptive students are likely to do the least damage in the low track.

So you find low-track teachers with a classroom full of students who have a history of school difficulties, school failures, or misbehavior. In those settings, even very skillful teachers often resort to classroom activities in which students are kept separate and quiet for purposes of control. These complex dynamics help perpetuate low-level curriculum for low-track students. That's one of the reasons I'm very suspicious about recommendations that schools simply "beef up" the low track: give students better teachers, more exciting curriculum, more interesting variety.

You mean, keep a tracked school but, within that system, just improve the quality of the bottom track?

Yes. That's been tried for many years without much success. And the reason is that you're still confronted with a situation where you've got a critical mass of students who know the school has identified them as not likely to succeed; you've also got students who have a history of misbehavior. And it just makes that kind of "beefing up"

more difficult to do. Plus you don't have the resources in these classrooms of other students who are eager and excited, who have retained some interest in school.

It seems as if more and more experts are critical of tracking, yet it remains one of the most entrenched of school practices. Why?

Well, I've thought about that long and hard and talked with lots of educators about why they believe this system is so persistent. At the root of the tracking problem, I think, are powerful norms in the culture of schools and in the society beyond the school: for example, about the nature of ability. The notion persists that ability is fixed very early in life, if not before birth, and that there's virtually nothing schools can do that might alter a student's fundamental capability.

Another is the persistent misunderstanding of the idea of the normal curve. It's not viewed as a statistical artifact that attempts to portray the distribution of certain characteristics of a population; it's seen as an accurate representation of the distribution of how well kids are likely to do in school. So these notions of ability and normal curves lead educators to say: "Well, the educationally sound thing to do is adapt our curriculum to the ways that students are."

Besides that, American educators seem to have a strong inclination to "be kind" to students: many feel it's unfair to expect high performance from students who can't do it; that it's frustrating and harmful to self-esteem.

Well, it would be foolish for anybody to say there aren't individual differences. The issue is how powerful are these differences in determining whether students do well in school? In countries like Japan and China, while ability is seen as part of the

equation, working hard and persisting at difficult tasks is seen as making the difference. And the expectation is that all students can do that. It's quite a different cultural norm.

Now, unlike Japan, which has a homogeneous society, we have enormous diversity, and, unfortunately, our perceptions of ability tend to run along lines of race and ethnicity. This makes it far more difficult for us than many Asian countries to adopt a norm that says that any child who works hard and sticks with it can do well. The interesting parallel, though, in terms of organization, is that in Japan they simply don't track students before the end of the 8th grade. They have very heterogenous classrooms; they have lots of peer learning activities going on. So even though they may end up with considerable variation in learning outcomes in their classes, there is this sense that they all can do it and they all can do it together.

So American schools need new norms?

I think we do need other norms if we wish to untrack schools. Cognitive psychologists are now saying that intellectual capacity is learned as children interact with other human beings and with the environment—that, in fact, in this way human beings are far more alike than they are different. They're saying that the normal curve is not a very accurate depiction of the potential for children to learn most of what schools would like to teach. The norm that educators need to buy into is that, through their interactions with students, schools really can make children smart. And that's a powerful shift from conventional beliefs.

There's another reason that tracking is so prevalent, and I think it's a political issue having to do with people who have precocious children and who have, over the last 40 years in particular, won special programs and special advantages for their children.

White and wealthier families, in particular, have fought to maintain a system that guarantees that their children will have a rich curriculum, extraordinarily well-qualified teachers, a peer group who is very much like them in terms of background and values and interests. The political pressure from those groups to maintain that system is extraordinarily great—the countervailing force that makes educators feel so very insecure.

It seems that students in the college-bound track and their parents are happy with the way things are. They're worried that if tracking ends, there would be more disciplinary problems in their students' classes, the pace would be a lot slower, and so on. Aren't those legitimate concerns?

They're extraordinarily legitimate concerns, and any strategy to develop alternatives to tracking has to take them into account, and has to put in place a whole array of new programs and policies—many of which are on the current school reform agenda.

We shouldn't lose sight of the fact that the fundamental goal of equalizing opportunity is not simply to mix students up, but to increase the quality of curriculum and instruction for *everybody* in the schools, even those who are now in the high track.

One thing we should keep in mind is that kindergartners coming to school show enormous interest in learning, and this cuts across socio-economic, racial, and ethnic lines. The willingness of 4- and 5-year-olds to work hard at learning is just extraordinary, both in school and out of school. But as kids go through school, if they don't have successful experiences and if they aren't considered shining stars, they learn that their effort does not pay off. So by high school we see a real diminishing of interest in school and willingness to do any hard work.

But is tracking to blame for that? Couldn't one argue that students have some degree of choice in what kind of classes they take? In most comprehensive high schools, they can select hard courses or easy ones.

Many high schools do use student preferences as one of the many criteria for course placement. But prerequisites are also a powerful factor. For example, in math, whether a student has had a pre-algebra class or whether she had an early algebra class in the 8th grade is more important than that student just saying, "I choose to take geometry as a 9th grader." And, of course, entry into those early prerequisite classes is often determined by the kind of math ability groups that a student was placed in during elementary school. It's a cycle that begins very early.

Another thing that places great constraints on students' choices is what educators tell them. I've studied three schools in the last two years, trying to understand what happens when a student's choice conflicts with what counselors or prior teachers think would be an appropriate course, based on the student's standardized test scores or performance. Often, that student is counseled out of his choice.

And then, probably the most pervasive factor is that kids and their parents learn early on from the judgments made about them which choices are appropriate for them. So students often choose exactly what the school would choose for them. They know where they're likely to succeed, where they're likely to have trouble. Parents and students usually agree with the school's notions about ability, whether or not ability can change, and whether hard work can make a difference.

What you're talking about involves a major change in expectations.

It comes down to rethinking our notions of who can learn. If we took seriously the idea that all students can really be smart, we wouldn't ration opportunities so early in the school experience, and, as a result, I don't think we'd see these big discrepancies in students' interests and in willingness to work hard when they're in high school. You can't very easily take children who have been socialized toward schooling in very different ways for eight years and then expect them all to achieve well in high school.

So schools somehow have to restructure to offer opportunities to more students?

It's an extraordinarily difficult promise to make, but it's one that schools absolutely have to make good on.

I've been interested recently in the reports that have come out from the National Center for Gifted and Talented Education about how bright students are languishing in regular classrooms, and I think they're absolutely right. I think *all* students are languishing in most regular classrooms. What's so exciting to me about these efforts to create heterogenous classrooms is that in order to do so, the curriculum has to be much richer, more problem-oriented, and more engaging than even the curriculum of the high track.

Students need a lot of opportunities to construct knowledge together as a group, to make meaning out of their experiences to make sense of what they're learning, to make connections. Frankly, I'm convinced that that's the best kind of curriculum for all students. ■

Jeannie Oakes is Professor in the Graduate School of Education at the University of California, Los Angeles, and a Consultant for the RAND Corporation. She may be reached at the Graduate School of Education, UCLA, 405 Hilgard Ave., Los Angeles, CA 90024. **John O'Neil** is Contributing Editor to *Educational Leadership.*

O'Neill, John (1992). "On Tracking and Individual Differences: A Conversation with Jeannie Oakes," *Educational Leadership*, 50, 2:18-21. Reprinted with permission of the Association for Supervision and Curriculum Development © 1992 by ASCD. All rights reserved.

Multiage Grouping

David Elkind

During the 1970s when British "informal education" was all the rage in this country, I visited a lovely, bucolic school in Oxfordshire that was more like a miniature farm than a school. One of the impressive features of the school was the mixing of age groups, which seemed quite natural and healthy. The younger children learned from the older children and the older children learned from instructing younger children. Likewise, the younger children who were more advanced were stimulated by being with the older children. Contrariwise, slower older children worked with younger children who were at or below their level.

When I returned to this country I was quite vocal about my new discovery only to be reminded that multiage grouping was hardly a British invention. The one room school house, so common in this country when we were a rural society, of necessity provided a multiage program. During the era of progressive education, many multiage groupings often worked on common projects. Finally, in many early childhood programs, and in a sprinkling of public and private elementary schools in this country, multiage grouping has been quietly practiced for many years quite independently of any influence from abroad.

In fact, if we think about it, multiage grouping is more natural and educationally beneficial than the rigid age grouping that dominates our schools. Age grouping is based upon physical time, whereas children grow on biological time and operate on psychological time. Biological and psychological times are variable while physical time is uniform. Within the same physical time period one child may grow two inches while another child gains only a quarter of an inch in height. Likewise, within the same physical time period one child will discover decoding while another continues to struggle with letter discrimination. Age grouping based on physical time denies the fact that children are organisms and that they operate on variable biological and psychological time, not uniform physical time.

Because it accommodates to the nature of children, multiage grouping could help solve many of the problems of the early education boom. Perhaps the most serious of these problems is that of the *age effect,* the fact that the youngest children in a kindergarten class routinely do more poorly than the older children. While retention, transition classes, and screening have all been used to solve this problem, the burden of these solutions falls upon the child. But the problem is not in the child but rather in the mismatch between the child and the curriculum.

Multiage grouping provides a classroom organization sufficiently flexible to accommodate children at different levels of maturity and with different levels of brightness. Moreover, the younger children will have the experience of being the older children when the older group moves on and a younger group moves in. Multiage grouping also encourages cooperation. There is a growing recognition, at all academic levels, that cooperation is much more effective than competition in improving academic achievement. Likewise, multiage grouping enables a teacher to use the knowledge she or he has gained about a child during the first year to plan learning experiences for the next year. Too often, in the strict age grouping arrangement, the knowledge a kindergarten teacher has acquired about her or his youngsters is lost when the children move on to first grade.

To be sure, there are some negatives and perceived negatives to multiage grouping. Teachers fear they may have to master the curriculum for two grade levels. At first this appears formidable, but once teachers realize that they already work with a number of reading and math levels, the majority prefer to work this way. There is always the danger that some rotten apples get into the barrel, which means that with multiage grouping a child can get stuck with a bad teacher for two years rather than for one year. And, finally, parents of the older children may be concerned that their youngsters are not being sufficiently stimulated because of the presence of the younger group in the class. None of these obstacles is insurmountable.

The first years of school are of critical importance not only for children's long-term academic achievement, but also for their abiding sense of self-esteem. In my opinion, the best strategy for dealing with the age effect and for giving the majority of children entering our schools a chance to develop a healthy and robust liking for themselves, for learning, and for schooling is multiage grouping at the K–1 level, and perhaps throughout the elementary school years.

> *The first years of school are of critical importance not only for children's long-term academic achievement, but also for their abiding sense of self-esteem.*

Multiage Classrooms: Children Learning at Their Own Speed

by Albert Shanker, President
American Federation of Teachers

The one-room schoolhouse offers a promising model for breaking the rigid structure of single-grade classrooms where teachers do most of the talking.

Teachers in one-room schools, who had to deal with students in seven or eight grades, couldn't spend their time standing up front and talking to all the students at once. Teachers helped students alone and in groups, and older students tutored younger ones. Students took initiative for their learning because they couldn't count on a teacher's guidance every moment of the day.

Cognitive psychology confirms that, what was a matter of necessity in rural America, is a better way of organizing learning. Children learn at different rates and in different ways, and they learn best when they're actively involved in their learning.

Multiage classrooms — especially at the elementary level — can be like modern one-room schoolhouses, with students of various ages and abilities working in different groups and different ways. With greater flexibility in how they group and teach their students, teachers in multiage classes can tailor instruction to the way children really learn.

Early childhood teachers know that an age difference of eight months or a year is enormously important in a child's development. It doesn't make much sense to group children according to their chronological age and then teach them as if they are a homogeneous group. The same is true with older students. Some might be three or four grades behind, while others can learn much more than students their age are usually taught. Furthermore, some students learn best by reading, while others need instruction that is more visual or hands-on.

By taking advantage of the normal differences among children, multiage classrooms lend themselves to the kind of teaching that worked in the one-room schoolhouse. Working alone and in large and small groups, students in multiage classes have to take responsibility for their own learning and that of their classmates. And without lectures and work sheets aimed at the whole group, students have more freedom to proceed at their own rate and in their own way. Teachers can take on the role of coach and mentor instead of being the source of all the answers.

Even if individual teachers were free to combine children of various ages, they'd have a hard time developing appropriate lessons for many different groups of students. Multiage classrooms have to be a part of broader school reform efforts because they involve fundamental changes in the way schools are organized.

But teachers and schools that try to make these changes will have a big advantage over the one-room schools of the past: technology, which will allow teachers to tailor instruction to individuals and groups of children. Much of the technology that can make multiage classrooms work already exists, but teachers need training in using technology and the best materials.

> *Few, if any, adults spend their days working with people who are exactly their own age, and there's no reason for children to do so.*

(A national technology clearinghouse could give teachers advice about what's best for a particular subject and a particular child's learning style.)

Few, if any, adults spend their days working with people who are exactly their age, and there's no reason for children to do so. Multiage classrooms acknowledge, and make use of, the similarities and differences between children that have nothing to do with age. Multiage classrooms that employ the best in technology can help make sure that all children learn at their own speed and in their own way.

Multi-Age Programs in Primary Grades
Are They Educationally Appropriate?

Elaine Surbeck

During a recent social gathering, the mother of a 1st-grader shared with other parents her experience in a multi-age classroom. Her child Hilary entered her first all-day schooling experience to find that she had been enrolled in a new program. A different teacher taught a different "subject" each day in a different classroom for six days. The routine would then repeat, so that the 25 6- to 8-year-olds who comprised this class rarely began school in the same room on the same day of the week, studying the same content. Not surprisingly, this mother and child did not easily adapt to the experience; the mother counselled the other parents to avoid "the multi-age classroom experiment" because it was just too confusing.

I was confused too! How could the implementation of mixed-age grouping be so far removed from what early childhood professionals advocate as appropriate education practice? While teaching an intensive graduate level course that focused on the multi-age early childhood program, I not only clarified misconceptions about mixed-age groups, but also discovered inappropriate reasons for implementing family grouping in the primary grades. Variously termed as vertical, family or mixed-age grouping, the nongraded multi-age grouping concept is increasingly viewed as a viable alternative to progression (or lack of it) through a series of homogeneous grades. Regardless of the term used, in a time of school reform, programs should be well conceived and carefully implemented if they are to function in the way they are intended.

According to Lodish (1992), multi-age groups are now mandated in three states (Kentucky, Mississippi, Oregon), with several other states (Alaska, California, Florida, Georgia, New York, Pennsylvania, Tennessee, Texas) considering similar legislation. Such state backing may be viewed as supportive of the developmental approach to education. When administrators and teachers, however, do not understand the rationale and theory that provide the scaffold for multi-age programs, classrooms like the one described are the result.

A similar problem exists when mixed-age groups are constituted to meet decreased or increased school enrollment, when the goal is primarily to improve the teacher/pupil ratio. The result may then become the creation of a "combination class" in which children in one class are treated as subgroups of two grades. It is critical that those individuals who design and implement the approach understand that vertical grouping is based on the following precepts:

- Heterogeneity within the group is valued for the natural learning environment it provides children; it is this planned pupil variability and diversity that optimize each child's opportunity to grow intellectually, socially and personally through interaction with mixed- (and same-) age peers (Katz, Evangelou & Hartman, 1990).

- This approach "functions meaningfully only when materials and activities are designed to meet individualized needs and are not dictated by grade" (Goodlad, 1984, p. 74). The curriculum is therefore more integrated, holistic and constructivist, focusing on broad concepts. Cooperative learning, inquiry and authentic educational experiences are strategies used to achieve goals sensitive to the developmental and personal needs and interests of students.

- The teacher or team of teachers strives to create a caring learning community, where learners have choices, and simultaneously acts as supportive experts and curious novices, in different contexts. In this climate, children's uneven development is not viewed as a deficit, but is accepted as a normal part of human growth. To create such an environment, teachers must have adequate knowledge of child development and education strategies that support children's learning styles.

In short, a solid commitment (and ability) to articulate the philosophy behind mixed-age grouping is the cornerstone upon which appropriate multi-age programs are created. If

Elaine Surbeck is Assistant Professor, Early Childhood Education, Arizona State University, Tempe.

that belief infrastructure does not exist, the program is likely to be inappropriate and, ultimately, to fail.

In addition to inadequate theoretical grounding, issues concerned with implementation strategies need examination. Ignoring or bypassing these areas can impede the acceptance, implementation and success of even the most well-conceived plans for mixed-age groups. In our metropolitan community, successful and educationally appropriate multi-age groups have resulted when the following occurred:

■ Teachers initiated the reform and participated in the implementation of a pilot phase of the program.

■ Teachers approached administrators with an articulate proposal including the following elements: a rationale outlining philosophy and research results on mixed-age program outcomes; budgetary needs or exchanges; implementation plans addressing changes in curriculum and assessment; plans for student selection; alternatives for grouping children (e.g., age range, size of groups, proportions of ages within a group); plans for parental involvement and considerations regarding teacher support needs (such as common planning and collaboration time).

■ Administrators and policymakers were informed early in the conceptualization of the program. Visiting successful program sites clarified their understanding of multi-age programs.

■ Planning time was adequate, approximately two years at least. During the planning phase, provision was made to observe in appropriately functioning sites. Opportunities were provided for teachers to collaborate in creating unique programs to meet the needs of specific populations and individual school sites.

■ Teachers were adequately trained in early childhood education and had experience in providing child-sensitive educational experiences. Teachers who had experience with children of various ages found the change from a "grade" to a multi-age program less stressful than teachers who had not taught before or who had experience at only one grade level.

■ Teachers were willing to engage in dialogue frequently with colleagues and administrators and to remain flexible during negotiation phases. Teachers and principals found it advisable to start with a pilot or small program, proceed slowly and resist the demand for immediate evaluation after the first year. According to Martinez (1991), vertical programs cannot be fairly evaluated for three to six years after their initiation.

■ Teachers learned that other teachers and colleagues were willing to participate in mixed-age groups only when they received individual support for taking a risk in changing their practice. For example, currently few (if any) materials are marketed for multi-age programs. Colleagues must be encouraged to see that this is as it should be: curricula should emanate from the unique make-up and interests of each group of children. The risk involves trusting that the content will emerge and become personalized. Textbooks and standardized materials will need to be replaced with authentic learning experiences.

■ Once the programs started, board members were invited to classroom events and children assumed the responsibility of sharing their learning with others. This worked well with parents also. Supportive parent groups evolved when parents had ample, timely information about the program, exercised the option to determine whether or not the child participated and were involved in the groups' activities in relevant ways.

Although mixed-age groups may be implemented without considering such issues, acceptance of such programs is much more difficult (and questionable practice may result) when these factors are ignored. Hilary's experience was, unfortunately, the result of common mistakes often made when programs are established before they are understood.

Clearly, the multi-age grouping approach is part of a much broader change in education. Neither a panacea nor the "final answer," it is, nevertheless, a step forward on a path toward a more effective educational experience for every child. Multi-age alternatives should be carefully implemented and reported in the research literature in a manner faithful to program integrity. Unless these groups are well conceptualized and adequately instituted, we must still ask, "Are they educationally appropriate?"

References
Lodish, R. (1992, May). The pros and cons of mixed-age grouping. *Principal, 71*(6), 20-22.
Katz, L., Evangelou, D., & Hartman, J. (1990). *The case for mixed-age grouping in early education.* Washington, DC: National Association for the Education of Young Children.
Goodlad, J. (1984). *A place called school.* New York: McGraw Hill.
Martinez, B. (1991). Nongraded elementary schools: Restructuring and the future of education. Unpublished paper, Morrison Institute for Public Policy, Arizona State University, Tempe, AZ.

The purpose of this column is to stimulate debate of timely issues affecting children, youth and families. The opinions expressed are those of the author and do not necessarily represent the position of Childhood Education *or the Association for Childhood Education International. Readers are urged to respond by submitting manuscripts or letters to: Dr. Joan Moyer, CE Issues Editor, Curriculum and Instruction/Early Childhood, Arizona State University, Tempe, AZ 85287-1711.*

Multiage: Why It's Needed

by Elizabeth Lolli, Principal
Central Academy Nongraded Primary
Middletown, Ohio

In light of the changing demographics of our society, and the change in societal expectations for public schools, it has become vital that educators rethink the structure of schools. Past practice has worked for a majority of children who came from a middle income, two parent home. However, growing numbers of children over the past several years have not met the expectations of the 1970 style curriculum and methodologies.

It is time to organize the structure of schools for all children. This organization must provide opportunities for children to grow and develop at a personal rate, not at the rate determined by a curriculum written for an "Ozzie and Harriet" population. What, then, is the structure schools should begin to explore?

A structure that comes from our American educational history is a multiage structure. The one-room schoolhouse of our past provided a multiage approach to education. Because of an influx of immigrants and a need to educate the masses, Horace Mann's idea from Prussia for a graded, age-based structure became the norm in public schools.

This structure served its purpose for the education of the masses. Now, however, the need for a more natural approach to grouping has surfaced. Children arriving at the classroom door in the 1990s and beyond need opportunities for socialization with many age levels, as well as individualized instruction. Multiage grouping can provide both.

For the sake of clarity, multiage groupings are purposeful, well-planned groupings of children, not combined classes with separate curriculums. A multiage classroom is organized with a mindful concern for heterogeneity in gender, ability, interests, and age levels.

The organization of a multiage classroom is first determined by the age levels served. Groupings must always remain flexible to enable the differences to be served each year. For example, one year groupings may be designed for 6-8 year-olds and 8-10 year-olds. The next year the school may need to have classrooms for 5-7 year-olds, 6-8 year-olds, and 8-10 year-olds. The most important tenet of multiage grouping is to maintain the flexibility of the age clusters.

Grouping children into the classrooms should be carefully completed. A placement test for reading, math, and composition should be administered to help teachers determine beginning points of instruction and to help those determining classroom lists to provide a heterogenous mix. Teachers should choose or write the placement tests. These tests should give teachers a clear idea of beginning points for each child.

Upon completion of the initial testing, staff members who will be working with the age cluster of children should discuss the results. Any insights or additional information needs to be recorded and later used by the child's teacher.

The person or persons responsible for designing classlists need to organize the classrooms to include even numbers of boys and girls, age, and ability levels. A grid to counter check potential oversights is a helpful tool (see figure A).

Figure A

	Teacher A	Teacher B	Teacher C
Boys 6	1	1	1
Boys 7	1		
Boys 8		1	
Girls 6	1		
Girls 7			
Girls 8			
Emergent B			
Emergent G			
Early B			
Early G			
Fluent B			
Fluent G			

Potential Problems:

After completing heterogeneous classlists, the staff should recheck information gained to safeguard against unbalanced ability levels, unequal numbers of boys and girls, and an over abundance of potential problems. This recheck will alleviate frustration and possible failure because of an impossible grouping.

Another major issue facing multiage teachers is the lack of a multiage curriculum. Simply combining two or three years of curriculum and cramming it into one year is not the answer. The curriculum needs to identify developmentally appropriate "benchmarks" which can be reached by most children at the end of a predetermined cycle. For example, by the end of the third year in school, a benchmark might be "a knowledge and practical application of at least 60 words." The benchmarks are determined at the district level and should include state or district mandated benchmarks, research-based benchmarks for the age level chosen, and teacher designed benchmarks. Every child will not reach these benchmarks at the same time or by following the same path. The benchmarks serve as long-range goals for each child regardless of the rate at which the child moves. This curriculum will, at first, have every possible item taught but will evolve into a truly multiaged curriculum as the staff becomes comfortable with multiage groupings and individualized instruction.

> **A** multiage classroom is organized with a mindful concern for heterogeneity in gender, ability, interests, and age levels.

Central Academy Nongraded Primary
GOALS

1. *To help children, through the use of appropriate instructional practices, reach their full potential.*

2. *To provide a caring and secure environment.*

3. *To develop and implement an individual education plan for each child which will allow for individual rates of learning.*

4. *To foster cooperation among students by teaching them to recognize and appreciate individual differences.*

5. *To elicit continued cooperation and support among students, parents, staff and community.*

6. *To develop a lifelong love of learning.*

7. *To instill an appreciation of written language through a literature-based methodology.*

8. *To utilize an integrated curriculum in relating school experiences to everyday life.*

9. *To involve the parents in the structure and implementation of their child's educational experiences.*

10. *To teach children to communicate through oral and written language.*

11. *To provide the opportunity for students to move from concrete to representational to abstract thinking.*

12. *To challenge students to become caring and responsible citizens in a global society.*

Questions and Answers about Multiage Programs

by Jim Grant

Q. Should a developmental K-3 program have four distinct grade levels?

A. A developmental approach can work in a K-3 program which has four and only four distinct grade levels, but there are other alternatives which can work better and should be considered.

An ungraded, multiage, continuous-progress program would be the ideal way to implement a developmental approach to early childhood education. This would allow children to develop and learn in a natural way, without being subject to the artificial constraints and pressures imposed by traditional grade levels. Unfortunately, most educators must find ways to make the developmental approach work within a more traditional grade structure.

A growing number of American schools are providing two-year combination grades as part of their early childhood programs. This sort of program helps to reduce the pressure on young children and provides a more heterogeneous learning environment, while still fitting into a traditional grade structure.

Many other schools have supplemented a traditional four-grade early childhood program with extra-year transitional grades, which provide the additional time to develop needed by many students to complete their curriculum. This approach has been used successfully across the U.S. for decades.

In schools which have only four distinct grade levels between kindergarten and third grade, students' needs for time flexibility can only be met by providing them with two years in the same grade. This approach can work satisfactorily, especially if the early year is provided as early as possible, but it is likely to be more stressful for children, their parents, and their teachers than the other alternatives.

The use of "lock-step" grade levels was brought to the U.S. from Prussia in the 19th century by Horace Mann. Unfortunately, this approach is simply not flexible enough to meet the needs of today's young children.

Q. Why are ungraded, multiage or combination-grade programs so advantageous?

A. Ungraded, multiage, and combined-grade programs reflect the way young children develop and learn, which does not fit neatly into the more systematic organization preferred by many adults. These programs are also better at accommodating the nation's diverse student population.

In an ungraded, multiage, or combined-grade program, children are expected and encouraged to learn at different rates and levels. This greatly reduces the pressure on young learners and makes academic failure far less likely to occur. It also creates an environment in which discipline problems and the formation of negative attitudes are far less prevalent, because students are accepted and supported at their

> *In an ungraded, multiage, or combined-grade program, children are expected and encouraged to learn at different rates and levels.*

current stage of development.

These programs also foster cooperative learning. Older students gain self-esteem by helping younger students, who then have good role models they can imitate. Children for whom English is a second language are particularly likely to benefit from this approach, as they can receive special assistance and support from other children who share similar problems and backgrounds. And, children with special needs are also more likely to flourish in an environment in which being different is the norm, rather than the exception.

Another advantage of ungraded, multiage and combined-grade programs is that they virtually require the use of learning centers, an integrated curriculum, cooperative learning, individualized instruction, and authentic assessments, all of which should be part of a developmental approach under any circumstances. The extent of student diversity in these programs is too great to allow extensive use of "lock-step" instructional methods geared to the whole class or a grade-level standardized test.

In addition to providing an environment which supports the natural diversity of young children, ungraded, multiage and combined-grade programs also help to prepare children for the natural diversity of the world they will encounter as adults.

Q. Are ungraded, multiage, and combined-grade programs easy to teach and administer?

A. No, educators have found that extra effort and extra funding are essential in order for these sorts of programs to achieve long-term success.

Teachers who are struggling to cope with the diversity of children at a single grade level might shudder to think about teaching two grade levels in the same classroom. Specialized training in working at several levels at the same time is needed, as is tremendous dedication to the job. A successful teacher in an ungraded, multiage, or combined-grade program must also have strong parenting skills, excel at classroom organization and management, and be a creative and motivational educator.

Even when a teacher meets all the requirements outlined above, team teaching and/or the use of trained aides may also be necessary to provide a sufficient amount of individualized instruction. Additional time is also needed for planning and the development of a flexible curriculum, as well as for record keeping.

Of course, all of this costs money. At a time when budget restrictions and cutbacks are the norm, and when many teachers already feel overwhelmed, finding funding or volunteers may not be easy. And, proponents of ungraded, multiage, or combined-grade programs may also encounter opposition from administrators and parents for philosophical reasons as well as financial ones. School officials may find these programs difficult to administer because they do not fit neatly into the traditional organization plan. Administrators may also feel uncomfortable with this sort of innovative approach, especially when many parents may have concerns about its effect on the students and prefer traditional grade levels instead.

While ungraded, multiage and combined-grade programs offer great advantages to students, no one should underestimate the difficulties they pose for educators.

Q. How should educators go about starting and implementing an ungraded, multiage, or combined-grade program?

A. Given the difficulties outlined previously, the best way to proceed is slowly and on a small scale.

Educators interested in starting an upgraded, multiage, or combined-grade program may first want to locate and visit a working model. Vermont in particular has a number of schools which have begun implementing these sorts of programs in recent years, and the programs can be found in many other states, as well. Educators should also read John Goodlad's *The Non-Graded Elementary School*, a book from the 1960s which has recently been reissued due to the renewed interest in this topic.

Once there is a small group of interested educators, an effort should be made to organize a school-wide task force, which would also include administrators and parents. The task force can then proceed to explore the availability of funding and personnel for a small pilot program, and prepare a proposal which could be submitted to the local school board. These activities should be accompanied by an intensive outreach program designed to educate teachers, administrators, and parents about the problems caused by traditional grades, as well as the advantages of ungraded, multiage, or combined-grade programs.

This sort of outreach effort should continue once the pilot program begins, and include frequent visits to the classes by supervisory personnel. The pilot program should be re-evaluated at regular intervals to make sure it is meeting the needs of the students, and follow-up studies should measure the progress made by children who participated in the program. Teachers in the following grades and parents of participants should also be surveyed in order to assemble as much information about the program as possible.

Once the benefits of the pilot program have been firmly established, efforts to expand it are far more likely to prove successful.

Q. Should young children be grouped by ability level on a long-term basis?

A. No, this process — also known as "tracking" — cannot be done accurately and is detrimental to students.

A developmental approach to early childhood education recognizes that young children grow and change rapidly and often unevenly so that judgments made about their abilities at one point in time may no longer be valid a short time later. In addition, tests and other measures of young children's abilities are likely to be inaccurate because young children are not good test takers and the full extent of their abilities is difficult to measure. Any long-term grouping of young children by ability level is therefore likely to be based on false premises.

The grouping of young children by ability level can also become a self-fulfilling prophecy. Children usually figure out which group they are in — no matter how creatively the groups are named. And, as young children are just forming their own identities and tend to place great faith in their elders, they often meet the expectations associated with their group. Children placed in a low-track group are likely to function at a low level, think less of themselves, and remain in a low-track group year after year, while those in a high-track group may feel great pressure to perform well and avoid being moved to a low-level group.

Students in low-track groups also tend to receive less intensive instruction and be taught with less interesting materials. This further reinforces negative self-images, makes it more difficult for them to do well in school, and increases the likelihood that they will remain low-track students as long as they remain in school.

Short-term groupings by ability level, need, or area of interest within a heterogeneous class may prove necessary for certain types of instruction. This practice is usually not harmful as long as the students understand it is based on what they can do in a specific area at a given time, and it is not a permanent judgment about their overall ability as human beings.

Q. **Are there other forms of tracking that should be avoided in addition to grouping by ability level?**

A. Yes, grouping by ability level is the most common form of tracking, but there are other forms that can be equally detrimental. At the same time, there are also helpful programs and practices which critics have labeled "tracking," but which in fact are distinctly different than tracking.

Another form of tracking which still occurs is "social tracking" — the grouping of students on basis of their neighborhood and/or their parents' income. If all the children from "the wrong side of town" are in one class, the likely expectation is that they will be wilder, less interested in school work, and less intelligent. Meanwhile, if another class is made up of children from the "nicer" neighborhoods, they are likely to be perceived and to perceive themselves as the exact opposite. This can lead to signifi-

cant differences in the way children are taught, and have profound effects on the children's self-images.

Similar groupings made on the basis of race and culture can have similar effects, as can grouping by sex and linguistic background. The key distinction in this regard is that tracking involves a long-term judgment about human potential, while other programs may group students on a short-term basis to provide intensive assistance in certain areas in order to help students fully realize their potential.

English-as-a-second-language and Chapter I programs, for example, are designed to help groups of children overcome disadvantages which may prevent them from doing well in school. Developmental extra-year programs are another example of a short-term, early intervention which helps children progress to the point where they can participate successfully in a heterogeneous classroom.

Early intervention programs are based on the assumption that participants may demonstrate very high levels of ability when their needs are met. This sort of program should not be confused with or mislabeled as tracking, which is based on the assumption that children's potential is limited and unlikely to change.

Q. **How should students be grouped within a developmental early childhood program?**

A. Each classroom of students should be as heterogeneous as possible. This grouping policy should not be limited to the random selection of students for a class, but instead should be a deliberate effort to maximize the diversity of the students in each class.

Within the classroom, students can be temporarily grouped for instruction on the basis of ability levels, areas of interest, and needs. These sorts of short-term groupings may often be the most effective way

to teach, especially when class sizes are overly large and there is a shortage of aides or volunteers. However, care should be taken to change the makeup of these groups on a regular basis, and to organize groups of students differently for various projects so that long-term tracking does not occur within a classroom.

Whole-class instruction should also occur on a regular basis. Even with a diverse class of students, this can be a very effective means of instruction when the teacher has had proper training and uses a process-oriented approach.

By combining whole-class instruction, short-term groupings, and individualized instruction, the teacher is educating her students as effectively and efficiently as possible, while also helping young children orient themselves. The other integral part of this approach is cooperative learning, in which students are encouraged to work together and teach each other. This is not only good for the students, it can also make the teacher's difficult job a little bit easier.

Diversity is not the easiest way, but it is the American way, and educators have a responsibility to make it a reality within our schools.

Excerpt from *Developmental Education in the 1990's* by Jim Grant. Published by Programs for Education, Rosemont, NJ.

THE WHYS AND HOWS OF THE MULTI-AGE PRIMARY CLASSROOM

By Kathleen Cushman

Y OU WOULD never know, talking to the teachers who do it, that running an elementary school classroom of mixed-age children is such a big deal. From the outside, to be sure, it seems a radical concept, ambitious and fraught with difficulties of every kind. Why else would the open-classroom mixed-age experiments of the sixties and seventies have dwindled so sharply in the past decade and a half? Why else are so few public schools now trying it, so few researchers studying it, and so many filled with mistrust at the whole idea of "family groupings" in a primary classroom?

Yet in Norma Leutzinger's combined first- and second-grade classroom at New York City's Central Park East II Elementary School, the concept fits as comfortably as a favorite suit of clothes. Around the room at groups of tables, twenty-eight children work quietly, reading books they have chosen or writing in their journals. They group and regroup frequently, at Norma's prompting: now into a fifteen-minute discussion with the whole class in a circle; now dispersing to chat while they choose materials to work with in groups of two and

---

Kathleen Cushman writes and edits Horace, *the journal of the Coalition of Essential Schools, a high school reform movement based at Brown University.*

three; now intent again at their tables as the teacher and her aide move from child to child to speak with them in lowered voices.

Leutzinger's class, which includes twenty-eight children ranging in age from six to nine by the end of the school year, is one of a small but increasing number of classes in this country where early grades are combined in different ways. We tracked down three of them to see what is going on, both in theory and in practice, when a school chooses a mixed-age alternative to the conventional single-grade system. What we discovered was a range of techniques loosely linked by a developmental, child-centered philosophy of learning but otherwise as idiosyncratic as American education itself. If this is a trend, it is one with room for individual variation; and the schools here represent not only different approaches but different stages of those approaches.

One way to structure classes is that of Central Park East, where teachers like Norma Leutzinger have a combined class of first- and second-graders or third- and fourth-graders, and children stay with the same teacher for two years. Aside from her students' forays outside the classroom for music and the arts, Norma is responsible for teaching all subjects herself, and she organizes

chief
field
piece
belief

ILLUSTRATED BY SUSAN DAVIS

the class differently for instruction depending on her goals. In social studies and science, the group often meets as a whole; but when it comes to math, she will teach two separate lessons at first- and second-grade levels. Language arts is so integral a part of classroom life that it cannot be categorized: sometimes the class meets together, sometimes in small groups, and sometimes on an individual basis.

Across the river in the Brownsville section of Brooklyn, children in a P.S. 41 class of seven- and eight-year-olds are working on simple addition, while in the classroom next door a class of eight- and nine-year-olds does higher-level math problems. But since the classrooms open onto a common hall—along with another room of special needs students ages six to ten—any student can easily move into another class for work in this subject. It takes joint planning to carry this off; the teachers in P.S. 41's "core teams" of three or four teachers share the same free period and lunch period, allowing them time to talk things through. They know all the children in their cluster of classrooms and work with them all at some point, possibly in a project that involves several classes together, or because children cross class lines for special instruction, say, in reading. And though children will not necessarily stay with the same teacher for two

years, the cluster technique de-emphasizes their grade level in favor of an identification with the core team as a whole.

AT P.S. 41, teachers work together to determine how best to share instruction of their different-aged children. But at Sands Montessori elementary school in Cincinnati, teacher Mary Motz knows beforehand exactly what the Montessori system expects in her classroom of six- to nine-year-olds. Montessori schooling is notable in the United States for the extent to which it puts into practice a comprehensive theory, complete with training and materials. Working on the floor around her classroom, some of Motz's students are absorbed in private tasks; others work in mixed-age groups of two or three, helping each other with different activities. All will work their way eventually through a series of learning tasks that make up the Montessori curriculum; and even though one younger child appears to be doing nothing at all with his materials, Motz is happy. "He's watching the children on the next mat," she whispers. "He'll be asking me if he can learn that next."

That expectation of continuous progress through a series of skills marks a few other well-organized educational systems here and abroad. Individually Guided Education (IGE), developed by the Wisconsin Research and Development Center for Cognitive Learning, provides guidance to participating schools that want a "continuous progress" method of learning in a nongraded class. And in Great Britain, where primary schools have been organized since the 1960s into mixed-age groupings, the system expects every seven-year-old, for example, to be able to demonstrate mastery of certain math skills before moving into the next level of mixed-age learning.

All these models depend, at their core, on a philosophy of learning based on the developmental theories of Jean Piaget, Jerome Bruner, and others. Children in the early years of school do not learn at the same pace, such educators agree. In fact, they enter school with a "mental age" that varies by as much as four years, and they progress at their own rate from a largely concrete way of learning and thinking to the more abstract one reached in later stages. Because the pace of this development is so varied, mixed-age advocates say, it makes little sense to sort and label children into fixed grade levels from an early age—especially if the result is retention and an early sense of failure for the child. Better to extend the age range of a primary class and thus provide a nurturing, success-oriented environment for children at widely different developmental levels.

By creating a model that expects diversity rather than uniformity among kids, many of the "problems" in a single-grade class lose their destructive grip over teachers and students both. More advanced students can learn together in mixed-age groups, and slow ones can be given the time they need to master skills at their own pace. At other times, children of different levels can be put in groups where they can learn from each other; the effectiveness of this strategy has been widely recognized in the trend toward cooperative learning and peer tutoring. Social skills grow in a mixed-age group, as children develop attitudes of responsibility and tolerance for those of different capacities. And in classes that stay with the same teacher for more than one year, proponents say, the teacher-student relationship can become so personal that both academic and discipline problems diminish.

The Open Classroom Reborn?

To many teachers who were around in the 1960s and early 1970s, mixed-age groupings sound suspiciously like the "open classrooms" of that era. And, in fact, such groupings only work if certain aspects of the open classroom are incorporated: a flexible use of space that uses "learning stations"; a wide variety of concrete materials available to children as they need them; a teacher's willingness to let children work in small groups rather than lecturing to them en masse; evaluations that record each child's progress through a continuum of skills. But the bugaboos that led many teachers to reject the early open classrooms are by no means ever present in the new mixed-age groupings. Most classrooms have walls, though some open the doors between them. Many teachers work in teams, but just as many classes are self-contained. Some mixed-age groupings take place for as little as an hour of shared time a day; others keep the mixed group together only for certain subjects; and

some keep them together all day. The classrooms visited here represent only a few of the ways teachers interested in a developmental, child-centered approach are moving toward mixed-age groups.

Central Park East is one of the few schools whose open classrooms survived the conservative reform wave of the late 1970s and 1980s, and its director, Esther Rosenthal, points to very practical reasons why the earlier trend toward mixed-age groupings failed. Unlike Great Britain's, most American teacher training programs did not teach developmental theories or provide model classrooms to practice them in, she says. By 1975, when a recession began to spark teacher cutbacks in districts across the nation, the newer teachers were the first to go, and many innovative programs died with their departure. The lack of bureaucratic support also made new ways hard for teachers: Everything from required testing to mandatory grade-level textbooks was organized to counter mixed-age principles. Little wonder, she says, that excitement about the idea among educators and researchers dropped dramatically by the mid-1970s. Still, education runs in cycles, she points out. "We are entering a new cycle with a more humanistic style. Pockets remained here and there, and now that movement is a-borning again."

IN MANY elementary schools, for instance, teachers excited by new pedagogies such as the whole-language approach to reading have begun turning to each other for new classroom structures in which these ideas can be carried out. This could mean teaming with another teacher to share ideas and resources—and even if that teacher is at another grade level, it could mean sharing students as well. The whole-language reading approach provides the flexibility to group children at different ability levels together, encouraging them to work with and learn from each other. Whether teaming is part of the picture or not, whole-language instruction can result, then, in a new openness toward mixed-age grouping.

In some schools, the push comes from another direction. At P.S. 41, the change to multi-age groups was regarded as a first step to getting teachers to try out new pedagogies. Once core teams of mixed-age groups were established, says Assistant Principal Gary Wexler, teachers found it both useful and necessary to personalize their classroom instruction. "Nongrading is the only way to *get* teachers to personalize, sometimes," he argues. "Because the only way nongrading can possibly work is to use cooperative learning, peer tutoring, learning centers." For P.S. 41, multi-age grouping is only one method of generating a spirit of enthusiasm and ownership among its teachers; and though the school's program incorporates only some aspects of the multiage theory, it clearly has succeeded on one level. The school is alive with cooperation and pride; around the lunch tables and in their common planning period, teachers talk continually about new ways to work with their students together.

Which Ages Go Together?

All these models rest on the principle that children do better when they work in small groups with flexible age boundaries—so that their success is measured not against others of the same age, but by their mastery of new skills as they become ready. How best to mix the ages to achieve this goal is another question. Most educators agree that between the ages of five and eight (grades K-3) children proceed through certain key developmental stages—and during this period they learn best by contact with as many sensory, concrete experiences as possible. But should the five-year-olds be put with the older children?

Few of the teachers combining grades 1 and 2 or grades 3 and 4 think so. "For the most part, the five-year-olds still belong in kindergarten with the babies," says Norma Leutzinger. "There's a big difference in what a five-year-old is ready for."

As she approaches six, a child makes a key transition, these teachers agree—not from a concrete mode of learning to a more abstract one (which happens later), but from a more individual way of learning to a group-centered one. Some schools acknowledge this by creating K-1 (or "transition") combinations where a child can comfortably work in both modes. As a child matures socially, he can work together with the class's older children.

Teachers and researchers also disagree about where the third-grader belongs. At the schools described here, most teachers felt strongly that by third grade a child has moved into a new mode of learning that calls for grouping with fourth-graders. Only in the Montessori elementary school was there a commitment to grouping six- to nine-year-olds (first- to third-graders) together in the same class. At Sands Montessori, for funding reasons, kindergarten makes a class of its own with five- and six-year-olds, though Montessori schools normally group three- to six-year-olds together.

"Montessori classes are divided into overlapping age groups [3-6, 6-9, and 9-12 years old]," says Sands principal Sandra Sommer, "to acknowledge the developmental passages that a child goes through around six years old and nine years old." By including six-year-olds both with younger and older children, Montessori acknowledges the "bubble" that includes some sixes with the fives and some with the older children. A similar process occurs at nine, Sommer says, and so narrow grade groupings of grades 1-2 and 3-4 are inappropriate.

"When you take an eight-year-old away from the sixes and sevens, you miss the beauty of the mixed-age experience," agrees Mary Motz. "By the third year in my class, the older child is very sensitive to the younger ones' progress. He can help check their work, for example, and by teaching a younger child he really shows mastery of the material." Children gain socially from the broader three-grade grouping too, she says, and self-esteem goes up. "A bright child in the middle year can go as fast as he wants, but a slow child in the middle isn't isolated as different."

Still, Motz says, teaching three grades in one classroom is unquestionably harder in some ways. She works all day on Saturday, she says, planning the week ahead: what to present to the whole group, which children need attention in which areas. And like all of the mixed-group teachers described here, she keeps meticulous progress records on each child through a combination of methods. Children keep journals that can be used to track their reading, writing, and language skills; and she records their mastery of specific skills in another log.

Discipline, a potential problem that scares off many teachers from combining age groups, seems less of a problem to Motz. In some ways, this is because she knows her students so well; when only a fraction of the class is new to the teacher each year, she has an automatic advantage. In fact, the theory is that mixed-age grouping fosters good discipline because older children take responsibility as leaders and models for the younger ones. Still, this does make work on the teacher's part; all the classrooms described here give a great deal of attention to routines that foster mutual respect and conflict resolution.

SUGGESTIONS FOR SUCCESSFUL MULTI-AGE CLASSROOMS

• Provide plenty of flexible space and divide it into functional areas or "learning centers."

• Supply a selection of concrete materials to foster math concepts and language play. You won't need twenty-five of everything, since most activities will only involve a few children at a time.

• Provide a wide variety of "real books" at every reading level. If you do use reading textbooks, do so only as a check.

• Structure into the day opportunities for older children to tutor younger ones. Pair a youngster at the early edge of acquiring a skill with one who is more confident but still needs practice. Or allow an older student to check a younger one's work.

• Involve students in making work plans or "contracts" on a daily, weekly, or monthly basis.

• Allow children to freely explore the room and to choose their activities individually or in groups.

• Structure the curriculum around themes that can integrate learning across content areas.

• Use plenty of support staff—in art, music, physical education, special needs. Be sure to include them in planning of curriculum themes.

• Don't sort, track, label, or retain kids. Break down the idea that June is "promotion" time. A child can remain in the group until his mastery of appropriate skills shows he is ready to move on.

• Try sharing responsibilities with another teacher if your subject matter expertise lies in different areas.

• Switch teaching assignments frequently in graded schools. This increases empathy and cooperation among teachers, familiarizes them with students of different ages, and helps them think of themselves as learners.

• Train student teachers in many grades, not just one. Include courses in early childhood development in their requirements for certification. □

K.C.

What To Do in Class

In a Montessori classroom, children of different ages learn together for both social and academic reasons. But how do they do it? How does a six-year-old work alongside a nine-year-old without one of them being bewildered and the other bored stiff?

The answer, say Motz and Sommer both, lies in the nature of the Montessori curriculum. It covers math, language, and cultural subjects in a series of concrete tasks—bead games, map puzzles, and the like—that can be taught to a larger group and then practiced again and again, with the teacher in smaller clusters and on one's own, until they are mastered. Motz and her students track their progress using monthly or weekly work plans, lists of activities from which the children can make their own choices. Through this tracking, teachers can help assure that each child is always working at the level he or she is comfortable with, prompted to try new things by curiosity about what is going on around him, and taught the necessary skills as the occasion arises. For a class of twenty-four six- to nine-year-olds, Motz makes up half a dozen such work plans or "contracts" monthly, some of which overlap in the academic areas they address.

Motz argues that the contract approach motivates children to acquire skills on their own, like math facts, that might otherwise be punishing rote routines. "The contract is actually unnecessary for most of the class, except as an aid to me," she confesses. "The children know that if they want to use a certain activity they need to take certain steps before they'll be able to. They have freedom; they're not told what day they have to do anything."

Contracts are also a key part of the IGE system, which organizes learning around a four-step cycle of assessment, selecting objectives, following a learning program, and then re-assessment. Using 9 x 12-inch "task cards" the teacher can record each child's progress in six or seven broadly defined areas (such as "letters"). Teachers use formal assessment methods to place children at the start and then move them ahead based on continuous, informal assessments of their mastery.

The Integrated Curriculum

Whatever their formal construct or rationale for teaching mixed-age groups, most teachers use another powerful classroom technique to pull together their learning objectives. Each year they select a theme—whales, for example, or "workers in the neighborhood," or "families from long ago"—and organize every aspect of the curriculum around it. Children practice language skills as they read about the theme and write about it; they measure and graph its component parts using math and science skills. Social studies material like history and geography is all tied in; and the whole class takes field trips together around the theme, practicing social skills along the way. In a class that stays with the same teacher from year to year, the theme shifts yearly; so teachers must plan on at least a two-year cycle.

Integrating a curriculum around a theme allows children of different ages and stages to work together in a group as well as to practice skills at different levels. "I might read an oversized picture book to the whole class," says Norma Leutzinger. "The older kids and early readers will be following the text, and the younger ones will get something from the pictures and the discussion, as well as from being read to aloud." Working together on a theme-related project, an eight-year-old may write down a story dictated by a six-year-old, type it, and bind it into a book illustrated by the nonreader, then give it back to the nonreader, who can use it to practice reading his own work.

The challenge of moving toward a mixed-age grouping can seem formidable when all the standard classroom materials are geared toward single-grade content areas. But in practice, say the teachers who do it, having to come up with theme-related activities and materials is a powerful spur to trying new ways of teaching. Because the children are still at a developmental age at which learning must be largely organized around concrete objects, useful learning materials can be as ordinary as bottle caps, bread tags, and popsicle sticks; and their collection can involve parents in the life of the classroom, too. And teachers learn from each other, sharing ideas as well as materials, planning together, and scheduling joint class activities. P.S. 41 encourages its teachers to visit other schools committed to mixed-age classes, like the model school at Bank Street College of Education.

Another good source of support, ironically, is the guidebook published by the Canadian province of Manitoba for teachers in small rural schools where mixed-age grouping is more necessity than choice. A down-to-earth manual crammed with ideas for themes, schedules, record-keeping and assessment, and dozens of other subjects, it is useful for long-range and short-term planning both. (For ordering information, call EDRS at 800-227-3742 and ask for ED300814.)

DIFFERENT WAYS TO GROUP CHILDREN OF DIFFERENT AGES

One key to the success of a multi-age classroom is a variety of groupings that afford students the opportunity to advance at their own pace, tutor others, and mix with different children. Some types of grouping are:

- **Problem-solving grouping,** in which learners are grouped around a common unsolved topic or problem; for example, a group discussion related to the main idea of a story.
- **Needs-requirement grouping,** in which students are instructed in a concept, skill, or value; for example, extra instruction in consonant blends.
- **Reinforcement grouping,** for learners who need more work in a specific area or task.
- **Interest grouping,** for learners who want, say, to read poetry out loud.
- **Learning-style grouping,** for those with a common pattern of learning, such as through manipulation of objects.

Adapted from Language Arts Handbook for Primary-Grade Teachers in Multi-Graded Classrooms, *Winnipeg: Manitoba, Department of Education, Canada, 1988.*

Who Most Benefits?

Do children in mixed-age groupings do better in the long run than those in single-age classes? Some categories of students do, some don't; but none seem to fare worse in mixed-age classes. The research on this question is somewhat inconclusive, partly because just what defines a "nongraded primary classroom" is often not clearly spelled out. Still, study results generally show a pattern of improved language skills among mixed-group students; in other academic areas, tests either favor mixed-age or show no difference. Nobody falls behind, these measures show; although those students on developmental and academic extremes benefit most—boys, blacks, the slow and the gifted, and children with low self-esteem. Some researchers report that such grouping is particularly effective for bright but immature children, who need both academic stimulation and a social environment more suited to a younger child. Others have shown that the longer children stay in nongraded classes the more their achievement scores rise in relation to their ability.

Most of the available research measuring these results is fairly old; but more recent research on how children learn tends to support the mixed-age structure as well. For example, children have been shown to adjust their language from an early age depending on who their audience is—so in a mixed-age class, a younger child could be stimulated to rise to the older children's level. Researchers have shown that in social situations, children spontaneously tend to choose mixed-age situations over same-age ones, lending weight to the argument that such arrangements foster social development. And peer tutoring has been shown to be a particularly effective learning technique between students of different ages—especially if the "novice" is already within a certain key range of the "expert" in her grasp of the topic. Finally, mixed-age groupings make it virtually impossible for a teacher to lecture on the same material to a large group, and research clearly shows that the more personal and individual the lesson, the more effective it is.

So Why Not?

Given all these advantages to mixed-age grouping, why are more schools not doing it? The most conservative answer is that such classes are not necessarily best for every student. Even the National Association for the Education of Young Children (NAEYC), whose 1988 position statement strongly advocates "developmentally appropriate" child-centered practice in the primary grades, recommends family groupings as only one of the desirable ways to achieve this. Classroom groups should vary in composition, the NAEYC says, depending on children's needs, and children should be placed where it is expected they will do best— "which may be in a family grouping and which is more likely to be determined by developmental than chronological age."

Some teachers shy away from mixed-age grouping at first, for understandable reasons. For one thing, over the last twenty years teachers have often been assigned to such classrooms simply to accommodate population overflows, not for pedagogical reasons—and so this has become the least-desirable assignment in the school, involving as it does two entirely separate preparations every day. The solution, say advocates, is to combine the class for many subjects and to adapt one's teaching style to a more individualized approach, rather than lecturing to two "classes" who vary considerably within themselves in any case.

The team teaching that often inspires mixed-age grouping can be difficult for some teachers. "You have to be realistic about the interpersonal stuff," says CPE director Esther Rosenthal. "With collaborative work, you have to be constantly talking about what you're doing, and it gets to be a strain." Other teachers who have teamed up agree that the right match of chemistry and teaching styles can make all the difference in how it works.

Teachers who are not trained to work with different ages at once may object to the idea. Few education schools offer courses that directly support this, and few open classrooms exist for practice teachers to learn in. As an interim step, therefore, some principals re-assign teachers annually to different grades until they are comfortable enough with several levels to combine them easily.

Until elementary teachers must study early childhood education before they work with the early grades—something that is required in Great Britain, and that NAEYC recommends—the skills to run a developmentally based mixed-age program may be lacking. So far, the U.S. educational establishment has simply not supported the development of mixed-age elementary teaching.

The bureaucracy of a central testing system also gets in the way of teachers trying out new ways. "To do this, you've got to trust yourself to introduce skills in your own way," says Norma Leutzinger. Though test results eventually prove that it works, she says, it takes a lot of confidence to change a traditional system.

Finally, a powerful system of textbook publishing that serves mainly single-grade classes impedes progress toward a more developmental approach. In the "scope and sequence" curriculum models of the last decade, children at every grade level were trained in carefully delineated subject areas before they moved on to the next grade. Mixing classes together, even if only for selected subjects, messes up that system. If it is to work, publishers will have to adapt—as they are beginning to already, prodded by the whole-language movement.

In the end, change may come bit by bit, as teachers find ways to team with each other comfortably, to give up absolute control at the head of the class, and to support new teachers on unfamiliar ground. The rewards are many, according to those who do it. "It's a whole different dimension," says Norma Leutzinger, "and it changes you. It's wonderful, but draining—just as intense as having a family. But then you see kids leave you, at the end of your two years together, with the confidence to stand up in front of the class and speak about something. And you see them come back, year after year, they visit your class, you read to them, and you play with them on the playground. I wouldn't do it any other way for the world." □

OFF THE TRACK

Children Thrive in Ungraded Primary Schools

EDUCATORS
NEED RESOLVE
TO CHALLENGE
ASSUMPTIONS,
APPLY NEW
THINKING

BY TREVOR CALKINS
Principal, Rogers School, Victoria, British Columbia

People change when they have to, and clearly we have to change the way we are delivering education in North America today.

In British Columbia, a Royal Commission concluded—after a thorough investigation of practices and attitudes in the educational, business, and parent communities—schools simply were not meeting the needs of the community or the learner.

Business leaders, attracted to new models, wanted to make paradigm shifts. They demanded higher-order thinking and problem-solving abilities in our graduates. *In Search of Excellence, Thriving on Chaos, The Aquarian Conspiracy,* and other popular works attacked our sacred cows. New knowledge about the brain and learning challenged us to reconsider our teaching techniques. Throughout Canada, particularly in British Columbia, whole language quickly was becoming the practice in the primary grades.

I believe we need to make two significant changes in education. First, we must personalize instruction. Then, we must give constructive feedback to the learner.

MAY 1992

Personalization

To make education more personal, we need to acknowledge children as important individuals especially when we assign children to classrooms and make sure each child has appropriate role models.

Each child should have:

• At least one friend in the class with whom she or he works well;

• A teacher who is aware of learning-style research and who will try to accommodate the student's style;

• A teacher skillful enough to adjust instruction to meet a variety of learning needs;

• A teacher with whom the child and the parents feel emotionally and socially comfortable;

• An opportunity to benefit from his or her leadership role and the challenge of working in a cooperative role; and

• An opportunity to feel intellectually challenged.

All these can be accomplished through multi-age classes that allow for greater choice in class placement and therefore, greater likelihood of successful placement.

For example, a school of 200 students, kindergarten to grade 7, with approximately 25 students at each grade level, could be organized into the following configuration:

• Division 1 and Division 2, grades K-2;

• Division 3 and Division 4, grades 2-4;

• Division 5 and Division 6, grades 3-5;

• Division 7 and Division 8, grades 5-7.

Depending on grade level, each child in the above organization has a minimum of two and a maximum of four divisions where she or he can be placed. In a traditional school organization, only one or two placement opportunities for each child is possible.

Sundry Advantages

A major advantage of multi-age classrooms is choice. Another is that students often can stay with their teacher more than one year. This provides for more effective communication in the second year and avoids the problem of spending the first term getting to know class routines.

Just as important, the teachers in this approach know they may have their students a second year, allowing them to plan effectively for continuous progress. Teachers become more interested in having happy, interested, knowledgeable, performing children because the relationship may be a long one.

Obviously, a school with 400 or 600 children has many choices when organized into the traditional single-grade classroom. But we often restrict those choices by tracking, based on reading and math scores.

John Goodlad and Robert H. Anderson described the ineffectiveness of tracking in 1959 and again in 1987 in their book, *The Nongraded Elementary School*. Tracking often ignores the social and emotional needs of students. Still, the concept of tracking for curriculum purposes is deeply embedded in our rational, self-organizing, pattern-making, and pattern-using brain.

We further restrict these choices by the way we organize the curriculum. Edward DeBono, in *I Am Right, You are Wrong*, makes a case that our dependence on scientific rationalism has made it difficult to look at the world and do anything other than analyze it into its component parts. The curriculum reflects this by being broken into subjects rather than being presented in its more

Susie Fitzhugh © 1992

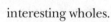
Each child should have at least one friend in the class with whom she or he works well.

interesting wholes.

In this model, math becomes a totally abstract, unconnected subject, divorced from everyday life. Science and history become lists of facts, instead of living, changing, interesting viewpoints on the world. We are caught in an endless vortex of analysis that prevents us from action.

In the business world, over-analysis, inaction, over-specialization, and ignorance of workers' social, emotional, and learning needs are excellent ways to go bankrupt. In the school system, it is all too often touted as the way to maintain standards.

Applying Feedback

In the traditional system, feedback most often is dispensed in the form of letter grades. Letter grades have a myth-like quality in the minds of many

In a Rogers School classroom, 5-, 6-, and 7-year-old children use hands-on methods to learn about math and science. Photos courtesy of Trevor Calkins.

educators, parents, and students.

The thought of not giving letter grades to children would have been simply horrifying to me in my former life as a high school math teacher and department head. More than a crutch, grades were the cornerstone of the program.

Grades provided parents, children, and me with a sense of comfort. Grades meant standards. Society knew where every student stood. Universities liked letter grades. Employers liked them. How else could society admit people to a university or decide who would get the job?

Only when I became an employer (a school administrator) did I start to examine the letter-grade construct. I soon realized employers are much more interested in dependability, perseverance, ability to work in groups, problem-solving, and creativity. Grades are very poor predictors in many of these areas.

We all know people who do well on multiple-choice tests and have few interpersonal and creative skills. The scholar often is portrayed in popular culture as a nerd with little common sense. While this is demonstrably unfair, voters seldom choose scholars to be leaders.

Grades are competitive and they do rank order. But do they serve us well? The Japanese have perfected this system, yet David Halberstam in *The Next Century* points out even the Japanese are looking to methods that will make their students more creative and less like automatons. Alfie Kuhn, in his book *No Contest,* shows letter grades and even praise can lead to less risk-taking and more conformist behavior.

Letter grades do rank order, but they do not necessarily demonstrate knowledge. So a student might have the best grade and only be the best in a bad lot. The system avoids demonstrations of knowledge and encourages the opposite through mass, multiple-choice testing that ranks order but not often indicates competence.

When grades do measure knowledge it is often limited in scope. There is clearly a correlation between well-written multiple-choice tests and intellectual ability. But we all know many people who do well on these tests and are unable to plan and allocate resources, form healthy interpersonal relationships, understand complex interrelationships, or work with a variety of technologies.

Neither is there any correlation between letter grades and integrity, self-esteem, or responsibility. (These skills are among those listed by the U.S. Labor Secretary's Commission on Achieving Necessary Skills as essential for success in the modern work force.)

A Quality Focus

Focusing on quality, rather than on grading, is one alternative.

In a quality-oriented system, you are forced to regard each child as an important individual who has social, emotional, and intellectual needs, so it makes sense to start expecting the best from each child. In a graded, tracked system, you assume that one-third will do poorly—and seldom do they disappoint you.

In a personalized, quality-oriented, system, teachers receive feedback through a variety of methods. They arrange for demonstrations, projects, essays, discussions, explanations, tests, and quizzes.

A portfolio of the student's work— a record of actual accomplishments— is kept. Sometimes the work selected is the student's choice, sometimes the teacher's or parent's. We look at the portfolio when we exhort the child to produce quality work.

Risk-taking is encouraged because everyone is interested in the process of accomplishing the task. Reflection is the key to succeeding the next time. Crises are opportunities for learning. Discipline is most often self-discipline. Feedback is continuous and comes from a variety of sources, including peers, teachers, parents, and community, and through self-reflection.

At report time, children show their parents what they can do and have done through an interview which, in itself, may well be a demonstration of knowledge. The student's written report is a list of accomplishments, projects currently under way, and next-term goals.

As a result, students work hard because they are interested and successful and have high personal standards. They are self-motivated and often work for the inherent satisfaction of the task. They take risks. They solve problems. They work well in groups and with their peers.

The focus is on getting the job done well, rather than competing with your fellow worker. These are the skills demanded by business, and they are the skills of successful workers.

Two Examples

At South Park Family School, an alternative elementary school in Victoria, British Columbia, the culture was ripe to accommodate the changes suggested by the Royal Commission.

The community was somewhat anti-establishment and was considered to be on the fringe educationally. The school population was small. Parents selected the school for the staff's commitment to active, child-centered learning, and to parent involvement.

They are self-motivated and often work for the inherent satisfaction of the task. They take risks. They solve problems. They work well in groups and with their peers.

Margaret Reinhard, co-author of *The Learner's Way*, transferred to the school and immediately helped set a tone of respect toward the learner and lifelong learning. Reinhard modeled what she wrote. Interest in her newly published book brought visitors to her classroom and her naturally collaborative nature brought the teacher across the hall into her fold.

Within two years, most of the school was working collaboratively. Teachers became more willing to investigate teaching methods. Parents became interested in educational change.

Then the Royal Commission came up with its "Year 2000" philosophy, and staff, parents, and students felt they had their ideas validated.

(Year 2000 is a futuristic, holistic, province-wide reform to the K-12 system. The curriculum is presented in five major strands: intellectual, social/ emotional, physical, artistic/aesthetic, and career. An integrated approach is intended.)

Change at South Park was easily accommodated because of its supportive community culture and its commitment to learning and collaborative, consensus decision-making.

The experience at South Park was very useful when I was asked to start a new school, with 200 students in kindergarten through grade 7 and with plans to accept 350. This privilege included the right to handpick a staff committed to implementing the British Columbia Year 2000 philosophy in a building that was designed for it. This was a principal's dream.

Unlike South Park, Rogers is a neighborhood, catchment area school. The community is relatively traditional and middle class with some government-subsidized housing. It has been served well in the past by three relatively traditional schools.

The problem for the staff at Rogers was to establish an environment and culture that would complement the Ministry of Education's Year 2000 framework, the school board's mission statement, and still reflect community values.

Our first effort at collaboration was at a public meeting where we explored 10 significant issues with parents. These included extracurricular activities, competition, grading practices,

length of the lunch break, French, music, and competitive sports.

Quickly, it became apparent grading practices would be an issue. Parents wanted personalized education, but they also appeared to want their children to be given letter grades.

We still weren't sure where we stood as a staff. We didn't have a letter-grade policy. We certainly didn't have a policy on quality. So at our first "meet-the-teacher" meeting in September, we asked parents what they wanted to see in their children's reports.

The parents responded that they wanted to know what their child could do including his or her strengths and weaknesses. They wanted the reports to be personal and individualized, and they wanted to know where their child stood in relation to other children of the same age. The task was daunting.

The staff soon realized individualization and personalization of instruction are difficult to implement—especially if we gave letter grades. Strengths and weaknesses are evident through letter grades, but personal action plans to resolve weaknesses are difficult to set in a rank-ordered system. Everyone cannot be at the top of the class.

Instead of grades, we needed a report that focused on strengths, outlined areas that needed work, and then set specific goals. We needed to let children know when they were doing their best. We needed to pay attention to detail (Tom Peters' "nuts and bolts of doing the job well").

The reports needed to enhance communication through collaboration with students and parents. Finally, the reports needed to encourage risk-taking. Interestingly, these needs parallel the characteristics of effective companies.

We took our concerns to the parent advisory council and they unanimously approved a strictly anecdotal reporting policy, much to our surprise. We then took the policy to parents at individual class meetings. We discussed the reasons for our policy, showed parents a sample of an anecdotal report, and asked them for input.

We didn't take a vote but asked for feelings. We did this by asking for a show of hands; five fingers meant you really liked the idea, four fingers you liked it, three fingers you were willing

In a quality system, you regard each child as an important individual who has social, emotional, and intellectual needs.

Above photos by Susie Fitzhugh © 1992

- *Involve parents in meaningful decisions.*

Listen to their fears. Remember they don't want their children used as guinea pigs and they, too, have experienced the negative effects of educational change. Respect their judgment. Provide them with research and give them time to reflect. Be prepared to live with rejection, but fight on for important beliefs.

- *Work hard at developing a collaborative atmosphere in the school.*

Encourage teachers to work in planning teams. Listen to your teachers and respect their concerns and fears. Encourage different adaptations to multi-age grouping, student assessment, anecdotal reporting, and parent involvement. See diversity as an asset.

- *Be aware of the change process for institutions and individuals.*

Read Michael Fullan on the change process. Don't expect everyone to change. Allow time for reflection. Truly believe that conflict and disagreement are a necessary part of good decision-making. Have a plan, but make it flexible. Remember, the objective is to change the culture, not to implement a single innovation.

- *Be aware of processes for building consensus.*

We want 100 percent, not 51 percent. Use Roger Fisher and Scott Brown's "Unconditionally Constructive Strategy" for "Building a Relationship That Gets To Yes." Develop strategies for balancing emotions with reason. Try to understand each person. Consult before deciding. Be reliable. Be open to persuasion, and try to persuade others. Accept everyone as worthy of consideration, care about them, and be open to learning from them.

- *Update your personal knowledge.*

Review current brain theory, management and leadership theory, learning theory, and motivational theory. We tend to operate on old models even after our beliefs change. Check your personal practices for consistency with beliefs. Understand that beliefs are very resistant to change and that work on practices is often a more effective way to implement innovations.

- *Try, try again.*

to give it a try, two you didn't like it and one you thought it was a terrible idea. In nine meetings, we had only three people give the idea a 2 or 1. More than three-fourths gave the idea a 4 or 5.

After sending home our first set of reports in November, we conducted a parent survey. The initial 30 percent response was strongly favorable. We pressed for a greater response and now have a 78 percent return. There is still strong support for the program. In January, we reviewed the survey results and came up with strategies for writing still better reports and for meeting the needs of a few dissatisfied parents.

The result is that we have implemented a highly controversial approach to grading in a relatively traditional middle-class, multicultural community, and have received high levels of support.

Surveys show that the reasons for this are: the quality of teaching, our openness during the process of making the decision, the feeling that the decision was not made ahead of time, the willingness to adjust, and the willingness to give comparative information in the interview, if the parent insisted. No parent insisted.

Future Implications

What are the lessons for school and district administrators?

TEACHERS NETWORKING
THE WHOLE LANGUAGE NEWSLETTER

Volume 11, Number 2   Richard C. Owen Publishers, Inc.   Spring 1992

Multi-Age Classrooms: Option to an Outdated System

by Linda Aulgur, Lynda Baker, and Kittye Copeland

Labeling citizens within a community on the basis of specific skills, ages, weights, or intelligence is unheard of. Why then do we structure our educational system in such a way? The system did not start out placing children in self-contained grade levels, but because of increasing school enrollments and the economics of organizing large numbers of children in one building, students were divided according to age. If all learners had similar background knowledge and experiences, had the same interests, and learned at the same pace, this kind of arrangement would work. However, this is by far *not* the case.

Lynda Baker, Linda Aulgur, Kittye Copeland

The notion that placing learners by age will ensure that they will be better educated has damaged many learners. Children who don't fit the age norm are labeled "slow," "below grade level," "above grade level," "immature," or even "learning disabled." Many young adults who are labeled and criticized throughout their educational experience as being "below the norm" drop out of the system feeling like failures. Why is this system of labeling and "herding" learners still in effect? Now is the time to look at the structure of learning systems that may be holding back the advancement of powerful lifelong learning.

Children do not need to be compared to other children of their age for assess-

Linda Aulgur, Lynda Baker, and Kittye Copeland are teachers at Stephens Elementary Children's School, Columbia, Missouri.

ment of learning. Doing so has turned education into a damaging contest instead of the support system students need to have the confidence to stay positive and successful in school. The power of not having to be judged by mythical grade levels is tremendous. Students in multi-age classrooms grow

in their academic ability year after year. With support and nurturing, they never feel like failures.

Social Nature of Learning

Whole language classrooms are based on the social nature of learning. Social learning is a child striving to make order of his environment by using language, both spoken and written, as a functional tool to make connections. As he utilizes his language, he comes to new understandings and connections about himself and his world. Multi-age

Whole language classrooms are based on the social nature of learning. Social learning is a child striving to make order of his environment by using language, both spoken and written, as a functional tool to make connections.

Multi-Age Classrooms

classrooms offer the essence of whole language learning to students, who come to value learning as a personal adventure.

The multi-age classroom is a secure environment that promotes a natural interaction which helps students meet the challenges they face as learners. The classroom becomes a community in which learning is considered a partnership; students encourage each other instead of competing with one another. The lesson of getting along with a variety of people in our daily lives is learned in a program that includes a variety of ages, abilities, and interests.

Peer teaching in the multi-age classroom makes it possible for less experienced students to have the aid of classmates who understand the learner's needs. More experienced, capable readers and writers work with those who have not yet become proficient. Those who had been considered "below grade level" in a traditional classroom become successful at helping other students. Students who are in the role of teacher gain as much as those who are receiving the tutoring. Students are getting multiple benefits, feeling safer, and are psychologically comfortable when their teachers recognize what they need in order to learn. The benefits of having experienced learners to act as guides for the less experienced learner is immeasurable. The group works as a team, helping each member move ahead by the support and trust each has for learning. Children come to realize that we all learn at different rates. No one is judged by what they *don't* know. They are valued because of what they *do* know, who they are, and for who they are becoming.

Curriculum for Lifelong Learners

Whole language advocates have been working to make it clear that curriculum developed for specific grade levels by

text or teachers creates barriers that make learning superficial, if not impossible. The notion that learning can be keyed to specific objectives by grade level is restrictive. Real learning takes place when children are taught *how* to learn, not *what* to learn.

One of the major responsibilities of the educational system is to motivate children to explore topics that interest them. Children need to be stimulated to ask their own questions, rather than answer those predetermined by others. Their ideas and questions then become the curriculum, in which students are helped to find ways of gaining information and answers. Children need to have options of studies, along with the guidance of the teacher and more experienced classmates.

Now is the time to look at the structure of learning systems that may be holding back the advancement of powerful lifelong learning.

The curriculum in a multi-age classroom is not built on predetermined grade level plans created by textbook companies or planned activities designed by state guidelines. The creators of these assume they know what children need to know and are ready to learn at a given age. We have found that because of the wide range of interests that children generate in the classroom, the curriculum becomes much broader than any that curriculum guides would provide.

The interests of the students and their needs, informed by current events, shape the classroom curriculum while stimulating each child to discover and accumulate knowledge about the subjects that will help them prepare for their role in the adult world.

How It Works

Our multi-age classroom contains children ages six to twelve. We also have Step Ahead, an afternoon program for kindergartners from other schools who mix with the older students and receive individualized learning experiences at their various levels.

The youngest children in the elementary class assume the role of mentors, tutors, and helpers for the Step Ahead children.

The older students become coauthors of stories and books with them and with the younger full-time students. They get valuable reading experience while reading aloud to them.

In our program, the teacher and experienced students demonstrate strategy lessons on note taking and revising to help other students become competent researchers. Notes are used to write drafts and produce final written reports. Oral presentations with visual aids allow children to share the knowledge, and even the youngest members in the class take notes. Students are encouraged to ask questions and add to the topic. The circle of strategies and interest in the work of fellow students is not affected by age. We have never seen the ages of the children make a difference in their ability to present or receive the information. In fact, some of the best articulated and orchestrated presentations have been by the youngest members of the group.

Personalized Writing

The same has been true when looking at the writing that goes on in a multi-age classroom. We have learned that children write in different voices when given the chance to choose, to write from their own background knowledge, and to write

Multi-Age Classrooms

for their own purposes. The students in our classrooms write for functional and useful reasons not determined by what age they are. They write to communicate their feelings, to get information, to respond to literature, to record events. Our children write to penpals in different countries and other grades, to college students, and to residents of retirement homes. We have heard from the recipients of the letters that they are always amazed because they could not tell from the letters the age or grade level of the writer.

Age has very little to do with the ability to write. In the multi-age program children are editors and collaborators, supporting each other in their goal to produce a finished piece. The class members are not concerned about who is older or younger. They give and take advice when needed.

Time to Build

One of the most important aspects of a child-centered curriculum is the valuing of and knowing the learner. Teachers are expected to know each student well enough to provide motivation for that child's learning. It is difficult to accomplish this goal in a nine-month grade-level classroom, for teachers need time to get to know the students.

Classrooms are more easily organized and predictable because the children carry on traditions and rituals that are hard to establish when they are together for only nine months. The members of a class have an appreciation for the history of that class. Teachers and children know each other well because of all the sharing and time spent together year after year.

The class is able to learn each others' strengths, needs, and interests. The school becomes an extended family and the focus of schooling becomes the act of communicating and learning.

The pressure of a rigidly planned,

nine-month timetable is removed, allowing projects and research to extend through summers and to continue for years. The extended time allows projects to be more in-depth and better quality. We have children who have written books with the same characters that have been developed for over three years. One club has continued its studies for five years. The members have adopted many endangered animals and raised money to support their cause, efforts that require time and persistence.

The class members are not concerned about who is older or younger. They give and take advice when needed.

Learners in Charge of Their Own Learning

Children are not valued only as decision makers in curriculum development; they are also valued as evaluators. We have found that in the multi-age setting, children are very proficient in giving solid suggestions to those who are less proficient or less secure in their work. Children evaluate on the basis of content, creativity, and effort, not just mechanics. As students become involved in conferencing with one another, they work with each other's strengths and needs instead of focusing on grades and grade level expectations. All evaluators would benefit from such a focus. Students are comfortable with each others' evaluations because they see it as good advice, not judgement.

One parent described her son's experience before he joined our class. The ten-year-old had previously been tested,

tracked, and ability grouped since kindergarten. In the fourth grade, he had slipped into "low" groups for every subject. His self-esteem had sunk to an all-time low, and he refused to be motivated to produce any work at all.

Upon arriving in our multi-age classroom, he was placed in the role of helping a younger boy write. Although his spelling and writing skills had been stifled, he took pride in correcting and helping the younger student. In turn, he was looked up to by the other student as a teacher. With this sense of achievement, he slowly began to focus on his own improvement. He knew that he was accepted the way he was, and would not be forced to work at a level for which he was not ready. As he was anxious to help the younger students, he began to look up information in resources to make sure he was correct. His own work rose accordingly. When the pressure of competing with twenty-six other students of his own age was released, he blossomed into a self-assured reader and writer.

Whole language programs treat reading and writing as a way to communicate with others, to help the learner find out what they do and do not know, and to appreciate learning as a way to enhance life. Our trust in how children learn has set us free to look at our children as capable learners not needing to be compared by arbitrary grade levels and judged by grades.

When a child asks why time at school goes so fast, a teacher must feel a sense of success. We feel fortunate that the question came from one of the six-year-olds in our first- through sixth-grade classroom. Time can go fast at school, but only when the students are enjoying learning with interest, intensity, and investment. We think a multi-age classroom system is the solution which will ensure children that the time is theirs to learn.

Reprinted from *Teachers Networking* by permission of Richard C. Owen Publishers, Inc., 135 Katonah Ave., Katonah, N.Y. 10536.

Bill Harp

When Your Principal Asks: What Can I Expect to see in Multi-Age Classrooms?

A new housing development is opening within your school's boundary and next fall will see an increase in enrollment. Like most things in school, the enrollment patterns are not highly predictable, but it looks like they will be uneven across grade levels. This has sparked considerable debate at faculty meetings and in the lounge. Should some teachers have "split grades" next year, or should the whole school move to multi-age classroom groupings? At one of the meetings the principal asks, "What can I expect to see in multi-age classrooms?"

An examination of the research on multi-age instruction reveals some common threads that seem to characterize such classrooms. Certainly, not all multi-age classrooms bear all of these characteristics nor are these characteristics absent from single-grade classrooms.

Outcomes-Based Instruction

When a teacher is dealing with a two- or three-year age range it is no longer possible to think in terms of "second grade" or "sixth grade" curriculum. Instead, curriculum outcomes must be specified in terms of specific processes and products children are expected to master. Often these processes and products are articulated along developmental lines. In reading, for example, the attitudes, understandings, and behaviors expected of emergent readers, early readers, and fluent readers are defined (Mooney, 1988). Children are observed, not in terms of the grade they are in, but in terms of which of these various developmental characteristics they exhibit.

Imagine how much more informative to the parent (to say nothing about how much more *informed* the teacher looks) to go to a parent conference and have the teacher say something like, "When we visited about Tricia in October, I observed that she was showing an interest in reading through her spontaneous play in the library corner, she was indicating an interest in seeing her words written down and reread to her, and she was responding to some environmental print. Now, in December, she has maintained all of those behaviors, and is choosing to reread some stories independently that we have read together, she is selecting books from the library corner during free times, and she is beginning to understand that letters represent sounds and that those same sounds are found over and over again in texts." Such outcomes-based instruction is far more informative to parents, teachers and children than saying something like, "Tricia has made good progress in reading. She has moved from pre-primer one to pre-primer three" (whatever that means!).

Peer Power

Peer power simply means learners helping learners. One is reminded of that old saying, "The best way to learn something is to teach it to someone else." This is the value of peer power.

In multi-age classrooms children are encouraged to learn to rely on peers for the assistance that traditionally would have been sought from the teacher. This peer power is played out in a variety of ways. Children ask a table mate or neighbor to help with reading and writing problems. Children are assigned editing groups in which the bulk of the editing work on writing pieces is done on a regular basis. Children who share strengths in a certain writing skill such as writing dialogue are assigned to a "Dialogue Committee" which reviews manuscripts singly for the writing of dialogue. Children work in interest groups on topics of their choice with outcomes agreed upon with the teacher.

Peer power may be invoked in other situations. The teacher may regularly assign "buddy reading," in which children daily pair up to practice oral reading. Such pairings may be used for peer tutoring in a variety of subject areas where a more advanced student is working with a developing learner (Limbrick, McNaughton, Cameron, 1985). The "bottom line" on peer power is that children are encouraged to come to a natural caring about and helping their fellow learners — something children are completely capable of if we create an environment that fosters this natural inclination.

In Joan Hagan's K-1-2 class at Horace Mann Whole Language Magnet School in San Jose, California, recently a morning meeting ended with four children explaining the projects they had each designed for their classmates. Children then selected their first project activity and effectively moved among them for about an hour. There was real peer power!

When teachers properly set the stage, the best in children comes out.

Cooperative Learning

Children are placed in cooperative learning groups on the basis of the teacher's knowledge of the children and their strengths. In putting a cooperative learning group together the teacher considers the strengths exhibited by each member as a learner in the selected curriculum area, for levels of independence/dependence as a learner, for strengths in problem solving, for strengths in group leadership and dynamics. Other strengths may be considered depending on the nature of the task before the group.

The cooperative learning group and the teacher identify the task or tasks to be accomplished. Usually a conference with the teacher underscores what the group knows about the topic or problem to be studied or solved, what they want to learn, and how they will go about learning. This conference usually includes reaching an agreement on the processes the group will use and the products the group will produce. The initial conference with the teacher, which can be a whole class discussion, may include decisions about what products are to be graded or evaluated and how, and whether processes will be evaluated. Timelines and individual responsibilities may be set at this initial conference, or these decisions may be made by the group independently of the teacher.

Effective Use of Homogeneous and Multi-Age Groupings

Richard Villa and Jacqueline Thousand (1988) report that a central characteristic of multi-age classrooms is the teacher's ability to organize effective combinations of homogeneous and multi-age groupings. While some doubt the real existence of a homogeneous group, it does seem clear that multi-age teachers know when to pull together a group of students with very similar educational needs and when to present instruction to whole multi-age groups. This simply describes good instruction in any classroom. The demands on the multi-age teacher to be a wonderful "kid

watcher" are enormous. The level of knowledge required about the children in this setting is believed to be far greater than in a single-grade classroom. But perhaps this is a "myth" of multi-age classrooms. The expectation is that in a multi-age classroom the teacher is expected to deal with these educational differences, and yet in a "traditional" sixth-grade classroom, these differences may be even greater.

Continuous Assessment and Parent Involvement

While not inherently unique to multi-age instruction, virtually every report on such successful instruction includes descriptions of continuous assessment and parental involvement. The teacher of multi-age children must be a true expert in watching the development of children.

Such an *informed* teacher looks at a child's oral reading miscues, for example, and sees a window through which he or she can explore and more deeply understand the child's use of the reading process and cueing systems. The uninformed teacher witnesses the same miscues and sees only mistakes.

Most parents want their children to succeed in school. They are deeply concerned about their children's growth and development. Successful multi-age programs have brought parents in as partners from the beginning. Parents are not only *informed* about school practice, but they have a *role* in the program. This partnership is usually easily formed when the school personnel explain the rationale for a program and the research supporting a program to parents.

The conversation with your principal ends with the agreement that much is known about the virtues of multi-age groups, much is yet to be learned, and that it is certainly worth a try.

References

Katz, Lilian G. *et al.* "The Case for Mixed-Age Grouping in Early Education." ERIC Clearinghouse on Elementary and Early Childhood Education, Urbana, IL; Washington, DC: National Association for the Education of Young Children, 1990.

Limbrick, Libby, McNaughton, Stuart, Cameron, Marie. *Peer Power* video tape. Wellington, New Zealand: Council for Educational Research, 1985. (available from Richard C. Owen Publishers, Inc.)

Mooney, Margaret. *Developing Life–long Readers.* Wellington, New Zealand: Ministry of Education, 1988.

Pratt, David. "On the Merits of Multiage Classrooms: Their Work Life." *Research in Rural Education, 3,* #3, Spring 1986, pp. 111-116.

Veenman, Simon *et al.* "Classroom Time and Achievement in Mixed Age Classes." *Education Studies, 13,* #1, 1987, pp. 75-89.

Villa, Richard A. and Thousand, Jacqueline S. "Enhancing Success in Heterogeneous Classrooms and Schools: The Power of Partnership." *Teacher Education and Special Education 11,* #4, Fall 1988, pp. 144-154.

Reprinted from *Teachers Networking* by permission of Richard C. Owen Publishers, Inc., 135 Katonah Ave., Katonah, N.Y. 10536.

35

The Country School Comes to Town: A Case Study of Multiage Grouping and Teaching

by **James K. Uphoff, Ed.D.**
Professor of Education, Wright State University, Dayton, OH 45435
Elected Member, Oakwood City Schools' Board of Education
and
Donna A. Evans
Classroom Teacher, First and Second Graders
Dayton City Schools, E.J. Brown Cooperative Elementary Magnet School

Some educational theorists and a growing number of ordinary people including teachers, parents, and politicians have been looking back to the old one-room country school with more than just fond nostalgia. As more and more research results show that cooperative learning, cross-age peer tutoring, process/project learning, and other methods pay major dividends in achieving cognitive, psycho-motor, and affective goals, people reflect back on the old rural school structure as having initiated many of these techniques. Older pupils helped their younger peers, younger children listened (and learned) to (from) the lessons being taught to their older peers. Working with the same teacher for several years in a row (sometimes eight) established closer affective relationships.

The Case for Mixed-Age Grouping in Early Education by Lilian G. Katz, Demetra Evangelou, and Jeanette Allison Hartman advocates a return to mixed-age grouping based on the type of research findings cited above. The authors' major problem is that there are almost no schools which have implemented such a major change long enough to have been studied carefully for current and future successes and/or failures. In other words, there are almost no long-term studies of what works and what doesn't. Thus, much of the rationale for such a massive change in today's elementary school structure is based upon research-based theory of component parts/methods, but not on the "total package" of the several parts being put together into a working whole.

Did multiage grouping always work in the past?

Definitely not. In the mid-60s through the mid-70s major efforts were made to have "continuous progress," "open space," and "multiage grouping." Most of these thrusts disappeared due to negative parental reactions and a major mismatch between these methods and the curricular expectations/materials of that period. Pacing children through workbooks and skill-drill pages did not lend itself to such methods. Many adults could not personally stand the noise and distraction of open space and assumed that their children had similar problems.

What is different now?

Major changes in curricular materials and methods have taken place since that time. The importance of whole language, manipulative math, hands-on science and social studies, literature-based reading, etc., to multiage programs is dramatic. For the first time instructional methods and materials which support the key elements of multiage teaching are available and have found growing acceptance by both the profession and significant publics (business, politicians, etc.). Never-the-less, help for the classroom teacher who is informed that the building will be moving toward such a program has generally been missing.

Case Study of the First Year of Teaching Grades One and Two Together

This case study presents a year-long summary of a teacher's first year teaching a mixed-age group in an urban magnet elementary school.

The setting: The second-grade teacher (author) and two of her colleagues were assigned both first and second graders in each homeroom. For the first year, mixed-age teaching was to be done in the homeroom for all subjects except language arts and math, which were to be taught by ability grouping and shared among all three teachers.

The author asked to work with her own group for all subjects and was allowed to include language arts. There were 11 second graders and 13 first graders in her room. She had previously used integrated units with whole language as her basic approach. She kept an extensive journal and copies of her plans, papers, projects, etc. From these documents and frequent discussions with her independent study professor, she has derived the following practical suggestions that may be helpful for teachers who are new to teaching mixed-age groups.

The teacher's basic concerns were: (1) Would she be able to meet the needs of all the children when the range of ability was so much wider than she had previously experienced? and (2) How would she adapt the curriculum so it would interest all age groups and yet challenge the most able students?

Organizing for Instruction

She worked with beginning readers in small groups of six or seven with close monitoring. She used many reading recovery techniques. Students at each level read many books. Other methods/practices included:

- Obtaining (sometimes scrounging) many books at a variety of levels
- Writing words and sentences
- Phonics instruction
- Matching individual words to words in a sentence
- Keeping word banks
- Writing group and individual books

More skilled readers were in larger groups of 10 to 12 each. Major methods/practices used with these pupils included:

- Author studies
- "Theme" books (friends, bears, bunnies, or books related to a unit under study)
- "Character" books (*Clifford, Curious George, Frog and Toad,* etc.)
- Poetry weeks
- Silent reading, book projects, and reading together

The teacher used whole class activities such as Big books, language experience writing, daily oral language, flannel board stories, and reading aloud to the children to help integrate children's learning

There seem to be clear-cut advantages, but also some problems to overcome. Moving to such a program design will require more work and genuine adaptability of teachers. But it also has the potential for providing them with more rewards.

experiences and build a total group spirit.

Peer tutoring was the key element that made the whole classroom work. At least one strong second grader was seated at each table of six first and second graders. Even though they did different work at times, older students helped the first graders and each other (1) find their place, (2) monitor their progress, and (3) understand something — perhaps explaining the directions differently than the teacher had done. The teacher showed students how to tutor so that they didn't just "tell the answer" to their peers. They grew much in their ability to function effectively in this role.

After much experimentation and struggle, the author established a writing workshop procedure. Students wrote right after lunch with the workshop regularly including the following elements:

- A rehearsal period of five to 10 minutes
- At least 10 to 15 minutes (sometimes more if interests were high) of silent writing with no talking allowed
- A five minute conference period in which students could ask each other or the teacher for reaction, help, etc.
- Sharing stories on an elective basis

Some writing also took place at other times, but this workshop method was used regularly and became the norm for the class.

The teacher regularly used cooperative group learning. Students worked on research projects

with a partner and did experiments and other projects as a group. Most activities were hands-on at the beginning of the year, but included more writing and reading as the year progressed. This method proved to be very helpful for all of the students.

Major Advantages and Disadvantages of Multiage Grouping

The teacher identified major advantages of the multiage classroom as follows:

- The students seemed to care more for each other and help one another more than she had experienced with single grade classes in her 15 years of teaching.
- The role modeling and peer tutoring definitely helped the first graders stay on task and helped the self-esteem of even the lowest ability second graders.
- All students, including the older ones, were more willing to seek and accept help from others.
- Because the first graders will remain with the teacher as second graders next year, they already know how the routine of multiage learning goes. The teacher expects the new year to start more smoothly.

The most significant problem experienced during the first year concerned the lack of flexibility in district policies. For example, the district provides field trips by grade level. First graders go to the art museum while second graders visit the museum of natural history. Finding ways to "get around" such district-wide policies is a major task if site-based management is to be effective and schools are to be able to function according to their individual needs and programs. All involved need to identify other such limitations as early as possible.

Planning for the Future

The experiences of year one and two workshops (Learning Styles and Portfolio Assessment) influenced major changes the teacher anticipated for the second year.

Specific changes planned for the second year included:

- Include more kinesthetic and tactile learning opportunities
- Develop more learning centers and use them regularly every day
- Have each student develop a personal portfolio to include many types of work and thus expand the assessment process toward a more holistic one
- Develop more hands-on and cooperative group activities/projects/etc.

For educators who are contemplating a change to multiage grouping, the author advises:

- Read as much of the research reports as you can find.
- Study the curriculum for each grade level included in your teaching assignment.
- Collect many materials and a very large selection of books.
- Become well acquainted with learning styles information and how to teach to the various styles.
- Think of ways peer tutoring can be used when planning lessons.
- Use hands-on and cooperative learning activities.
- Find a fellow teacher with whom to work.

Adopt an attitude of a learner for yourself. This will help reduce the chances of being overly self-critical. Look for ways to change and improve via self-analysis. Consider change to be the norm, not the exception. Keeping a journal can be of major value especially if both the successes and the failures are recorded.

The author found that her journal documented the increasingly successful experiences and that the process of writing about her frustrations and problems helped her formulate better solutions. Occasionally rereading the journal helped the teacher see progress and renew her motivation.

Summary

There is growing interest in the multiage classroom and there are increasingly more materials and methods which will work well with such increased diversity. There seem to be clear-cut advantages, but also some problems to overcome. Moving to such a program design will require more work and genuine adaptability of teachers. But it also has the potential for providing them with more rewards such as whole child growth and achievement rather than only test-score growth.

The authors welcome feedback, ideas, experiences, etc., from teachers and administrators alike. The lack of such "how it was done" information is one of the major problems faced by those who want (or are told) to implement a multiage learning environment. The authors hope that this article will help many avoid the effort involved in re-inventing the wheel.

Reference

Katz, L.G.; Evangelou, D; & Hartman, J.A. *The Case for Mixed-Age Grouping in Early Education.* Washington, DC: NAEYC, 1990.

Voices

But change in education is difficult. It means doing things differently, not just doing longer or harder what we already do. Change is difficult also because we tend to confuse what is familiar with that which is natural. Change is inhibited more by tradition and inertia than by mandates and regulations. "Letting go" of some practices is proving to be more difficult than "adding" new ones. And since most of us were schooled in the very type of institutions that we are trying to change, too many of us hold suspect any school that does not resemble the school that we remember.

Adam Urbanski, President
Rochester Teachers' Association
(quoted in Education Week, October 23, 1991)

Reprinted with permission.

The Gift of Time

In this novel approach to teaching, primary graders move ahead by staying right where they are

BY DIANA MAZZUCHI AND
NANCY BROOKS

Diana Mazzuchi and Nancy Brooks teach at Academy School, Brattleboro, VT.

"Two years in the same class works wonders with children who are shy."

Have you ever said to yourself, "If I could just have that child for two or three more months . . . he (or she) is just beginning to get it."

As first grade teachers, we said that to ourselves every June. One year, we decided to do something about it. We approached our principal and got permission to try something new: We would keep our first grade students for a second year as second graders.

Here's how it works: When Nancy finishes in June with her first graders, she takes her class on to second grade in September, while Diana begins with a new class of first graders. The following year, Diana takes her first graders on to second grade, while Nancy begins with a new group of first graders.

Actually, it's a lot simpler than it sounds. And it has been successful. In fact, it's been so successful that we've now completed three two-year cycles, and we wouldn't want it any other way.

Other benefits. Keeping children for two years in the same classroom is very different from a multi-age classroom. In Vermont, groups of two or more grades in one classroom have long been a fact of life for many schools. We've both taught mixtures of grade levels in one classroom, and although there are advantages to such an arrangement, the two-year span offers other benefits. For one thing, a child's development is seen in a less fragmented way and in a more natural setting when it occurs over time.

Also, a two-year span provides a child with greater continuity in experience, both socially and academically. The opportunities to make personal connections with others and with ideas over time are especially valuable for emotional and intellectual growth.

Many children find the consistency that comes with two years with the same teacher and students extremely valuable. For example, by the time Genny was six and a half, she had lived in two states, one foreign country and had attended a total of seven day care facilities. She had never been to kindergarten, nor to an American classroom before. It took the first year for Genny to adjust and begin to read in English. Socially, the other children went from seeing Genny as almost an "alien" to accepting her and liking her and recognizing her strengths. In the second year, she blossomed because all those involved—the teacher, the children, the parents and Genny herself— had time.

Working wonders. Two years in the same class also works wonders with children who are shy. We've had numerous students come out of their shell in the second year because they felt confident about themselves and secure within the group. Holly is a good example. A bright but extremely quiet child, Holly would participate in oral activities within a group, but rarely shared personal opinions of a risk-taking nature. In the second year, however, she was leading many groups in story theater activities and sharing aloud her opinions about books she had read.

Jolie was another two-year student. She was so shy that she rarely spoke, except in a whisper and then usually just to her teacher. An eighth grader now, she is frequently teased about the "good old days" when she didn't talk. It's hard to get her to be quiet now.

39

Working closely with the same classmates for two years gives children a sense of security.

Visitors to this Academy School classroom are amazed at the level of intensity shown by the children.

Another shining example is Anna. Within the whole group, she would never volunteer anything unless called on, and then only in a very quiet voice. Changes were first noticed in small group project time, when the group would choose activities to do in the listening, game, art and writing areas. In the beginning, Anna went along with whatever the group decided. She was encouraged to speak up and slowly she spoke more and more.

Her mom shared a story of Anna's visit to the doctor. The doctor kept talking over her head to her mom. Anna interrupted, "Hey! Aren't we talking about *my* ears?" At that point, the doctor apologized and included Anna in the conversation. Obviously, Anna felt empowered to speak up for herself.

Support from parents. A two-year teaching span has still other advantages. The teacher definitely gets to know her or his students and their parents. The children and parents, for their part, get to know the teacher. We have much greater support from parents whose children are in the second year. The parents are more comfortable with us. They know our philosophy of education and how it applies to teaching their children.

During the first year, we work hard to

Many children in the two-year program become close friends, even to the point of regarding the class as a family unit.

communicate with the parents. We invite them to share in the learning experiences of their children. We send them newsletters which explain various aspects of the curriculum. The result is that in the second year, we have parents participate in events for the first time. We have greater support for fund-raising, and we have more volunteers in the classroom.

As any teacher knows, it takes time to find out the interests, learning style and abilities of each student in the classroom. All aspects of classroom planning are affected by this knowledge. As a result of having the same child for the second year, the teacher already has this information in depth and can build on it. At the beginning of the second year, the children and teacher immediately get into where they left off last spring.

As far as the curriculum is concerned, we're able to spread certain themes over a longer period of time, allowing each child opportunities to build conceptual knowledge and develop attitudes and behavior for maximum learning. For example, if we study "The Family and Its Needs" in first grade, then in second grade we might study how the neighborhood contributes to the needs of the family.

Frequently, children bring up activities and experiences from the previous year that relate to present activities. We're able to help children carry over information and make connections because we know what concepts and skills our children have to build on.

Familiar figure. For many children, the end of the first grade can be very scary. They're leaving a familiar figure and are not sure until sometime in August (when a letter informs parents and children) just who their teacher will be for the following year. Our children, however, know who they're going to have. They leave the classroom on the last day of school, waving happily and yelling, "See you next September!" To make the bond just a little firmer, we correspond with each child over the summer.

Each teacher has her or his own style, and for many children, making the transition from one teaching style to another can be difficult—especially during the primary years. In addition to a new teacher, there are new routines, new expectations and often new classmates to adjust to. The two-year span, however, enables the child to establish more firmly an identity in what is often a large, institutional setting.

Visitors to our classroom on the first week of second grade are amazed at the level of intensity and focus of our second graders. Relationships have deepened and matured. Kyla remarked to her father how much

another child's reading had improved. "He can really read some things he couldn't read before," she said. She took pleasure in the other child's growth. This kind of group support contributes to problem-solving in the classroom and carries over onto the playground. There's a great deal of evaluation, in the most positive sense, that goes on in the second year.

One mother told us that for her second-year child, the class had become a family unit. When her son had been ill for several days, almost everyone in the class sent him a get-well card. Because her child was diabetic, a sense of security was necessary for him to be able to feel comfortable dealing with his diabetes in the classroom. As a result of the security he felt in the classroom, the mother said, her son had become very independent and competent.

Another child in the same class had to deal with the death of his father. The whole class shared in his sense of sadness and tried to help him through it.

"Gift of time". The most important benefit of the two-year span is the "gift of time" it gives to many children. All children do not learn in the same way or at the same pace, of course. However, that's sometimes forgotten when children do not learn at the pace expected of them. As a result, the children are penalized in some way.

In our two-year span, if a child needs more time to gain understanding, we can build in helpful activities over a longer period of time. There are many cases where a child is reading six months below grade level at the end of first grade. Because he or she is going on with the same teacher, retention is not an alternative. Then, a "miracle" happens! By giving the child the security and comfort of the same group, as well as "the gift of time," the child is able to read at grade level with true comprehension by the end of the second year.

Our approach has been so successful that it's being given serious consideration by other primary teachers in our school. In fact, two teachers are thinking about trying it out with third and fourth graders. We feel that keeping a class for two years would work at all grade levels. The children become such a strong, established group that they deal with any issues that come up in a loving, supportive way. ↓

Reprinted with permission of the publisher, Early Years, Inc., Norwalk, CT 06834.
From the Feb. 1992 issue of *Teaching / K-8.*

41

Teaching K-8, the magazine "for teachers who make things happen," pays a visit to the Pikeville Elementary School in Pikeville, Kentucky...

Ungraded Primaries Begin To Take Over In Kentucky

The Kentucky Educational Recovery Act, KERA, marks the state's solid mandate for massive systemic changes.

Cooperative Learning *becomes an accepted way of life as children in ungraded classes, working independently, amicably help each other.*

PHOTOS: JOHN FLAVELL

Last March we journeyed deep into the coal country of the Appalachian Mountain Range, to Pikeville, Kentucky. We met change.

More to the point, and the reason for our visit, we met ungraded primaries.

We also met KERA, a relatively new acronym for the Kentucky Education Reform Act, passed by the legislature on July 13, 1990. KERA has become part of the language as Kentucky's parents and educators talk about educational change and goals.

To call it "landmark legislation" is probably one of the few times that appellation has been accurately applied. Many feel the legislation's six major goals (described in a box accompanying this article), while assuredly destined to play a major role in Kentucky school reform, may also become the model for similar laws in other states.

Now, lest your eyes glaze over and you conclude this is just another dull article reporting on a politically motivated move by Kentucky's legislature, with little chance of success, have faith. This is systemic change, and it's happening now. It's the law.

We couldn't possibly go into all of the implications of KERA; it takes volumes. Rather, we want to zero in on two aspects of the legislation which can have important and immediate implications for teachers everywhere.

One aspect is School-Based Decision Making (SBDM), which has been defined in Kentucky as "...a decentralized, shared decision making process in which the local school becomes the place where most of the decisions about schooling take place."

The other aspect is the ungraded primary, and more about that in a moment.

But first: School Based Decision Making. The shared decisions start with a six-person School Council composed of three teachers (elected by the teachers), two parents (elected by the parents) and the school's principal. The Councils possess wide powers, many formerly held at state/district levels.

Which brings us to Pikeville, with a population of about 6,300. It's a small town, nestled in a sharp bend along the Levisa River at the eastern end of Kentucky. The Pikeville Indepen-

Teresa Venters, reading to a group of her 5's & 6's, comments, "It was tough at first; now I'm so excited!"

Phyliss May, who has taught kindergarten for the last 10 years, says of ungraded primaries: "This is the way to go. Look at my 5's & 6's; you can't tell the difference."

Chester Bailey has been elementary principal in Pikeville for 21 years.

Ungraded classes provide great experience for student teacher, Donna Nezbeth.

Maria Shockey, technology coordinator, says, "IBM's TLC fit like a glove."

Cooperative Learning, says Jennifer Waddell, seemed "stress-free" for her 7's & 8's.

dent School District has one K-6 elementary school (enrollment 770) and one combined junior/senior high (enrollment 610).

The elementary school's principal for the last 21 years, Chester Bailey, began using "school-based decision making" long before the process became fashionable.

"He is a master at it," one of the school's 48 teachers commented, "always encouraging our input into how the school functions. He's so reassuring, and everyone has ownership in the final decision."

Sometimes calling the process by its more well-known label, site-based management, Mr. Bailey affirms, "It's not new to this school."

What's new to the school, however, is the ungraded primary, which was introduced as a pilot program into Pikeville Elementary School during the 1991-92 school year. It involved four teachers, teaching four classes.

Two of those classes were for children ages 5 and 6, the other two were for children ages 7 and 8 (although one teacher indicated the age range in her class was closer to 7-10).

This school year, 1992-93, all 20 of the K-3 classes are ungraded. Indicating the pilot pro-

Betty McGuire, former grade three teacher, is looking forward to teaching 7 and 8 year olds this fall.

IBM's "TLC" program gets high marks from technologist Maria Shockey (see story).

Kentucky's Six Educational Goals

1. Students shall use basic communication and mathematics skills for purposes and situations they will encounter throughout their lives. The emphasis is on the use of basic skills in real-life situations.
2. Students shall apply core concepts and principles from mathematics, the sciences, the arts, the humanities, social studies and practical living studies.
3. Students will become self-sufficient individuals.
4. Students will become responsible members of a family work group or community.
5. Students will think and solve problems in a variety of situations they will encounter in life.
6. Students will connect and integrate experiences and new knowledge from all subject matter fields with what they have previously learned and build on past learning experiences to acquire new information through various media sources.

gram last year had been very successful, Mr. Bailey said, "We now have the infrastructure in place, we've learned a lot, we've done a great deal of planning; now we're ready to implement the change.

"We also have the backing of our School Board and our superintendent, John Waddell. They've always been very supportive, which I believe is why we've come so far here in Pikeville."

It is logical to assume that the past experience of Mr. Bailey and the staff in school-based decision making helped all of the staff establish the pilot program in the ungraded primary. But there was another ingredient: staff development.

"That is what the teachers always want and deserve," Mr. Bailey said. "It became particularly important," he continued, "as we worked to establish ungraded primaries.

"As you know, most teacher training at the college level is quite traditional. Ungraded primaries, on the other hand, are different in their approach. Therefore, we knew we must provide professional staff development of the highest order."

At the Pikeville Elementary School, ungraded classrooms are called "families;" beginning at the kindergarten level, a child remains in the same family unit, composed of a class for 5's and 6's, and another for 7's and 8's, until she or he moves into 4th grade. During the pilot year (last year) the families (there were two) were called The Voyagers and The Rocketeers. This year they are one family, Alpha, because they were first!

This year, as all primary levels became ungraded, there are five Families: Alpha, Challengers, Crusaders, Pathfinders and Pioneers.

The family unit gives children a sense of security — they know which teachers they'll have for the entire four years, K-4. Incidentally, the names seem to establish a team-like enthusiasm and loyalty — i.e., "Rocketeers don't quit!"

The family aspect also provides teachers with a sense of community, as well as the obvious opportunity to plan together, talk together about the needs of the individual children, get to know the children well, individualize instruction and coordinate their curriculum over a four-year span.

"Teachers are sharing together as they never shared before," said Anne Keene, Instructional Supervisor for the Pikeville Independent School District, adding, "A great deal of research and planning went into the program. It is very well designed, very organized, even though the children have more freedom.

"It is also developmentally appropriate for how young children learn. They are constructing new knowledge by discovery.

"We held several parent-awareness sessions before we launched the program. We also called the parents, explaining the program, one-on-one.

Principal Bailey, *Glenda Adkins, his daughter, grandson James, and Mr. Bailey's wife, Sylvia, a teacher for 25 years. This year both Glenda and Sylvia are teaching ungraded lower primary.*

More Information

You may contact both of the following individuals/ organizations for more information about non-graded primaries in Kentucky:

Marlene McCullough, Kentucky Department of Education, Capital Plaza Tower, 500 Mero Street, Frankfort, KY 40601, (502) 564-3064

Anne Keene, Pikeville Independent School District, P.O. Box 2010, Pikeville, KY 41502 (606) 432-8161

"There were also several non-agenda parent meetings when we said, 'We're here for issues and answers.'"

As a result of this preliminary work, parents were overwhelmingly supportive. But how about the teachers? Were they supportive?

The answer seems to be "yes," but not without some thoughtful observations.

Phyliss May, who has been teaching kindergarten for 10 of her last 20 years as a teacher, said, "Its hard on us, because it's hard to teach an old teacher new tricks. The assessment part was particularly hard for me.

"But," she added with a knowing smile, "I love it. This is the way to go. Look at my fives and sixes — you can't tell the differences in ages, and watch how the little ones learn from the older ones. The younger ones don't mind it at all.

"Yes, I love it, and before I retire this is the way I'm going to spend the last five years of my teaching career. I'm glad to see Kentucky going this way."

Almost wistfully, she added, "I'm going to hate to lose my six-year-olds at year's end," adding in the same breath, "But I have 15 children coming back to me for another year!"

And therein lies one of the obvious reasons why teachers are so supportive of ungraded primaries; the children and teachers are together for two years and, because of the "family link," closely involved with each other over a four-year span,

Technology played a role in developing the ungraded program. During the year of planning before implementation of ungraded primaries, teachers realized that IBM's program, "Teaching and Learning With Computers" (TLC) — see Teaching K-8's cover story, October 1990 — might play a role, especially in the upper primaries.

Said Maria Shockey, technology coordinator: "Long before ungraded primaries, we had started with IBM's Writing To Read and were looking for the next step. So, we pulled in TLC. It worked so beautifully in the classroom; it gave the teachers a little more security, and gives the children a wonderful opportunity to work independently.

"Thus, as we looked at the ungraded primary, we realized TLC fit like a glove. It's an asset because it provides us with so many resources at so many different levels. Now we're using technology the way it should be used, the way it's meant to be used, in an integrated fashion.

"It's another tool available to us. Our computers are used all day long."

Dema Litafik, teaching the 7's and 8's, was asked how well she was coping with the ungraded class. Her thoughtful answer, after a pregnant pause, was "Well, quite well. At first it was stressful, and it took a lot of planning.

"But there is such an observable difference, especially with the 7's. I have them doing long division for the first time in my life, and that includes almost 20 years as a teacher."

Teresa Venters echoed comments of the other teachers. During her first year with an ungraded class of 5's and 6's, she said, "I love the ungraded classroom. It was tough at first, because I didn't know what I was doing.

"Now I'm so excited!"

Every two weeks Ms. Venters sends home a progress report on each child, indicating "Steady progress" or "Improvement needed." The one-page report covers everything from reading development, mathematical development, science, social studies, writing and language development, to evaluations of the child's classroom habits — "listens to and follows directions," "uses time productively," "respects the feelings and rights of others."

Jennifer Waddell, who had 7's and 8's in last year's pilot program, commented that the children seemed to be doing more learning cooperatively.

"They'll get one partner, or two partners, and really work well together. The children don't even know they're learning. I feel very good about the ungraded primary.

"It's stress-free, there is a lot of movement, a lot of interaction going on. I'm glad I had the opportunity to take the first step."

Elsewhere on these pages we have provided addresses so that you, or your school, may obtain additional information. ↓

ALLEN RAYMOND

Warm up to Cooperative Learning

PHASE ONE

BUILDING TEAM SPIRIT

Here are some shared exercises to try during the first few weeks of school:

In the Bag

Tape a paper bag to the edge of a table. Place a paper cup on the table and let small groups of kids work together to blow the cup into the bag. Although it sounds easy, this activity really takes effort and cooperation on the part of all members of the group. It's a great metaphor for the types of skills students will need to use later in the year.

Getting Connected

Pass out 3-by-5-inch strips of oaktag. Direct children to write their names and illustrate with symbols of their interests and hobbies on one side of their strips. Have the members of each small group link their strips into loop chains with tape or staples, making sure the decorated sides are on the outside. Then have the groups link their chains. Display the chain around the room or on a bulletin board labeled "We're All Connected."

Or use the chain as a prop for an introductory activity. For instance, have kids stand in a circle holding the chain. Pick a student to introduce him- or herself and the person immediately to his or her right, adding a bit of information about that person. For instance, "My name is Karen and this is Nick, who loves to play soccer." Continue going around the circle. Be sure to include yourself in the chain!

Go Fish

This exercise will graphically demonstrate how teaming up to arrive at a shared goal is more beneficial than competing *against* one another.

You'll need a couple of bags of goldfish crackers. Divide the class into groups of three. One student in each group is the monitor. The other two

face each other, right elbows on desk, right hands clasped in the posture of an arm wrestle (in fact, this is an arm wrestle, but don't tell kids that). Tell students the rules: For two minutes, every time the back of your partner's hand touches the desk, the monitor will give you a goldfish.

Giving no further directions, time the paired students for two minutes. Frequently, you will see the time elapse with just one or two wins, but a wise pair will figure out that if they alternate back and forth, they'll *both* win several crackers. Discuss with students other times when cooperation might be mutually beneficial.

Group Journals

Chances are, you already have students keeping personal journals. You can also use journals to help them reflect upon their experiences working in groups.

Have each group make a journal by stapling pieces of lined paper together.

THE ELEMENTS OF COOPERATION

I make sure that every cooperative lesson I plan includes these collaboration elements:
• plenty of face-to-face interaction between group members;
• lots of practice using social skills, such as sharing, encouraging, and taking turns;
• positive interdependence (The lesson should require the cooperation of all group members. If it's something students can better do alone, then it probably isn't worth doing as a group.);
• opportunities for teacher observation and reflection on the process as it happens; and
• opportunities for group processing and celebration (Children should have time to discuss what happens in their groups and any problems they encounter).

MICHELLE STANSBURY
Littleton, Colorado

After finishing a cooperative activity, each child in the group should write a sentence reflecting on the team experience—noting accomplishments and analyzing setbacks. Tell them that instead of using specific names, they should try to focus on terms like *I*, *We*, and *the group* (this cuts down on the temptation to use the journals as a vehicle for tattling and keeps kids focused on their individual role in the group effort). Once each child has recorded his or her thoughts, everyone in the group should read the entire entry. You may want to collect journals occasionally, to see how groups are progressing.

Kindergarten Huddle Groups

This is an especially good activity to use with kindergartners. Just remember when forming groups that children of this age work better in threes (in groups of four, they tend to pair off instead of working as a team). I call these teams *huddle groups*.

Before starting the activity, ask kids to think of some words people can use to encourage one another, such as, *It's okay* or *try again!* Then let each group choose a puzzle to work on together. After groups have completed their puzzles, come together as a class to discuss some of the feelings they had while working together and what problems they encountered. Brainstorm solutions to these problems together. You might want to write some of the solutions on chart paper for students to refer to in the future.

APPRECIATING DIFFERENCES

Children need to understand how individual differences can enrich group efforts. Use these activities to help promote that understanding.

The Peanut Scramble

Bring in a bag of unshelled peanuts (apples work, too). Give each child one

When they play "Go Fish," students learn how compromise can benefit everyone.

peanut to study closely for several minutes. Then have students pile their peanuts on a table and close their eyes while you mix them up. After a few minutes, have them take turns looking through the pile to find their original peanut. Amazingly, students almost always find the right one! Remind kids that although these objects could be classified as peanuts, each has its own unique characteristics, just as all humans have unique qualities.

It's All in a Name Tag
On the first day of school, have kids make special name tags on which they list not only their names, but where they were born, two favorite activities, favorite places to visit, and two adjectives describing themselves. Next ask kids to jot the names of their classmates on a pad with two columns labeled Similar and Different. Let them spend 10 minutes mingling with their classmates, writing down one similarity and one difference between themselves and each person they meet. After they've collected as much data as time allows, bring the class together to discuss some of these similarities and differences.

PHASE TWO

READY FOR THE REAL THING
Once kids are ready to try more substantial cooperative projects, you'll want to use these strategies to make sure plans go smoothly.

A Kids-Eye View
Do a sociogram of the class to find out how kids view each other from a social perspective. By telling you who the class leaders and loners are, this activity helps enormously when you start to set up cooperative groups.

To do a sociogram, give students each a sheet of lined paper and ask them to fold them in half lengthwise. Have kids list three people in the left-hand column who they think would make good work partners. On the right-hand side, ask them to write reasons for each choice. Tell kids that the lists will be completely confidential and they are not to disclose what they wrote to anyone else.

By repeating the activity throughout the year, you not only have information for forming new groups, but can find out how the isolates are faring and how the dynamics of the class are changing.

Role Cards
When beginning to work in cooperative groups, children must learn how to fairly divide roles and tasks. By teaching

them how to make and use role cards you can save valuable time and avoid potential conflicts later on.

You can use role cards repeatedly throughout the year for some regular activities; make up others as children take on new projects. For instance, during writer's workshop, children can use cards labeled Encourager, Reader, Questioner, and Editor for group sharing. When you make up the cards, write a few sentences outlining each role and then laminate them. Teach kids how to shuffle, deal the cards, and pass them to the right after the first person has shared and everyone's done his or her part. This way, everyone gets a chance to play different roles.

For other, less frequent projects, keep plenty of blank oaktag cards available so children can make up their own role cards. When they're working in groups, allow them to brainstorm the roles necessary to carry out a project and jot each of these on a card. They can use the shuffle-and-pass method they've learned in writer's workshop to fairly distribute the roles. After some practice, kids will automatically use this strategy.

DEALING WITH GROUP CONFLICT
In the heat of an argument, tempers often flare before logical problem solving can occur. Have students use the following steps to analyze a conflict so they can learn from it. With regular practice, students will use the strategies automatically. Walk younger students through the method orally; older ones can work with partners or write down their reactions on paper individually. The steps are:
• This is what happened.
• This is what I did.
• Here are five other ways I could have responded.
• This is what I might try next time.

COOPERATIVE ACTIVITY RESOURCES
Cooperative Learning: Where Heart Meets Mind by Barrie Bennett, Carol Rolheiser-Bennett, and Laurie Stevahn (Interactive Resource Books, 1991). More than 350 pages of activities and resources for the cooperative classroom. $25. Call Jennifer Loates at (416) 619-0161 for information.

Building a Caring, Cooperative Classroom by Jim Bellanca (Skylight Publishing, 1991). Jam-packed with fun activities to build team spirit. $15.95. To order, call (800) 348-4474.

Our Cooperactive Classroom by David Johnson, Roger Johnson, Judy Bartlett, and Linda Johnson (Interaction Book Co., 1988). Reproducible thinking skill activities for children to do in groups.

$10 plus shipping & handling. Call (612) 831-9500.
Tribes: A Process for Social Development and Cooperative Learning by Jeanne Gibbs (Center Source Publishing, 1987). This book includes ways to teach kids to listen, exercises for greater self-awareness, and techniques for creating a unified class. $19.95 + $2.25 shipping and handling. Call (707) 577-8233 to order.

Contributors to this article include: Carol Pelletier, Middleboro, Massachusetts; Susan Whalen, Greenwich, Connecticut; Michelle Stansbury, Littleton, Colorado; Judy Lee Dunn, Cardiff, California; Becky Brandl, Sioux City, Iowa; and Jeannette Fields, Cherokee, Iowa.

PHASE THREE

COOPERATION ALL YEAR LONG

Here are some simple ways to add a cooperative flavor to basic subject areas.

Math

Make memorizing multiplication tables a team effort with this idea:

Let kids average the scores of group members whenever they take a timed test. (Students as young as third grade can learn how to do this fairly easily.) Challenge groups to beat their team score each day (or however frequently they take tests). Encourage students to celebrate their groups' improvement even if it's only by a few points. This takes the pressure off one student to compete against the others.

Spelling

Every Monday, give kids a basic spelling-list pretest. Let them replace every word they already know how to spell with a challenging word from a special bonus list you've posted on the board. This usually results in a different spelling list for each student. Have them study their lists in pairs throughout the week and test each other on Friday. (You should score them.) Then, as a class, brainstorm strategies students learned from their partners for remembering tricky words. Keep a running list of strategies on chart paper.

Geography/Social Studies

• Before a unit of study involving many geographical locations, make a list of countries (or other geographical features) you'd like kids to locate on a map. Remember that you can use geographical locations related to historical people (for instance, birthplaces) and events as well.

On individual index cards, write the name of the country and put a colored dot in the top right corner, using only as many colors of dots as you have groups, and only as many dots as members in each group. Distribute cards and have kids use a textbook map or atlas to locate their country, city, or state.

Have kids form groups based on their colors and let them point out the locations of their areas to the rest of the group. Then randomly call on members of each group to show where various places are located.

• Use this cooperative activity to help kids review what they've learned after a unit of study:

On the chalkboard, write one concept or historical figure students have studied, such as Thomas Jefferson. Have groups write the topic vertically down the page. Then ask them to use textbooks and notes to find a key word or phrase that starts with each letter of the topic (they're not allowed to use articles like *the* to start their phrases).

Spelling is one subject area in which kids can cooperate on a regular basis.

Let each group write their completed acrostic on the chalkboard. Encourage individual students to make their own acrostics, adapting the best key words from other groups, if necessary. These are great study helps.

Reading

Reading is a natural for cooperative learning.

• Even kindergartners will enjoy getting in groups to share favorite parts of the books they're reading. Ask them to take only two or three minutes per person, so the entire process takes a total of about 10 minutes. Students love talking about their books, and this activity motivates them to try titles they might not otherwise have read.

• Get kids in the habit of shared-paired reading. It's an excellent way to improve comprehension.

First ask kids to brainstorm ways two people can read aloud to each other; for instance, by taking turns reading sentences, paragraphs, pages, and chapters. Tell students that they should stop after every chapter to discuss or ask questions about the story or to look up any unknown words. Next, take some time to model comprehension strategies. Pick a volunteer to read a few pages with you in front of the class. When you stop to discuss the book, focus on the actions of a particular character, a feeling you had while reading a scene, or a reflective response like: I wonder if James will run away from his mean aunts. You may have to model these strategies on several occasions and should monitor pairs closely at first to get them really interacting with the story (and each other). After a while, they'll use the strategies automatically.

Science

Use this activity before kids do their first experiment or project in a group. It's a great way to teach about the importance of effective verbal communication.

Divide the class into groups of three. Give each group 25 gumdrops and 50 toothpicks. Tell students that they will have three minutes to plan a device to improve the environment. When time is up, they will get two minutes to construct the device, *without talking*.

During the construction phase, expect to see signs of frustration—frantic hand signals, exasperated shaking of heads, even angry glares. When time is up, ask a spokesperson from each group to explain the creation. Many times, students will disagree about the purpose and function of their inventions. At the end of the explanations, ask:
• Was this task difficult? Why?
• What were people feeling as they tried to work?
• What would have made your jobs easier?
• Did your invention turn out as your group planned it?

Encourage children to think about what would have happened if they had been able to talk to one another during the task. ∎

From *Instructor Magazine*, Sept. 1992. © 1992 by Scholastic, Inc. Reprinted by permission of Scholastic, Inc.

COOPERATIVE LEARNING

"It is not enough to simply tell students to work together. They must have a reason to take one another's achievement seriously."

Robert Slavin

Robert Slavin: Cooperation in the Content Areas

Recent research conducted by Robert Slavin and his colleagues at Johns Hopkins University has focused on cooperative learning methods designed for specific subject areas at specific grade levels.

One such comprehensive cooperative learning model, called *Team Assisted Individualization* (TAI), was developed for use with mathematics in grades 3 through 6 and combines cooperative learning with individualized instruction. TAI allows each student to progress at his or her own rate and to work on the skills he or she needs most. At the same time, however, every student is part of a team. Students earn points for their teams as they progress through individualized learning modules.

Teammates help each other with problems and check each other's work against answer sheets. Ultimately, students take final unit tests without teammate help. Student monitors score the tests.

While students take responsibility for managing the flow of materials and checking each other's work, the teacher is free to spend class time providing lessons for small groups of students drawn from the different teams.

Slavin and his colleagues have also developed a comprehensive program for teaching reading and writing in the upper elementary grades, called *Cooperative Integrated Reading and Composition* (CIRC). According to Slavin, research supports the notion that complex, comprehensive approaches that combine cooperative learning with other instructional elements can increase achievement and that cooperative learning programs can be used as the primary instructional method in certain content areas—not just as add-on strategies for the teacher.

For more information on TAI and CIRC, contact Robert Slavin, Director, the Elementary School Program, Center for Research on Elementary and Middle Schools, The Johns Hopkins University, 3505 N. Charles St., Baltimore, MD 21218.

What Research Says

Cooperative learning works, and it's here to stay!

After nearly two decades of research and dozens of studies contrasting the achievement outcomes of cooperative learning and traditional methods, America's leading researchers on cooperative learning agree that cooperative methods can—and usually do—have a positive effect on student achievement. However, most researchers also agree that achievement depends on certain essential features, such as positive interdependence (students believe they are responsible both for their own learning and for the learning of the other group members) and individual accountability (each student demonstrates mastery of the assigned work).

Here, we offer brief snapshots of what three leading researchers have to say about some of the bigger issues in cooperative learning.

The Johnsons: Grading

According to David W. Johnson and Roger T. Johnson, grades and other rewards can be effective tools in ensuring positive interdependence. Here are just some of the techniques the Johnsons recommend for grading in cooperative situations:

1. *Individual score plus group bonus points.* Group members study together and ensure that all have mastered the assigned material. Each then takes a test individually and is awarded a score. If all group members achieve over a preset criterion of excellence, each receives a bonus.

2. *Individual score plus bonus points based on lowest score.* The group members prepare each other to take an exam. Members then receive bonus points on the basis of the lowest individual score in their group. This procedure emphasizes encouraging, supporting, and assisting the low achievers in the group.

3. *Group score on a single product.* The group's product (essay, presentation, report, exam, or worksheet) is evaluated and all group members receive the awarded score. When using this method with worksheets, sets of problems, and so on, group members should reach consensus on each question and be able to explain it to others.

4. *Randomly select one member's paper to score.* Group members all complete the work individually and then check each other's papers to certify that they are perfectly correct. The teacher then picks one paper at random, grades it, and all group mem-

"It is important that students perceive the distribution of grades and other rewards as fair, otherwise they may become unmotivated and withdraw psychologically or physically."
David and Roger Johnson

bers receive that score.

5. *Average of academic scores plus collaborative skills performance score.* Group members work together to master the assigned material. They take an examination individually and their scores are averaged. At the same time, the teacher observes their work and records frequency of performance of specified collaborative skills. The group receives a collaborative skills performance score, and the teacher adds it to their academic average to determine their overall mark.

For more information on grading in the cooperative classroom, contact David and Roger Johnson at the Cooperative Learning Center, University of Minnesota, 202 Pattee Hall, 150 Pillsbury Dr. SE, Minneapolis, MN 55455.

Spencer Kagan: Structuring Social Interaction

Kagan's structural approach to cooperative learning is based on the way social interaction is organized in a classroom. Structures usually involve a series of steps, with proscribed behavior at each step. There are a number of different structures, as well as variations among them, because the structures have different functions. Unlike activities, structures can be used repeatedly with almost any sub-

"Structures are like tools in a tool box. Teachers use the tools to design exciting lessons. Part of the art of teaching is choosing the appropriate structures for the goals at hand. "
Spencer Kagan

ject matter, in a wide range of grade levels, and at many different points in a lesson plan. But every structure incorporates the most important principles of cooperative learning: positive interdependence, individual accountability, and simultaneous interaction.

SAMPLE STRUCTURES
Following are just a few examples of the many structures available to teachers who use this approach.

Structure: Round-robin
How It Works: Each student, in turn, shares something with his or her teammates.
Academic Function: Expressing ideas and opinions; creating stories
Social Function: Equal participation; getting acquainted with teammates

Structure: Partners
How It Works: Students work in pairs to create or master content. They consult with partners from other teams. They then share their products or understanding with the other pair in their team.
Academic Function: Mastery and presentation of new material, concept development
Social Function: Presentation and communication skills

Structure: Think-Pair-Share
How It Works: Students think to themselves on a topic provided by the teacher; they pair up and discuss it. They then share their thoughts with the class.
Academic Function: Generating and revising hypotheses, inductive reasoning, deductive reasoning, application.
Social Function: Participation, involvement.

ALL TOGETHER NOW
A cooperative learning teacher who is fluent in many structures can competently move in and out of them as needed to reach certain learning objectives. According to Kagan, the teacher's ability to use a range of structures increases the range of learning experiences for students and results in lessons that are richer in the academic, cognitive, and social domains.

For more information on the structural approach to cooperative learning, write Spencer Kagan, Director, Resources for Teachers, 27134 Paseo Espada, #202, San Juan Capistrano, CA 92675. ∎

Teacher Education and Special Education, 1988, 11(4), 144-154

INCLUSIVE EDUCATION

Enhancing Success In Heterogeneous Classrooms And Schools

The Powers Of Partnership

RICHARD A. VILLA

JACQUELINE S. THOUSAND

Richard Villa is the director of pupil personnel services for the Winooski School District in Winooski, Vermont. Jacqueline Thousand is an assistant professor at the Center for Development Disabilities of the University of Vermont in Burlington.

ABSTRACT

The purpose of this article is to identify and describe practices associated with successful schooling o. students in heterogeneous groupings. Included are descriptions of outcomes-based instructiona. models; instructional models using peer power; effective use of heterogeneous and multi-aged groupings; strategies for redefining the school organizational structure; and training content that creates common conceptual frameworks, knowledge, and language among local school staff.

The purpose of this article is to identify and describe those practices that appear to be associated with successful schooling of students in heterogeneous groupings. Before discussing these practices, it is important to clarify what we view as fundamental characteristics of successful heterogeneous public schools, schools in which all students are educated together.

First, these schools are comprehensive. They are comprehensive in that they actualize the "zero reject" principle (Lilly, 1971) by welcoming and educating *all* students in their own home schools; they accommodate the unique variations in students' educational needs through responsive and fluid instructional options rather than pigeonholing students into one of several standing, standard programs (Skrtic, 1987). They are comprehensive in that they expand the body of decision makers concerned with individual student, instructional, and organizational issues to include not just a small, select group of administrators and instructional personnel, but members of the broader school and general community (e.g., parents, students, paraprofessionals, school nurses, guidance counselors, lunch room staff, community members, generic human service agency personnel, community employers). They are also comprehensive in that they look beyond academic achievement as the major or sole criterion of school success and promote the mastery of social and life skills requisite to success in work, recreational, and community life beyond high school.

The second characteristic of successful heterogeneous schools is the effort put forth to ensure that school personnel are prepared to implement effective instructional practices. Exemplary educational practices from both general and special education are merged in order to take advantage of the knowledge base and demonstrated benefits of both sets of practices.

51

This article is structured to provide brief descriptions of educational practices that seem to promote student success in heterogeneous schools. These practices are derived from the results of research and model demonstration efforts as well as the authors' first-hand experiences in Vermont schools that have made the commitment to educating *all* of their students in heterogeneous groupings. First, outcomes-based instructional models are reviewed. Next, strategies for the effective use of *peer power* and homogeneous and multi-age groupings are examined. A discussion of strategies for redefining professional roles and creating opportunities for collaborative teaming follows. The article closes with a presentation of training topics that promote heterogeneous grouping of students and create common conceptual frameworks among school personnel.

INSTRUCTIONAL PRACTICES

Outcomes-Based Instructional Models

In a recent summary of research on approaches for adapting curriculum and instruction to accommodate individual student differences in regular classrooms, Glatthorn (1987) identified outcomes-based instructional models, cooperative group learning models, and computer-assisted instruction as three specific approaches that have strong support of quality research. Two of these approaches, outcomes-based instructional models and cooperative learning models, are discussed in this article. The components of outcomes-based instructional models will be described first.

Common to most outcomes-based models is a sequence of six teacher behaviors (Block & Anderson, 1975; Brookover et al. 1982; Vicker, 1988). First, teachers use diagnostic procedures to determine whether students have the prerequisites for the lesson or unit. Additional instruction on the prerequisites is offered to students who need it. Second, teachers create an atmosphere of anticipation or readiness to learn by giving the students a brief description of what they will learn, why they are learning it, and what they will be able to do with the new learning. Next, teachers provide "best shot" instruction; they select and implement the instructional strategies they judge to have the best chance of enabling all students to attain the lesson's objectives. Following best shot instruction, teachers structure opportunities for guided practice in which each student's progress is monitored. The objective here is to assure that students have the skills and pro-

cedural knowledge to successfully engage in independent practice.

The fifth teacher behavior involves the administration of a formative assessment or test to determine whether students have mastered the lesson's or unit's objectives. Students who need additional instruction receive it, while those who have mastered the objectives go on to enrichment activities. The sixth and final teacher behavior involves the summative assessment of student's mastery of a cumulative set of objectives from a number of lessons or units.

Because outcomes-based instructional models have been effective in responding to individual student differences within regular education, they need to be examined and considered for use by school personnel who want to become truly heterogeneous in their educational practices. The special education administrator of an outcomes-based school district in Vermont that has had success educating all of its students in regular education settings has pointed out how outcomes-based models can promote heterogeneous schooling:

> An underlying assumption or philosophical orientation of outcomes-driven schools is that all children can learn that which we think is important for them to learn, given time and the appropriate resources. My school district embraces this philosophy, and it has shaped our practices. It challenged us to look at segregated services for students eligible for special education, and we found them totally unacceptable. (Schattman, 1988)

Instructional Practices
Utilizing Peer Power

A major resource that can facilitate the education of all learners within regular education is "peer power." Schools that effectively use peer resources do so in a variety of ways — through peer tutor and peer buddy systems, cooperative learning models, and the inclusion of peers on the individualized educational planning teams of students with identified handicaps.

Peer Tutor Systems   Same-age and cross-age peer-tutoring systems are two forms of peer power upon which heterogeneous schools capitalize. In a review of the literature regarding peer tutoring, Pierce, Stahlbrand, and Armstrong (1984) have cited benefits of peer tutoring to tutees, tutors, and instructional staff. What follows is a discussion of some of these benefits.

Benefits to Tutees.   Clearly, students who receive tutoring receive increased individualized instructional attention as a consequence of the one-to-one teaching arrangement with a peer; and research has consistently demonstrated that students make significant academic gains as a result of tutorial sessions with same-age or cross-age peers. In addition, there is the opportunity for a positive personal relationship to develop between the tutor and the tutee; and the tutor may become a positive role model, demonstrating interest in learning and desirable interpersonal skills. Finally, success experienced by the tutee in the tutorial situation promotes enhanced feelings of self-esteem (Pierce et al., 1984).

Good and Brophy (1984) have suggested that peers trained as tutors may be more effective than adults in teaching particular content, such as mathematical concepts (Cohen & Stover, 1981). They further speculate that their superior effectiveness lies in their tendency to be more directive than adults; their familiarity with the material and their resultant understanding of the tutee's potential frustration with the material; and their use of more meaningful and age-appropriate vocabulary and examples.

Benefits to Tutors. There is an old adage, "If you can teach it, you know it." For the tutor, the act of teaching and the preparation required to effectively teach a concept or skill can lead to a higher level of reasoning and a more in-depth understanding of the material being taught (Johnson, Johnson, Holubec, & Roy, 1984). Like the tutee, the tutor's self-esteem may be enhanced, in this case by assuming the high status role of teacher (Gartner, Kohler, & Riessman, 1971). The social skills of the tutor also may be increased as a direct result of the modeling, coaching, and role playing of effective communication skills (e.g., giving praise, giving constructive criticism) that they are expected to use in tutorial sessions (Pierce et al., 1984).

Benefits to Teachers. Peer-tutoring partnerships are a cost-effective way for teachers to increase the amount of individualized instructional attention available to their students (Armstrong, Stahlbrand, Conlon, & Pierson, 1979). By using same-age and cross-age tutors, teachers can add instructional resources to the classroom without adding additional adult personnel.

Arranging Peer-tutoring Systems. Peer-tutoring systems can be established within a single classroom or across an entire school. Systems that have been demonstrated to be effective have well-developed strategies for recruiting, training, supervising, and evaluating the effectiveness of the peer tutors (Cooke, Heron, & Heward, 1983; Good & Brophy, 1984; Pierce et al., 1984). Frequently the tutor and supervising teacher formulate and sign a contract that spells out in detail the performance expectations of the tutor and the supervisor. At the high school level, courses may be taught and credit given for peer-tutoring service.

Peer Support Networks and Peer Buddies Historically, some students, particularly students with disabilities, have been excluded from certain aspects of school life (e.g., school clubs and other cocurricular activities, school dances, attendance at athletic events). Peer support groups or networks have been established in some schools and have proven to be effective in enabling these students to participate more fully in the life of their schools.

The purpose of a peer support network is to enrich another student's school life. A student who has helped organize a peer support network describes the goal of peer support as follows:

> Peer support is a bunch of kids working together to break down the barriers that society has built into the public's idea of what the norm is. Teachers and peers need to be trained; they need to understand that the goal of peer support is not competitive academics. The goal is to belong, to meet new people, to learn to break down the barriers. Budelmann, Farrel, Kovach, & Paige, 1987)

Peer support networks are composed of students who have volunteered, been recommended by teachers or counselors, or been recruited by other students in the network to serve as "peer buddies." Students and school personnel have stressed the importance of trying to include as peer buddies those students who are active in school activities or who are perceived as having high social status among their peers. Peer support networks are effective because the peer buddies *are* active in school activities and have a social network and, therefore, *can* facilitate the introduction, inclusion, and active involvement of students who typically might not be invited or volunteer to participate in a nonacademic school function.

Peer buddies are different from peer tutors in that their involvement is primarily nonacademic. The diversity of support peer buddies can provide other students is limitless. For example, a peer buddy might assist a student with physical disabilities to use and get items from his or her locker or "hang out" in the halls with a student before or after classes. A peer buddy might accompany a student to a ballgame after school or speak to other students, teachers, or parents about the unique physical, learning, or social challenges that he or she sees their friend facing and meeting on a daily basis.

The benefits of peer-tutoring programs cited above also apply to peer support systems. Peer buddies assist the person with whom they are paired and the larger school community to acquire skills to more effectively communicate and interact socially with one another. In the words of a speech and language pathologist actively involved in organizing a peer support system in her school,

> The most crucial contexts in which to learn social skills are the places where all students learn these skills — on the athletic field, in the hallways, in the lunch room, and in the classroom. These are the places where social communication happens for teenagers; these are the places where the most appropriate peer models are. (Harris, 1987)

Some school systems explicitly teach students the skills required to establish a social support system or a network of friends. In structured class settings, students are taught how to seek, develop, and maintain friendships through the use of direct instruction, modeling, and role play situations. They rehearse skills such as initiating a conversation, reciprocating in a conversational exchange, making nonverbal behavior consistent with verbal behavior, interpreting others' body language, and various problem-solving strategies. Peer buddies are included in this instruction, receiving feedback from teachers on their own performance, and providing models and specific feedback for the students with whom they are involved.

Peer support networks have helped to make heterogeneous schools places where students' learning is expanded to include an understanding of one another's lives. Two high school seniors who have served as a peer buddies for several years have nicely summarized this notion, stating:

> I learn from my new friends too. I have learned that all high school students have the same needs — friends, social life, and the opportunity to get involved. No high school student should be limited or isolated from these needs. We all feel the same feelings. (Budelmann et al., 1987)

Cooperative Learning Models As previously noted, cooperative learning models have been cited as one of three approaches with strong support of quality research for adapting curriculum and instruction to accommodate individual student differences in regular classrooms (Glatthorn, 1987). Several groups of researchers and practitioners (Aronson, Blaney, Stephan, Sikes, & Snapp, 1978; Johnson & Johnson, 1987b; Slavin, 1983; Sharan & Sharan, 1976) have studied and implemented cooperative group procedures in kindergarten through high school classrooms.

Benefits of Cooperative Learning Models. The benefits of the use of cooperative learning groups have been well documented. Cooperative learning experiences with heterogeneous groups of learners tend to promote higher achievement than competitive or individually structured learning experiences (Johnson & Johnson, 1987c; Johnson, Maruyama, Johnson, Nelson, & Skon, 1981). This has been found to be true across grade levels, subject areas, and different types of learning tasks (e.g., concept attainment, retention, verbal problem solving, motor performance). Furthermore, students who participate in cooperative learning experiences, compared with competitive and individualistic ones, like their teachers and the subject area better (Johnson & Johnson, 1987c).

Cooperative learning experiences, compared with competitive and individualistic ones, also promote higher levels of self-esteem as well as positive relationships, acceptance, support, trust, and liking among students who are different in ethnic membership, gender, social class, and the need for special educational services (Johnson & Johnson, 1987c; Johnson, Johnson, & Maruyama, 1983).

The Role of the Teacher in Cooperative Learning Models. When implementing cooperative learning, the teacher becomes more a facilitator of learning or a manager of the learning environment than a presenter of information (Glasser, 1986). As a facilitator or manager, the teacher is responsible for five major sets of strategies (Johnson et al., 1984):

> 1. Clearly specifying the (academic and collaborative) objectives for the lesson
> 2. Making decisions about placing students in learning groups before the lesson is taught
> 3. Clearly explaining the task, goal structure (positive goal interdependence), and learning activity to the students
> 4. Monitoring the effectiveness of the cooperative learning groups and intervening to provide task assistance (such as answering questions and teaching task skills) or to increase students' interpersonal and group skills
> 5. Evaluating students' achievement and helping students discuss how well they collaborated with each other. (p. 26)

Responding to Individual Differences Through Cooperative Learning. One question often asked by teachers new to cooperative learning is "How do I integrate a low-achieving student or a student with a handicap into heterogeneous cooperative learning groups?'' Several strategies have proven to be effective (Johnson & Johnson, 1987b). One strategy is to assign the student a specific role that promotes participation and minimizes anxiety about collaborating with more capable students. Examples of appropriate roles are praising members for participation, summarizing group answers, and checking that all members can explain the group's answer. A second strategy is to pretrain these students in select collaborative skills so they have unique expertise to bring to the group.

A third set of strategies involves adapting lesson requirements for individual students. This can be done in a number of ways. Different success criteria can be used for each group member; the amount of material each group member is expected to learn can be adjusted; or group members can study and coach one another on different problems, lists, reading materials, words, and so forth. If a test is given, the entire group might receive bonus points based upon the extent to which members exceed their individualized success criteria.

Peer Membership on Individualized Educational Planning Teams Peers also have proven to be invaluable members of individual educational planning teams for students with identified handicapping conditions. They are particularly helpful in identifying appropriate social integration goals to be included on a student's IEP. A special education administrator who now routinely includes peers in IEP development has stated:

> Although we have emphasized socialization and inclusion for years, it never really took off until we turned to the students and asked for their help. We previously were leaving out of the planning process the majority of the schools' population. (DiFerdinando, 1987)

Students also have been enlisted to assist in planning for the transition of students with handicaps from more segregated to regular education settings. Recently, the entire student body of a small junior high school met with school staff in small groups to plan the transition of a student with multiple handicaps from a segregated residential facility to their seventh grade. The advice they gave was enlightening, ranging from suggestions for an augmentative communication device that they felt would best help the new student communicate his needs to what kind of notebook he should have to "fit in" (Scagliotti, 1987).

Effective Use of Homogeneous and Multi-Age Groupings

Homogeneous grouping, also known as ability grouping, clusters students of similar "ability." Although this practice is one of the most controversial issues in education, its use is widespread in American schools. Elementary school teachers frequently form homogeneous reading and math groups within their classrooms based upon student performance, even though research "evidence on the effects of regrouping within grade levels for reading and mathematics is unclear, and there is no methodologically adequate evidence concerning the use of reading groups" (Slavin, 1987, p. 321). Special education "pull-out" services, where students leave their classroom for separate instruction, is another example of ability grouping, the efficacy of which is currently in question (Madden & Slavin, 1983; Reynolds, Wang, & Walberg, 1987; Stainback & Stainback, 1984, 1985). At the secondary level, between-class ability grouping (e.g., tracking, streaming) continues to be practiced despite nearly 60 years of research and widespread agreement that this practice does little to foster student achievement (Kulik & Kulik, 1982; Slavin, 1987; Wilson & Schmits, 1978) and "strongly influences students' future education and career options" (Brookover et al., 1982, p. 110).

Given that American schools and school teachers seem to be inclined to group student homogeneously in spite of evidence questioning the practice, the question becomes, "Is there a place for homogeneous grouping in schools?" In his recent review of the effects of ability grouping on the achievement of elementary school students, Slavin (1987) answered this question with a *qualified* yes.

Based upon his careful review of the research, Slavin recommended that teachers use *only* those grouping methods that have been demonstrated to be effective. He particularly cautioned educators to avoid class assignment by ability group, as it fails to facilitate student achievement and "seems to have the greatest potential for negative social effects in that it entirely separates students into different streams" (Slavin, 1987, p. 321). The two homogeneous grouping that have been found to be effective, at least at the elementary level, are within class ability grouping for upper-elementary mathematics and the Joplin Plan in reading. (See Provus, 1960, for a description of the effective use of regrouping in mathematics.)

In the Joplin Plan (Floyd, 1954) students are regrouped only for reading instruction. They are regrouped across grade levels and age rather than within grade levels in order to create homogeneous

55

reading groups. Like multi-aged nongraded classrooms, the Joplin plan breaks with the American school tradition of assigning students to instructional groups or classes exclusively according to age. Many Joplin-like plans actually combine multi-aged nongraded classroom groupings with regrouping for reading. In Joplin-like plans students and teachers are randomly assigned to heterogeneous multi-aged nongraded classes. Homogeneous reading groups are created by regrouping students from the various ungraded classes.

A major advantage of the Joplin Plan and Joplin-like plans over traditional within-class ability groupings is the potential for increasing the amount of direct instruction each student receives. For example, in a traditional class with three reading groups and 45 minutes of daily reading instruction, each group receives only 15 minutes of instruction from the teacher. With the Joplin Plan, all students have teacher contact for the full 45-minute period.

In theory, teachers group students according to performance or ability in order to more closely match the pace and content of their instruction with the learning characteristics of different students. However, in practice, ability grouping frequently is misused or abused. Noting this, Slavin wisely cautioned that research-based ability grouping plans be used *only* when the following conditions can be met (Slavin, 1987):

1. The grouping plan measurably reduces student heterogeneity *in the specific skill being taught;*
2. The plan is flexible enough to allow teachers to respond to misassignments and changes in student performance level after initial placement; and
3. Teachers actually vary their pace and level of instruction to correspond to students' levels of readiness and learning rates. (p. 322)

Slavin has also recommended that students be regrouped for no more than two subject areas, thus allowing them to spend the majority of their school day in heterogeneous groupings. This increases the likelihood that low-achieving students or students with handicaps will have a heterogeneous student group as their primary reference, avoiding the potential detrimental psychological effects of being associated with a low ability track or a special class (Rosenbaum, 1980; Schafer & Olexan, 1971).

Research comparing the effects of various ability groupings and alternatives to ability groupings has yet to be conducted. Therefore, at present, models that do have a solid research base, such as cooperative learning models and outcomes-based instructional models, seem to have the greatest potential for accommodating student heterogeneity (Glatthorn, 1987; Slavin, 1987).

REDEFINING PROFESSIONAL RELATIONSHIPS

"Achievement of the goals of an organization is highly related to the structure of the organization" (Brookover et al., 1982, p. 78). Given that schools are organizations and that their goal is to educate all learners in heterogeneous environments, their organizational structure must promote or, at the very least allow for, heterogeneity.

A number of characteristics of the organizational structure of the traditional American school stand in the way of heterogeneous schooling: stratification of students through pull-out special education service delivery models, ability groupings, and tracking systems; reliance upon a lock step curriculum approach in which students' grade level rather than their assessed individual needs determine what they are taught (Stainback & Stainback, 1985); and an implicit expectation that teachers are to work alone.

Schools that are educating all of their students in heterogeneous environments have attempted to eliminate these and other organizational barriers by redefined professional roles and creating opportunities for collaboration.

Redefining Professional Roles and Dropping Professional Labels

"I used to think of myself as a speech and language pathologist; but now I think of myself as a teacher who happens to have training and expertise in the area of communication" (Harris, 1987). This statement was made by an educator who works in a school system in which the roles and responsibilities of regular and special education have continuously been redefined over the past 5 years. The redefinition of job functions was viewed as necessary in order for this system to make the shift from categorical educational programs (e.g., regular classroom, special classes, pull-out services for speech and language and compensatory education services) to a single unified system where broad-based support ultimately would be available to all teachers and any of their students (Villa, 1988).

Job titles and the formal or informal role definitions that accompany them determine the way in which a person behaves within a school (Brookover et al., 1982). For example, the title "resource room teacher" may carry with it a set of expectations that (a) this teacher works in a separate room, (b) students must leave the regular classroom to get this person's services, and (c) only those students identified as eligible for special education can or will be allowed to benefit from this person's expertise. This person, however, may have a great deal of training and expertise in assessing students' strengths and needs, task and concept analysis, designing and implementing classroom and behavior management programs, and other areas that, if shared with classroom teachers, might help them to maximize their responsiveness to the diverse educational needs of students.

Suppose the "resource room teacher" label were dropped and this person's role was redefined to be a support person expected to provide technical assistance to any number of educators in the building through modeling, consultation, team teaching, and inservice training. Such a change in job definition should result in an exchange of skills, thus increasing the number of students whose needs may be met in heterogeneous classrooms. There is considerable evidence that a consultative, training-based intervention model is effective in maintaining students in general education settings (Idol, Paolucci-Whitcomb, & Nevin, 1986; Knight, Meyers, Paolucci-Whitcomb, Hasazi, & Nevin, 1981; Lew, Mesch, & Lates, 1982; Miller & Sabatino, 1978). The steps for implementing this so-called "consulting teacher" model have been described by Idol et al. (1986).

The Winooski School District is an example of a Vermont school district that has taken a number of steps to redefine roles and responsibilities of school personnel in order to successfully educate all students in general education settings. First of all, a single department of pupil personnel services has been created to unite guidance, health, gifted and talented, special education, compensatory education, and early childhood services and personnel. The former special education administrator directs this department and collaborates with the other administrators to jointly supervise and evaluate *all* district instructional personnel. These changes have eliminated the preexisting departmental boundaries that had administratively separated programs and have facilitated the coordination of services and sharing of professional expertise.

Second, the roles of professional and paraprofessional personnel in the new department of pupil personnel services have become primarily consultative in nature. Whereas they historically had delivered services exclusively through pull-out programs, they now are expected to consult and team teach with general educators. The elementary communication specialist, for example, has "come out of the closet" and now delivers speech and language instruction mainly by team teaching with classroom teachers.

In a final move to alter professional roles and responsibilities, the special education classes for students with moderate and severe handicaps were closed. Students who would have been in these classes now are educated in age-appropriate classrooms and integrated community and vocational settings. The responsibility for supporting these students is distributed among a cadre of educators who collectively have skills in health, vocational education, communication, counseling, and functional education (i.e., domestic, community, recreational, vocational) as well as traditional (e.g. reading, math) curriculum domains.

Montlake, a Seattle elementary school of 243 students, is an example of a school that has dramatically altered the job responsibilities of its school staff in order to improve education for all students (Olson, 1988). Pull-out programs for special instruction have been eliminated, and the librarian and the former special education and compensatory education teachers now teach reading and math groups along with the other teachers in a multi-aged arrangement. In the afternoon, students are regrouped by grade level, and teachers cover social studies, science, and other subject areas. According to the principal, because teachers now share students, they work more cooperatively and feel more responsible for the whole school. In addition, discipline problems have declined, teacher morale has improved, and students' standardized test scores have increased.

By redefining instructional roles, the Winooski and Montlake schools have allowed for more creative use of the human resources that always were present within these schools. In carrying out their new job functions, educators model collaboration for their students. "The integration of professionals within a school system is a prerequisite to the successful integration of students. We cannot ask our students to do those things which we as professionals are unwilling to do" (Harris, 1987).

Expecting and Creating Opportunities for Collaboration

Establishing a Collaborative Teaming Process. A key to successfully meeting the educational needs of all students is the development of a collaborative relationship among the school staff so that expertise may be shared. "A teacher is more willing to share responsibility for a student who presents challenges when that student comes with a team to support him" (Tetreault, 1988).

In a number of Vermont schools a problem-solving and decision-making process referred to as "collaborative teaming" is employed to promote the sharing of expertise (Thousand, Fox, Reid, Godek, & Williams, 1986). Collaborative teaming is a process in which team members work cooperatively to achieve a common, agreed-upon goal. The process involves the application of the principles of cooperative group learning, as forwarded by Johnson and Johnson (1987b, 1987d), to adult planning groups. In the words of a collaborative team member,

> We've taken the technology of cooperative group learning for kids and applied it to our adult teams. We meet as cooperative groups. Everyone shares in the common goal, that goal being the most appropriate education for the students we serve. (Cravedi-Cheng, 1987)

In a collaborative team, members perceive themselves as positively interdependent, as "sinking or swimming together." They also are expected to exhibit certain interpersonal and small group skills that have been related to successful cooperative group work (Johnson & Johnson, 1987a). For a team to be optimally effective in planning and problem-solving, its members need to learn and practice these skills. Skills include basic group management skills that result in an organized team with an established set of expectations, leadership behaviors that help the team to accomplish its tasks and maintain positive working relationships, and skills for managing conflict or creating constructive controversy.

Members of collaborative teams frequently are at different levels in terms of their competence and confidence in performing collaborative skills. However, all of these skills can be taught and learned. In some school districts, direct instruction in collaborative teaming skills has been arranged for staff. Teachers also have chosen as annual professional growth goals the development of specific collaborative teaming skills.

A speech and language pathologist has enumerated the ways in which collaborative teaming contributes to successful heterogeneous schooling, pointing out both teacher and student benefits:

> As individuals we bring to our teams a wide range of values, experiences, training, resources, strengths, and weaknesses. We share our diversities and work toward meeting mutually defined goals. We've created an interdependence among ourselves as professionals. When we meet there is shared leadership, a division of labor, an atmosphere of trust, and effective communication. The result is a professional support network through which we meet the needs of learners and grow as professionals (Harris, 1987).

Collaborative teaming empowers teachers and students by enfranchising them through their participation in decision-making processes (Johnson & Johnson, 1987d; Slavin, 1987; Thousand et al., 1986). It facilitates the distribution of school leadership responsibilities beyond the administrative arm of the school to the broader school community. Thousand and colleagues (1986) offered an expanded description of the collaborative teaming process and strategies for implementing the process in heterogeneous schools. Readers who wish to learn more about specific collaborative skills are referred to *Joining Together: Group Theory and Group Skills* (Johnson & Johnson, 1987a).

CREATING COMMON CONCEPTUAL FRAMEWORKS, KNOWLEDGE, AND LANGUAGE THROUGH TRAINING

The way in which teachers choose to interact with students depends, at least in part, upon the conceptual frameworks and terms they use to think and talk about students (Smith, 1988). Smith has argued that what instructional personnel need is "shared meaning" — a common knowledge base, conceptual framework, and language for communicating about students and learning. In addition, this shared meaning needs to be based upon sound theory and research. "In order to establish and maintain constructive dialogue between and among professional groups about intervention methods, we must identify and communicate the notion of best practice in intervention based on known theory" (Smith, 1988, p. 8). In short, for school personnel to be most effective in their collaborations with one another and their instruction of students, they need to share common concepts, vocabulary, and training in instructional strategies that are founded in sound research and theory.

Lyon (1988; Thousand, 1988) has pointed out that teaching is a complex act that requires quality models and intensive guided practice and feedback across a number of teaching situations and conditions for teachers to translate demonstrated assessment and instructional techniques into productive, effective teaching. Lyon also discussed survey results that revealed regular and special educators' dissatisfaction with preservice training experiences. Teachers feel they have been ill-prepared to effectively adapt their own instruction to accommodate students who fail to learn from their typical "first shot" instruction.

Taken together, Smith's (1988) and Lyon's (1988) observations point to the need for staff of heterogeneous schools to acquire the conceptual frameworks, language, and technical skills to communicate about and implement assessment and instructional and collaborative teaming practices that research and theory say will enable them to respond to the unique needs of a diverse student body.

One content area in which all school staff need instruction is collaborative teaming (Johnson & Johnson, 1987a, 1987d; Thousand et al., 1986). As already discussed, school personnel need to become skillful in implementing a collaborative teaming model and using interpersonal and small group skills to function optimally as collaborative team members.

A second content area involves knowledge of current best educational practices in heterogeneous schooling. Training here would examine the characteristics of schools that *general education* researchers have found to be more effective than others in promoting students' learning and development (Brookover et al., 1982). It also would examine that which *special education* researchers promote as best educational practice (Fox et al., 1986). Armed with this information, instructional personnel would be equipped to articulate the demonstrated benefits of these practices and argue for the establishment and merger of exemplary practices within their school.

A third content area covers a variety of instructional practices that enable teachers to effectively accommodate a heterogeneous group of students. Training includes outcomes-based instructional models (e.g., Block & Anderson, 1975; Hunter, 1982); cooperative group learning models (e.g., Johnson et al., 1984; Slavin, 1983); computer-assisted instruction (e.g., Heerman, 1988); an assessment model that enables teachers to discuss learner characteristics and make decisions about their own instructional behavior (e.g., Lyon & Moats, in press; Lyon & Toomey, 1985); classroom management strategies (e.g., Becker, 1986); methods for teaching positive social skills and reinforcing students' use of these skills in school (e.g., Hazel, Schumaker, Sherman, & Sheldon-Wildgen, 1981; Jackson, Jackson, & Monroe, 1983); and the use of peers as tutors, buddies, and members of educational planning teams.

It is important to emphasize here that, whatever the training content a faculty member elects to include as its course of study, the principles of effective instruction should be followed in the delivery of the content; that is, faculty and field placement personnel need to model multiple and diverse examples of the desired knowledge or practice, provide guided practice in the application of the knowledge or practice, and arrange for coaching and feedback in the actual school situations in which the knowledge or practice is expected to be employed (Joyce & Showers, 1980).

SUMMARY

The educational practices presented in this article appear to influence the success of students and educational personnel in heterogeneous schools. We encourage teacher education faculty members to carefully examine the practices and beliefs that promote or impede continued progress toward meeting the diverse needs of all students. We further encourage faculty members to embrace the belief that there *are* actions each individual can take to positively influence the learning environment of all students, for "we know that a school can change if the staff desires to improve or modify beliefs, structures, and instructional practices" (Brookover et al., 1982, p. 35). The quality of professional preparation provided to this generation of teachers will be determined by the collective responsible actions of the diverse group of teacher educators, public school personnel, and parents who commit to being life-long learners in order to reap the promises offered by research, current best educational practice, and creative problem solving.

REFERENCES

Armstrong, S.B., Stahlbrand, K., Conlon, M.F., & Pierson, P.M. (1979, April). *The cost effectiveness of peer and cross-age tutoring.* Paper presented at the international convention of the Council for Exceptional Children. (ERIC Document Reproduction Service No. ED 171 058).

Aronson, E., Blaney, N., Stephan, C., Skies, J., & Snapp, M. (1978). *The jigsaw classroom.* Beverly Hills, CA: Sage Publications.

Becker, W. (1986). *Applied psychology for teachers: A behavioral cognitive approach.* Chicago: Science Research Associates.

Block, J., & Anderson, L. (1975). *Mastery learning in classroom instruction.* New York: Macmillan Publishing.

Brookover, W., Beamer, L., Efthim, H., Hathaway, D., Lezzotte, L., Miller, S., Passalacqua, J., & Tornatzky, L. (1982). *Creating effective schools: An inservice program for enhancing school learning climate and achievement.* Holmes Beach, FL: Learning Publications.

Budelmann, L., Farrel, S., Kovach, C., & Paige, K. (1987, October). *Student perspective: Planning and achieving social integration.* Paper presented at Vermont's Least Restrictive Environment Conference, Burlington.

Cohen, S.A., & Stover, G. (1981). Effects of teaching sixth-grade students to modify format variables of math work problems. *Reading Research Quarterly, 16,* 175-200.

Cooke, N.L., Heron, T.E., & Howard, W.L. (1983). *Peer tutoring: Implementing classwide programs in the primary grades.* Columbus, OH: Special Press.

Cravedi-Cheng, L. (1987, October). *A special educator's perspective on teaming to accomplish cooperation between and among regular and special educators for the provision of services in the least restrictive environment.* Paper presented at Vermont's Least Restrictive Environment Conference, Burlington.

DiFerdinando, R. (1987, October). *An administrator's perspective on the value of peer support networks.* Paper presented at Vermont's Least Restrictive Environment Conference, Burlington.

Floyd, C. (1954). Meeting children's reading needs in the middle grades: A preliminary report. *Elementary School Journal, 55,* 99-103.

Fox, W., Thousand, J., Williams, W., Fox, T., Towne, P., Reid, R., Conn-Powers, C., & Calcagni, L. (1986). *Best educational practices '86: Educating learners with severe handicaps.* (Monograph No. 6-1) Burlington: University of Vermont, Center for Developmental Disabilities.

Gartner, A., Kohler, M., & Riessman, F. (1971). *Children teach children: Learning by teaching.* New York: Harper and Row.

Glasser, W. (1986). *Control theory in the classroom.* New York: Harper and Row.

Glatthorn, A. (1987). How do you adapt the curriculum to respond to individual differences? In A. Glatthorn, *Curriculum renewal* (pp. 99-109). Alexandria, VA: Association for Supervision and Curriculum Development.

Good, T.L., & Brophy, J.E. (1984). *Looking into classrooms* (3rd ed.). New York: Harper and Row.

Harris, T., (1987, October). *A speech and language pathologist's perspective on teaming to accomplish cooperation between and among regular and special educators for the provision of services in the least restrictive environment.* Paper presented at Vermont's Least Restrictive Environment Conference, Burlington.

Hazel, J.S., Schumaker, J.B., Sherman, J.A. & Sheldon-Wildgen, J. (1981). *ASSET: A Social Skills Program for Adolescents.* Champaign, IL: Research Press.

Heerman, B. (1988). *Teaching and learning with computers.* San Francisco: Jossey-Bass.

Hunter, M. (1982). *Mastery teaching.* El Segunda, CA: TIP Publications.

Idol, L., Paolucci-Whitcomb, P., & Nevin, A. (1986). *Collaborative consultation.* Rockville, MD: Aspen Publishing.

Jackson, N.F., Jackson, D.A., Monroe, C. (1983). *Behavioral social skill training materials — Getting along with others: Teaching social effectiveness to children.* Champaign, IL: Research Press.

Johnson, D.W., & Johnson, R. (1987a). *Joining together: Group theory and group skills* (3rd ed.). Englewood Cliffs, NJ: Prentice-Hall.

Johnson, D.W., & Johnson, R. (1987b). *Learning together and alone: Cooperation, competition, and individualization* (2nd ed.). Englewood Cliffs, NJ: Prentice-Hall.

Johnson, D.W., & Johnson, R. (1987c). *A meta-analysis of cooperative, competitive and individualistic goal structures.* Hillsdale, NJ: Lawrence Erlbaum.

Johnson, D.W., & Johnson, R. (1987d). Research shows the benefit of adult cooperation. *Educational Leadership, 45*(3), 27-30.

Johnson, D.W., Johnson, R., Holubec, E., & Roy, P. (1984). *Circles of learning.* Arlington, VA: Association for Supervision and Curriculum Development.

Johnson, D.W., Johnson, R., & Maruyama, G. (1983). Interdependence and interpersonal attraction among heterogeneous and homogeneous individuals: A theoretical formulation and a meta-analysis of the research. *Review of Educational Research, 53,* 5-54.

Johnson, D.W., Maruyama, G., Johnson, R., Nelson, D., & Skon, L. (1981). Effects of cooperative, competitive and individualistic goal structures on achievement: A meta-analysis. *Psychological Bulletin, 89,* 47-62.

Joyce, B., & Showers, B. (1980). Improving inservice training: The messages of research. *Educational Leadership, 37,* 379-385.

Knight, M., Meyers, H., Paolucci-Whitcomb, P., Hasazi, S., & Nevin, A. (1981). A four year evaluation of consulting teacher services. *Behavior Disorders, 6,* 92-100.

Kulik, C.L., & Kulik, J.A. (1982). Effects of ability grouping on secondary school students: A meta-analysis of evaluation findings. *American Educational Research Journal, 19,* 415-428.

Lew, M., Mesch, D., & Lates, B.J. (1982). The Simmons College generic consulting teacher program: A program description and data-based application. *Teacher Education and Special Educational, 5*(2), 11-16.

Lilly, M.S. (1971). A training based model for special education. *Exceptional Children, 37,* 745-749.

Lyon, R. (1988, March). *What we know and don't know about learning disabilities.* Paper presented at the First Vermont Symposium on Learning Disabilities, Rutland.

Lyon, R., & Moats, L. (in press). Critical factors in the instruction of the learning disabled. *Journal of Consulting and Clinical Psychology.*

Lyon, R., & Toomey, F. (1985). Neurological, neuropsychological and cognitive-developmental approaches to learning disabilities. *Topics in Learning Disabilities.* Montpelier: Vermont Department of Education.

Madden, N.A., & Slavin, R.E. (1983). Mainstreaming students with mild academic handicaps: Academic and social outcomes. *Review of Educational Research, 53,* 519-569.

Miller, T., & Sabatino, D. (1978). An evaluation of the teacher consultant model as an approach to mainstreaming. *Exceptional Children, 45,* 86-91.

Olson, L. (1988, April 13). A Seattle principal defies the conventional wisdom. *Education Week,* pp. 1, 22-23.

Pierce, M.M., Stahlbrand, K., & Armstrong, S.B. (1984). *Increasing student productivity through peer tutoring programs.* Austin, TX: Pro-Ed.

Provus, M.M. (1960). Ability grouping in arithmetic. *Elementary School Journal, 60,* 391-398.

Reynolds, M.C., Wang, M.C., & Walberg, H.J. (1987). The necessary restructuring of special and regular education. *Exceptional Children, 53,* 391-398.

Rosenbaum, J.E. (1980). Social implications of educational grouping. *Review of Research in Education, 391,* 361-401.

Scagliotti, L. (1987, December 20). Helping hands: School works to overcome student's handicap. *Burlington Free Press,* Section B, pp. 1, 10.

Schafer, W.E., & Olexan, C. (1971). *Tracking and opportunity.* Scranton, PA: Chandler.

Schattman, R. (1988, January). Full integration. Paper presented at the Wisconsin's Administrator's Training Project Conference, Milwaukee.

Sharan, S., & Sharan, Y. (1976). *Small-group teaching.* Englewood Cliffs, NJ: Educational Technology Publications.

Skrtic, T. (1987). An organizational analysis of special education reform. *Counterpoint, 8*(2), 15-19.

Slavin, R.E. (1983). *Cooperative learning.* New York: Longman.

Slavin, R.E. (1987). Ability grouping and student achievement in elementary school: A best-evidence synthesis. *Review of Educational Research, 57,* 293-336.

Smith, C. (1988, March). *What's in a word? On our acquisition of the concept language learning disability.* Paper presented at the First Vermont Symposium on Learning Disabilities, Rutland.

Stainback, S., & Stainback, W. (1985). The merger of special and regular education: Can it be done? *Exceptional Children, 51,* 517-521.

Stainback, W., & Stainback, S. (1984). A rationale for the merger of special and regular education. *Exceptional Children, 51,* 102-111.

Tetreault, D. (1988, March). *The Winooski model.* Paper presented at the Portsmouth School District Integration Workshop, Portsmouth, NH.

Thousand, J.S. (1988). Addressing individual differences in the classroom: Are we up to the job? — A conversation with Reid Lyon, PhD. *Teacher Education and Special Education, 11,* 72-75.

Thousand, J., Fox, T., Reid, R., Godek, J., & Williams, W. (1986). *The homecoming model: Educating students who present intensive educational challenges within regular education environments.* (Monograph No. 7-1). Burlington: University of Vermont, Center for Developmental Disabilities.

Vicker, T.R. (1988). Learning from an outcomes-driven school district. *Educational Leadership, 45*(5), 52-55.

Villa, R. (1988, January). *Full integration.* Paper presented at the Wisconsin's Administrator's Training Project Conference, Eau Claire.

Wilson, B.J., & Schmits, W. (1978). What's new in grouping? *Phi Delta Kappan, 59,* 535-536.

Reprinted with permission of *Teacher Education and Special Education*, 1988, Vol. II, Number 4.

Questions About Implementing Mixed-Age Grouping

by Lillian G. Katz, Demetra Evangelou and
Jeanette Allison Hartman, coauthors of
The Case for Mixed-Age Grouping in Early Education

Research indicates that cross-age interaction among young children can offer a variety of developmental benefits to all participants. However, merely mixing children of different ages in a group will not guarantee that benefits will be realized. Four areas of concern are the optimum age range, the proportion of older to younger children, the time allocated to mixed-age grouping, and the appropriate curriculum. None of these concerns has been examined by empirical studies. We attempt here a preliminary exploration of questions.

What is the optimum age range?

Although no systematic evidence has been found concerning the beneficial effects of the age range within a group, experience suggests that the range is likely to affect the group in several ways. We hypothesize that there is an *optimal* age range and that children too far apart in age will not engage in enough interaction to affect each other. If the age span within a group goes beyond the optimal range, then the models of behavior and competence exhibited by the oldest member may be too difficult for younger members to emulate. Indeed, there may be a risk that the eldest children will

intimidate the youngest members. Furthermore, we suggest that customary age-segregation practices provide too narrow a range of competence for maximum learning across much of the curriculum. For example, in a class composed entirely of three-year-olds, the children may not be able to engage in play as complex as they would engage in if in a class including four-year-olds. However, in many schools and child care centers, the mixture of age groups is more likely to be determined by the actual enrollments than by empirically-derived formulae.

Research is needed to illuminate the dynamic factors that operate in various age ranges. Comparative studies of classes with a two - versus a three-year age spread could identify the effects of age range on the frequencies, structure, and content of cross-age interaction. It would also be useful to know whether the types and frequencies of prosocial behavior (e.g., nurturance, leadership, tutoring) that older children exhibit in interactions with younger ones are related to the spread in ages. Of course, in many situations, the age range may not be a matter of choice, but rather a function of demographic factors beyond the school's control. The advantages or risks associated with age ranges are not clear from any available data.

What is the best proportion of older to younger children in a class?

There is at present no empirical basis on which to predict what proportions of older to younger children within a class are optimal. Real conditions are unlikely to allow teachers to have one-half the class age four and the other half age five. It seems likely that if the class consists of five four-year-olds and 15 five-year-olds, the youngest members might easily be overwhelmed by their older classmates. However, if the proportions are reversed, might the demands of the younger children overshadow the needs of the older ones, and the acceptance of behavior appropriate from the younger children give the older ones license to behave in these less mature ways as well? In either case, the teacher's role includes not only fostering cooperative and constructive interaction across the age groups, but also minimizing the potential risks of the uneven distribution of the age groups and the kinds of behavioral characteristics associated with them. We have only indirectly related evidence on these issues — from cross-cultural studies on peer interaction (Whiting &Whiting, 1975). The Whitings' classical study describes a wide age range of peer interaction found in other cultures. The Whitings report that prosocial behaviors tend to emerge, and relationships among children of all ages are characterized by cooperation.

What proportion of time ought to be spent in mixed-age groups?

There is as yet no evidence to indicate what proportion of the time children spend in an early childhood setting should be spent in mixed-age groups. However, we might consider possible mixtures of ages in early childhood settings and elementary schools. An ideal elementary school that has provisions for four-year-olds could be organized to provide an early childhood section or department for children four to six years old. (The National Association of State Boards of Education, 1988, recommends a unit composed of four- to eight-year-olds.) In such an early childhood department, the children might spend all of their time in mixed groups, depending to a large extent on the nature of the curriculum. If the curriculum is mainly informal and includes spontaneous play, learning centers, project work, and individual assignments as needed, children's progress in acquiring basic literacy and numeracy skills will not be jeopardized.

Another plan might be to set aside particular periods during which the teacher offers specific learning and instructional activities for small, flexible subgroups of children with relatively homogeneous abilities, knowledge, or competence. Members of these groups might work on specific individual assignments and receive systematic instruction as needed. While these small groups are receiving special instruction (see Katz & Chard, 1989. pp. 10-11), others in the class can continue to work on projects or play together in spontaneous groups.

On the other hand a school might want to have a home room for several periods of the day. For example, the children might be in mixed-age groups during an opening period, an extended lunch and rest time at midday, and perhaps during the last half-hour of school. The main advantages to the age mixture in this arrangement stem from opportunity for social interaction rather than from various kinds of cross-age tutoring or mixed-age project work.

The teaching staff of an early childhood department can allocate some time each day that cooperative learning groups use to work on assigned learning tasks. We suggest that the staff plan together the allocation of time and their own efforts in such a way that a balanced grouping results. When such a balance exists, mixed-and same-age groups have the opportunity to form spontaneously, and the teacher can organize assigned groups (more or less mixed in age) for specific instructional purposes. Each child would spend her first three years in the department, participating in a variety of peer groups. In this way, the uneven development and progress of many young children could be addressed by the flexibility of placement both in same-age and within mixed-age groups.

Efforts to maximize family grouping seem to be especially appropriate in child care centers in which many young children spend the majority of their waking hours. A class in a center could be composed of three-, four-, and five-year-olds. The early part of their day could be spent participating together in the morning meal.

Maximizing the advantages and minimizing the risks of mixed-age grouping and making proper use of time will depend largely on the judgment and skillfulness of the teacher.

The children could take a real role, appropriate to their level of competence, in setting the table and cleaning up after the meal, and could undertake real household chores before starting to play. Of course, the group does not have to be mixed in age to create this kind of family or community atmosphere. This plan would enhance the homelike quality of child care settings and reduce the temptation to "scholarize" the lives of very young children in child care. If, as is often the case, their siblings are enrolled in the center, increasing the opportunities for sibling contact is desirable. Many young children in institutions may find contact with siblings during the day a source of comfort.

Thus far, there is no data that suggests the optimal allocation of time to mixed-versus homogeneous-age grouping. There is therefore no reason to believe that time must be allocated to either one or the other age-grouping arrangement. Maximizing the advantages and minimizing the risks of mixed-age grouping and making proper use of time will depend largely on the judgment and skillfulness of the teacher.

What about curriculum and mixed-age groups?

One of the possible benefits of mixing ages in the early childhood classroom may be a reduction of teachers' and administrators' tendency to adopt a unidimensional curriculum consisting of exercises and assignments that all children must complete within a given time. Instead of a formal academic curriculum for a whole class or age cohort, we recommend an informal curriculum with ample group project work, opportunity for spontaneous play and systematic instruction for individual children as needed.

Unless the curriculum has a significant amount of time allocated to informal group work and spontaneous interactive play in naturally occurring groups, the benefits of the age spread are unlikely to be realized. Katz and Chard (1989) propose that the curriculum for all young children should include opportunities for children to work on extended group projects in which individuals contribute differentially to the effort at many levels of competence.

If a class includes five-and six-year-olds in a family grouping arrangement some fives will be closer to six-year-olds than to other fives in a given skill and will profit from small-group instruction that involves six-year-olds as well. Similarly, some six-year-olds may benefit from small-group experiences that involve certain activities with five-year-olds for a while. The composition of the groups can be fluid, depending on the tasks and the rate of progress of each child.

One of the important potential advantages of a mixed-age early childhood department is the minimization of grade retention and repetition. Any child who had spent two or three years in such a department and was still judged unlikely to profit from the subsequent grade, which might be called Year 1 of primary school, could be referred for special services. Any curriculum for which more than 10% of the age-eligible children are judged unready is probably inappropriate (Katz, Raths, & Torres, 1987; Graue & Shepard, 1989).

Summary

Although mixed-age grouping is a straightforward concept, the practical details of implementation are not well researched. Experience and some research, however, suggest that 1) an optimum age range is larger than the customary range in current classrooms, yet not so wide that children cannot share interests, 2) the proportion of older to younger children should be large enough to keep the older children from regressing, 3) no particular proportion of time needs to be allocated to mixed- and same-age grouping, and 4) an informal, multidimensional, non-age-based curriculum is most appropriate to a mixed-age group.

References

Graue, M.E., & Shepard, L. (1989). Predictive Validity of Gesell School Readiness Tests. *Early Childhood Research Quarterly*, 4, 303-315.

Katz, L.G., & Chard, S.C. (1989). *Engaging Children's Minds: The Project Approach*. Norwood, NJ: Ablex.

Katz, L.G., Raths, J.D., & Torres, R.D. (1987). *A Place Called Kindergarten*. Urbana, Il: ERIC Clearinghouse on Elementary and Early Childhood Education.

National Association of State Boards of Education (1988). *Right from the Start: The Report of the NASBE Task Force on Early Childhood Education*. Alexandria, VA: Author.

Research in Rural Education, Fall 1990, Vol. 7, No. 1, pp. 1-8

A Review of the Quantitative Research on Multigrade Instruction

Bruce A. Miller[1]
Northwest Regional Education Laboratory

Note: This article is part of a larger publication entitled The Multigrade Classroom: A resource Handbook for Small, Rural Schools. This article and the handbook from which it comes are publications based on work sponsored wholey, or in part, by the Office of Educational Research and Improvement (OERI), Department of Education, under Contract Number 400-86-0006. The content in these publications do not necessarily reflect the views of OERI, the Department, or any other agency of the U.S. Government.

ABSTRACT

This paper examines the quantitative research literature regarding the effects multigrade classroom organization has on student cognitive and affective outcomes. Findings indicate that student achievement is neither better nor worse in multigrade classrooms. However, areas relating to student affect significantly favor the multigrade environments. But quantitative studies only reveal one dimension of multigrade instruction. Research is needed that provides a rich, detailed description of multigrade classroom life in, especially high performing classrooms.

INTRODUCTION

The multigrade classroom has traditionally been an important and necessary organizational pattern of education in the United States. In 1918, there were 196,037 one-room schools, representing 70.8 percent of all public schools in the United States. By 1980, less than 1,000 of these schools remained (Muse, Smith & Barker, 1987). The number of multigrade classrooms consisting of two grades or more is considerably higher. For example, in a study of multigrade classrooms of only two grades, Rule (1983) used a sample from a suburban district outside of Phoenix, Arizona. Of the 21,000 elementary students in the district, approximately 17 percent were in combined classrooms. Many school districts combine classrooms as a cost-cutting measure. Thus, the multigrade classroom still holds a significant place in schools, especially in small isolated rural districts.

The multigrade classroom has also had a significant place in mainstream urban and suburban districts. In the 1960s and 1970s, the ungraded school, open education, and individualized instruction became driving forces in school organization. Energized by developmental theories of learning, a large influx of federal money and student-centered models of instruction, the multigrade classroom became a major educational innovation.

This resulted in numerous studies conducted to assess the effectiveness of multigrade classroom instruction. Interestingly, when educators described these changes in school organization, they often used the image of the one-room school with its multiage "family" groups, student-centered learning and cooperative atmosphere. For the most part, efforts to recapture the ideal of the one-room school were unsuccessful. Only a small proportion of the multigraded "experiments" of the 1960s and 1970s remain.

We have learned a great deal from these innovative efforts. Working in an open, multigrade school requires serious, ongoing teacher training and a commitment to hard work. Most teachers receive training for teaching single grade classrooms

1Bruce Miller is a Rural Education Specialist in the Rural Education Program, Northwest Regional Educational Laboratory, 101 S.W. Main St., Suite 500, Portland, OR 97204.

organized around whole-class and/or small ability-grouped instruction. When placed in an open, multigrade setting, teachers discover that the time requirements and skills needed to be effective are simply not part of their training and experience.

In addition, a long tradition of graded schools has created powerful expectations for administrators, teachers and parents regarding how schools should be organized. Graded instructional organization is a norm expected of schools which creates a handicap for anyone (whether out of necessity or by theoretical design) seeking to operate a multigrade school. Although the large scale innovations of the '60s and '70s have virtually ended, the multigrade classroom remains a powerful reality for many small, rural school districts in the United States, as well as for many schools throughout the world.

For most rural educators, multigrade instruction is not an experiment or a new educational trend, but a forceful reality based on economic and geographic necessity. In a society where educational environments are dominated by graded organization, the decision to combine grades is often quite difficult.

Within this context, many teachers, administrators and parents continue to wonder whether multigrade organization has negative effects on student performance. Therefore, an overriding question in the minds of many educators and parents faced with the reality of multigrade classroom organization is, "What effect does multigrade instruction have on student performance?" The purpose of this research is to answer that question.

Research studies focusing on multigrade instruction, especially in rural settings, are quite rare. Through contacts with rural educators both in the United States and abroad, and through computer searches of ERIC, Psychological Abstracts and the Social Science Citation Index, a body of research literature was collected. Only quantitative studies were reviewed. In other words, only studies designed to determine whether there were statistically significant differences between elements or variables in a school or classroom were selected. The research was then organized and reviewed according to cognitive and affective outcomes. However, it should be kept in mind that no distinction has been drawn between studies of rural and metropolitan multigrade classrooms. This was due to the fact that so few empirical rural studies could be located. In addition, the underlying purpose of this research review was to describe how multigrade students perform in relation to their single-grade counterparts.

QUANTITATIVE STUDIES: STUDENT ACHIEVEMENT

Table 1 provides an overview of quantitative studies that were designed to ascertain the differences in student achievement between students enrolled in single and multigrade classrooms. Nearly half of these studies were conducted during the '60s and '70s when there was a large interest in team teaching, individualized instruction and multigrade instructional grouping. These studies are unique in that the programs were driven by a theoretical design rather than economic necessity.

In many cases this would suggest a difference in attitude and belief by those working in these settings. The remainder of the studies focus primarily on combined classroom situations. Research literature on the rural one or two-room school is quite limited, primarily consisting of descriptive, survey and self report/opinion types of information.

The studies summarized in Table 1 indicate that there is little or no difference in achievement in students in single or multigrade classrooms. Two studies (Knight, 1938; Chace, 1961) found that multigrade students performed consistently higher in mathematics, reading and language than did single-grade students. However, the differences were not statistically significant. In eight studies (Drier, 1949; Adams, 1953; Way, 1969; Harvey, 1974; Adair, 1978; MacDonald & Wurster, 1974; Lincoln, 1981; Pratt & Treacy, 1986) researchers found no difference between student performance in the multigrade or single-grade classrooms. Only in the studies that reported mixed results do we find significant differences.

Yerry (1964) investigated the differences between students combined in grades 1-2, 3-4, and 5-6 with students from single-grade classes. Differences between levels within the multiage group were also compared. At grades 2, 3 and 6, there were no significant differences from single-grade students. But at grades 1 and 5, significant differences favoring multigrade classes were found for some subjects (arithmetic, language, and total achievement for both grade 1 and grade 5). Milburn (1981) found significant differences for vocabulary that favored the multigrade students, but when analyzed by age, it was found that lower-level multigrade students performed better than their single-grade counterparts. At the upper levels there was little or no difference.

Table 1
Research on Multigrade Classroom Instruction: Student Achievement

| | | Comparison Groups | | | | | | | |
Study	Unit of Measurement	Multigrade N	Level	(Organization)	Single Grade N	Level(s)	Measure	Subjects	Results
Knight (1938)	Classroom (no. of students not specified)	7 / 7	4th / 4th	(3-4 combined) / (4-5 combined)	6 / 6	4th / 4th	Achieve. test / Achieve. test	Reading, Math, Language, Spelling	T / T
Drier (1949)	Students	923	6th	(1-6 mixed)	599	6th	Achieve. test	Reading, Math, Language, Spelling	N
Adams (1953)	Students	150	5th	(4-5 combined)	150	5th	Achieve. test	Reading, Math, Language	N
Chace (1961)	Classroom (No. of students not specified)	3	3 to 6	(mixed)	57	3 to 6	Achieve. test	Reading, Math, Language	T
Yerry (1964)	Students	500	1 to 6	(1-2) (3-4) (5-6)	500	1 to 6	Achieve. test	Reading, Math, Language	M+
Way (1969)	Students	135	1 to 5	(combined)	671	1 to 5	Achieve. test	Reading, Math, Language	N
Harvey (1974)	Students	31	K	(K-1 combined)	152	K	Achieve. test	Readiness Achievement	N
MacDonald and Wurster (1974)	Students	Not Specified	2nd	(1-3 mixed)	Not Specified	2nd	GATES Reading test	Reading	N
Adair (1978)	Students	500*	1st	(K-1 combined)	500*	1st	Achieve. test	Reading, Math, Listening, Word Analysis	N

| | | Comparison Groups | | | | | | | |
Study	Unit of Measurement	Multigrade N	Level(s)	(Organization)	Single Grade N	Level(s)	Measure	Subjects	Results
Milburn (1981)	Students	125	1 to 6	(4 classes w/ 3 yr. span per class)	125	Not Specified	Achieve. test	Reading, Math	M+
Lincoln (1981)	Students	402	2nd	(combined)	402	2nd	Achieve. test Aptitude	Reading	N
Rule (1983)	Students	3,360*		(2-3)	3,360*	2 to 6	Achieve. test	Reading, Math	M+
Pratt & Treacy (1986)	Classroom	13 / 2	1 to 2 / 2 to 3	(combined) / (combined)	13 / 10	1st / 2nd	Observation & document analysis	Students Learning	N

+ = Statistically significant   T = Trend favoring multigrade, but not significant   M = Mixed results   N = No difference
*N includes total sample

Rule (1983) compared student achievement for 3, 360 students in grades 3, 4, 5 and 6 across three settings:

- students who came from multigrade classrooms of two grades (for example fourth and fifth or third and fourth)

- single-grade classrooms in schools with multi grade classrooms

- single-grade classrooms in schools with only singe-grade classes

In addition, students were grouped and compared according to high, medium to high and average achievement. Only reading and mathematics performance were analyzed.

Results were mixed. For reading, only one analysis produced significant differences between single and multigrade classrooms. High performing fourth grade students from multigrade classrooms had significantly better scores than high performing students from single fourth grade classrooms.

In general, multigrade students scored higher in reading on standardized achievement tests than did single-grade students. However, for math achievement, the results are nearly reversed.

High-achieving third graders in single-grade classes scored significantly higher than their multigrade counterparts. Of the 12 analyses conducted, four favored multigrade classes and eight favored single-grade classes. Rule (1983) concludes her study with several implications for the practitioner contemplating combined classrooms:

1. Multigrade classes do not appear to affect reading achievement negatively; rather, they may actually enhance it for average to high-achieving students.

2. Student mathematics achievement might be negatively affected by placement in a multigrade classroom, especially for grade 3.

3. If one is contemplating combining classes, the average/high-achieving students appeared to be the best configuration for all grades in reading and for grades 4, 5, and 6 for math.

Rule's (1983) research does not yield information regarding low-achieving students or mixed-ability group students since nearly all students placed in the multigrade classrooms were selected because of their high achievement. In other words, when school officials combined classes they tended to select the higher achieving students for placement as a means of reducing the achievement disparity in the multiage classroom. It was believed this would simplify the work demands on the teacher. In addition, Rule did not include first or second grades as part of her sample.

The most comprehensive study of multigrade classrooms reviewed was conducted by Pratt and Treacy (1986) in Australia. Their study sought to identify differences between single and multigrade primary classrooms in rural and urban settings. Teacher interviews, structured classroom observations, analysis of student work and a student attitude measure were used for data collection. Unlike the research previously reviewed, Pratt and Treacy placed a heavy emphasis on the classroom context, thus providing an excellent picture of student and teacher behavior across a range of single and multigrade classrooms at the primary level.

Pratt and Treacy (1986) found that there was no indication that academic progress or social development were affected by how students were grouped (i.e., multigrade vs. single grade). Their review of student academic work indicates students from both types of classrooms were progressing at nearly the same rate. Interestingly, larger differences were found within classroom types than between them. In other words, when they observed how individual classrooms were organized, regardless of whether they were single or multigrade, they observed a great deal of variation in student at-task behavior. More research of this type is sorely needed to provide practitioners with detailed information on what actually occurs in the classroom.

QUANTITATIVE STUDIES: STUDENT ATTITUDES

Where the multigrade classroom has the greatest impact on student performance is in the affective domain (Pratt, 1986; Ford, 1977). Results generally favor the multigrade classroom when measures of student attitude toward self, school or peers are compared across a range of schools and geographic areas. Table 2 provides an overview of key studies on multi-

Table 2
Research on Multigrade Classroom Instruction: Student Attitude

Study	Unit of Measurement	Comparison Groups					Measure	Topics	Results
		Multigrade			Single Grade				
		N	Level	(Organization)	N	Level(s)			
Chace (1961)	Classroom (No. of students not specified)	3	3 to 6	(mixed)	57	3 to 6	-California Test of Personality	Personality & Social Development	+
Yerry & Henderson (1964)	Students	600	1 to 6	(1-3, 4-6)	600	1 to 6	-Ohio Social Accept. Scale	Friendship	N
							-Text Anxiety Scale	School Anxiety	N
Mycock (1966)	Students	150-180		(K-3)	150-180	(K-3)	-Text Anxiety Scale	School Anxiety & Social Adjustment	N
							-Sentence Completion	Teacher-Child Relations	+
							- Drawing Test		
							- Student Observation	Range of Social Interaction	+
							-Aspiration	Levels of Aspiration	+
Junell (1970)	Students	54	(Not specified)		96	(Not specified	-Bill's Index of Adjustment & Values	Self Concept Self Acceptance Ideal Self	T
							-Borg's USU School Inventory	Attitude Toward School	+
							-California Test of Personality	Belonging	
									N
							Freedom from Withdrawal		
							Freedom from Antisocial Tendencies		
Schroeder & Nott (1974)	Students	140	(1 to 5)	(Not specified)	140	(1 to 5)	-Bonnie Myer's Attitude Toward School	Attitude Toward School	+
Papay, Costello, Hedl, Spielberger (1975)	Students	133	1 to 2	(Mixed)	133	(1 to 2)	-State-Trait Anxiety Inventory	Trait Anxiety State Anxiety	+ +
Schrankler (1976)	Students	990	K - 6	(Mixed & K-1, 2-3, 4-6)	Not specified		-IOX Measures of Self Concept & Attitude Toward School	Self Concept Attitude Toward School	+ +
							-Parent Approval Index	Perception of Approval	+
							How About You? What Would Your do?	Perception of School Success Expectations of Success	+
							-School Sentiment	Dimensions of School	+
Milburn (1981)	Students	125		(4 classes w/ 3 yr. span)	125	(K - 6)	-Piers-Harris Self-Concept Scale	Self Concept	T
							-NFER Attitude Survey	School Attitudes	T
Sherman (1984)	Students	87	3 to 5	(Mixed)	87	3 to 5	-Sociogram	Social Distance	+
Pratt & Treacy (1986)	Classroom	13 2	1 to 2 2 to 3	(Combined) (Combined)	13 10	1st 2nd	-How You Feel About School Inventory	Attitude Toward School	N

+ = Statistically significant   T =Trend favoring multigrade, but not significant   M = Mixed results   N = No difference
*N includes total sample

grade instruction, with only the affective measures displayed. Of the nine studies reviewed there were approximately 23 separate measures of student attitude. Sixty-five percent of the measures favored the multigrade classroom at a significant level, 13 percent indicated a trend toward multigrade students out-performing their single-grade counterparts, and 22 percent revealed no differences between classroom types. Only one measure favored the single-grade classroom.

How do multigrade students feel about school and themselves, and do they feel different about their fellow students than do single-grade students? Five different measures of attitude toward school were used. Four of the five studies (Schroeder & Nott, 1974; Schrankler, 1976; Milburn, 1981; Junell, 1970; Pratt & Treacy, 1986) favored the multigrade students (three at the significant level) and one indicated no difference. Clearly, multigrade students have more positive attitudes toward school.

When measures of attitude toward self were administered the results were nearly the same. Schrankler (1976) found multigrade students to have significantly higher self-concept scores than students in single grades. Milburn (1981) and Junell (1970), using different measures of self-concept, found that multigrade students out-performed single-grade students, but not at a statistically significant level.

When assessing student social relationships and sense of belonging, the overall trend favors the multigrade students. Sherman (1984) discovered that multigrade students felt closer to their multiage classmates than did single-grade students. Chace (1961) and Mycock (1966) found that multigrade students had significantly better teacher-child relationships and better social development than single-grade students. Yerry and Henderson (1964) and Junell (1970) found no differences between single and multigrade students in terms of friendships and belonging.

In terms of anxiety toward school, multigrade students fared slightly better than single-grade students. Papay, Costello, and Spielberger (1975) used the State-Trait Anxiety Inventory to measure student anxiety levels. Multigrade students had significantly less anxiety than single-grade students. However, in studies conducted by Yerry and Henderson (1964) and Mycock (1966), no differences were found.

The most significant differences between single and multigrade classrooms were found in measures of self-concept and related measures of self-perception. Most studies favored the multigrade setting. Three

studies indicate that multigrade students have better self-concepts than single-grade students (Junell, 1970; Schrankler, 1976; & Milburn, 1981).

One interesting finding emerged from the Schrankler (1976) study. When 10-year-olds were asked about their expectations for success, the results indicated that single-grade students had significantly higher expectations than multigrade students. However, when 11-year-olds were asked to describe their perceptions of how successful they were in school, the results favored the multiage classroom. These seemingly contradictory results provide an excellent illustration of the problems researchers face in assessing student attitudes.

Variation in grades, time of year, quality of instruction and socio-economic status, to mention only a few key variables, mediate student perceptions. Educational researchers studying student attitudes often have difficulty setting up studies where these variables can be adequately controlled. One compensation strategy is the aggregation of studies across setting and time. Practitioners can have greater confidence when many studies indicate similar results.

Viewed as a whole, the ten studies presented (Table 2) clearly indicate that students in multigrade classrooms tend to have significantly more positive attitudes towards themselves and school. A trend toward more positive social relationships was also indicated.

CONCLUSION

Twenty-one quantitative studies comparing the effects of multigrade with single-grade classroom organization were reviewed. Table 1 provided an overview of 13 experimental studies assessing student academic performance, while Table 2 presented 10 studies that focused on student attitudes. Clearly, these studies indicate that being a student in a multigrade classroom does not negatively affect academic performance nor student social relationships and attitudes. In terms of academic achievement, the data clearly support the multigrade classroom as a viable and equally effective organizational alternative to single-grade instruction. Some research evidence does suggest there may be significant differences depending on subject and/or grade level. Primarily, these studies reflect the complex and variable nature of school life. However, there are not enough of these studies to make safe generalizations regarding which subjects or grade levels are best for multigrade instruction.

When it comes to student affect, the case for multigrade organization appears much stronger, with multigrade students out-performing single-grade students in over 75 percent of the measures used. One wonders, then, why we do not have more schools organized into multigrade classrooms.

One response to this question is that "We have nearly always organized classrooms by grade levels—that history and convention dictate graded classrooms." This response seems a bit ironic, given the early dominance of the multigrade school in American education. However, there is a related but more compelling answer that can be found in the classrooms themselves and in information drawn from classroom practitioners.

The quantitative studies reviewed focused on numerical student outcome data (i.e. test scores). Detailed contextual information describing what actually occurs in the classroom was not collected in these studies. We do not learn how teachers plan, prepare and teach with multiple grades. As a result, we do not know how teachers feel and respond to being assigned to a combined classroom. How are students grouped? Are classroom management and organization different? Are there different strategies for teaching specific subjects? These are just a few of the important questions that must be understood in light of the multigrade environment in order to understand why multigrade classrooms are not more prominent. To respond to these questions will require qualitative methodology, one preferably linked to student outcomes through quantitative measures. Clearly, we need more rural research that links qualitative and quantitative methods — studies that describe the rich context of rural classroom instruction along with related cognitive and affective outcomes.

REFERENCES

Adair, J. H. (1978). An attitude and achievement comparison between kindergarten and first grade children in multi and single grade classes. *Dissertation Abstracts International, 39,* 659A-660A.

Adams, J. J. (1953). Achievement and social adjustment of pupils in combination class enrolling pupils of more than one grade level. *Journal of Educational Research, 47,* 151-55.

Chace, E. S. (1961). *An analysis of some effects of multiple-gradegrouping in an elementary school.* Unpublished doctoral dissertation, University of Tennessee.

Day, B., & Hunt, G. H. (1975). Multiage classrooms: An analysis of verbal communication. *Elementary School Journal, 75,* 458-464.

Drier, W. H. (1949). The differential achievement of rural graded and ungraded school pupils. *Journal of Educational Research, 43,* 175-185.

Ford, B. (1977). Multiage grouping in the elementary school and children's affective development: A review of recent research. *The Elementary School Journal, 78,* 149-159.

Harvey, S. B. (1974). A comparison of kindergarten children in multigrade and traditional settings on self concept, social-emotional development, readiness development, and achievement. *Dissertation Abstracts International, 35,* 3340-A

Junell, J. S. (1970). *An analysis of the effects of multigrading on a number of noncognitive variables.* Unpublished doctoral dissertation, University of Washington.

Knight, E. E. (1938). A study of double grades in New Haven City schools. *Journal of Experimental Education, 7,* 11-18.

Lincoln, R. D. (1981). *The effect of single-grade and multi-grade primary school classroom on reading achievement of children.* Unpublished doctoral dissertation, University of Connecticutt.

MacDonald, P. A., & Wurster, S. R. (1974). *Multiple grade primary versus segregated first grade: Effects on reading achievement.* Bethesda, MD. (ERIC Document Reproduction Service No. ED 094 336)

Milburn, D. (1981). A study of multi-age or family-grouped classrooms. *Phi Delta Kappan, 64,* 306-309.

Muse, I., Smith, R., & Barker, B. (1987). *The one teacher school in the 1980s.* Las Cruces, NM: ERIC Clearinghouse on Rural Education and Small Schools.

Mycock, M. A. (1966). A comparison of vertical grouping and horizontal grouping in the infant school. *British Journal of Educational Psychology, 37,* 133-135.

Papay, J. P., Costello, R. J., & Spielberger, C. D. (1975). Effects of trait and state anxiety on the performance of elementary school children in traditional and individualized multiage classrooms. *Journal of Educational Psychology, 67,* 840-846.

Pratt, C. & Treacy, K. (1986). *A study of student grouping practices in early childhood classes in Western Australian government primary schools.* (Cooperative Research Series #9). Nedlands, Australia: Education Department of Western Australia.

Pratt, D. (1986). On the merits of multiage class rooms. *Research in Rural Education, 3,* 111-115.

Rule, G. (1983). Effects of multigrade grouping on elementary student achievement in reading and mathematics. (Doctoral dissertation, Northern Arizona University). *Dissertation Information Service No. 8315672.*

Schrankler, W. J. (1976). Family grouping and the affective domain. *Elementary School Journal, 76,* 432-439.

Schroeder, R., & Nott, R. E. (1974). Multi-age grouping—it works! *Catalyst for Change, 3,* 15-18.

Sherman, L. W. (1984). Social distance perceptions of elementary school children in age-heterogeneous and homogeneous classroom settings. *Perceptual and Motor Skills, 58,* 395-409.

Way, J. W. (1969). *The effects of multiage grouping on achievement and self-concept.* Cortland: State University of New York, Cortland College, Institute for Experimentation in Teacher Education.

Yerry, M. J., & Henderson, E. (1964). *Effects of interage grouping on achievement and behavior: End of year report.* (Experimental Program No. A-27-63). Bethpage, NY: Plainedge Public

Journal of Research in Rural Education, Winter 1991, Vol. 7, No. 2, pp. 3-12

A Review of the Qualitative Research on Multigrade Instruction

Bruce A. Miller
Northwest Regional Educational Laboratory

ABSTRACT

This paper examines the qualitative research literature regarding multigrade classrooms. The paper is organized in two parts: the first section, based on interviews and surveys, provides an overview of the problems and needs of rural school teachers in multigrade classrooms; the second section reviews studies and teacher reports describing how instruction is conducted in multigrade classrooms as compared with single-grade classrooms. The author suggests far-reaching implications for teacher preparation, classroom organization, and student learning in multigrade classrooms.

QUALITATIVE STUDIES: A VIEW FROM THE INSIDE OF THE MULTIGRADE CLASSROOM

The multigrade classroom has a long history in the United States dating back to the 1800s. It wasn't until the industrial revolution that educators began to think of instruction in terms of the graded classroom. Currently, most educators view school organization around the concept of gradedness. However, the multigraded classroom remains, to this day, an integral part of both rural and metropolitan education. As Miller (1989) has pointed out, the multigrade classroom became a driving force during the 1970s movement in open education and continues to this day in many rural schools. In addition, the 21 quantitative studies reviewed by Miller indicated that students in multigrade classrooms performed academically as well as students from single-grade classrooms. In terms of affective measures, however, multigrade students out-performed their single-grade counterparts at a statistically significant level. Clearly, multigrade classroom instruction is a viable alternative to single-grade organization.

The review of qualitative literature that follows has been divided into two sections. The first section provides an overview of the problems and needs of rural school teachers in multigrade classrooms. Primarily based on surveys and interviews, this literature describes how teachers and administrators view the job demands of the multigrade classroom. The second section reviews studies and teacher reports describing how multigrade instruction is carried out in the multigrade classroom.

ESTABLISHING THE NEEDS OF THE MULTIGRADE TEACHER

Imagine you have recently graduated from a university in a rural state. You would like to live and work in the small city where the university is located, but so would nearly every other graduate. You apply to the local school district, but are told that there is a long waiting list. Feeling anxious about a job for the fall, you also apply to many of the small rural schools around the state. It is in one of these schools where you eventually find a teaching job.

During your job interview with the local school board and superintendent, you are told you will teach the second grade. Moreover, when you report to work, your assignment has slightly changed and you find yourself responsible for a combination classroom of second and third graders. The principal apologizes for the change, but mentions that enrollment has dropped for the third grade, thus necessitating a combined class.

Bruce Miller is a Research Associate in the Rural Education Program, Northwest Regional Educational Laboratory, 101 S.W. Main St., Suite 500, Portland, OR 87204.

You are also told that you will only have an additional eight students, bringing the enrollment to thirty-two. Some extra aide help is hinted at.

While attending the university, you learned that a combined classroom was a distinct possibility in a rural school. However, the majority of your classes focused on instructional strategies for single-grade classrooms. Fortunately, you did have several methods courses and practicum experiences in grouping students for reading and math. As you face the task of preparing for the opening day of school, you decide to use what you know about grouping. A roster of students is reviewed as well as the previous year's cumulative folders. Unfortunately, this information is not very helpful.

Based on what test results you could locate, you discover there is an achievement span of five grades in reading and four grades in math. You decide to combine several levels in order to reduce the number of groups. Next, you begin planning for language arts, social studies and science. Should you teach separate groups by grade level for each subject? What happens if some second graders get third grade science and social studies? Will they have to repeat this content in third grade? And what about art, physical education and spelling? By this time, your anxiety has risen and you decide to take a break and ask another teacher for some help. Maybe ask the principal. You think to yourself, "Maybe I should just keep these concerns to myself. After all, I am a certified teacher trained to teach all K through 8 grades . . . what if the students are poorly behaved. . .don't like me . . . what if . . .?"

This fictitious teacher's thoughts and feelings are not too dissimilar from what many teachers, new or experienced, might feel as they approach the realities of teaching a multigrade classroom. As anyone who has taught knows, the greater the student diversity in the classroom (multiple achievement levels, developmental differences, differences in socio-economic status, etc.), the more one needs to plan and organize if individual student needs are to be met.

Bandy (1980) conducted a study of the characteristics and needs of country school teachers in British Columbia, Canada. A random, stratified sample of 50 principals and 500 teachers was surveyed. This was followed by open-ended interviews with 32 teachers drawn from a representative sample of 15 small rural schools. Interview data were then cross-checked with findings from the questionnaires.

Principal comments indicated that the most important factor to successful multigrade instruction was the teacher's ability to plan and organize. Most principals felt that the multigrade classroom was no problem to their teachers. Interestingly, over 90 percent of the teachers surveyed said they had multigrade classroom experience which suggests a highly skilled cadre of capable multigrade teachers. Many principals also mentioned that there were advantages to multigrade classes such as individualized instruction, tutorials by older students, and a greater opportunity for teachers to be innovative. However, principals said that the extra time needed in preparation and planning lessons was a definite disadvantage.

Teachers were asked to compare single and multigrade classrooms on a range of items. For example, they were asked to indicate whether it was "easier" or "more difficult" to motivate students in a multigrade classroom. Over half said it was more difficult. Teachers also believed that "assisting individual children" and "planning" were more difficult in the multigrade classroom. However, maintaining classroom control and student learning were seen to be about the same. The area believed to be the most difficult (84 percent) was "planning science and social studies without repetition." Clearly, teachers in this study believe it is more difficult to teach a multigrade classroom.

During interviews, teachers mentioned that special training for multigrade classrooms was critical. The most frequently mentioned need was having a practicum in a rural school. This was followed by developing skills in curriculum development (unit planning), class organization, individualizing instruction, and collecting resources and materials.

Table 1 provides an overview of the implications, by respondent group, for multigrade instruction drawn from the Bandy (1980) study. Many other studies, conducted both in the United States and abroad, produced similar findings.

Pietila (1978) describes the changes that have occurred in the combined classrooms of Finland. Combined classrooms of grades 1-6 in a one-teacher school are very rare. As late as 1950, there were more than a thousand of these schools. But the instructional problems were so great that the Ministry of Education eliminated nearly all of them.

Because the small, rural schools play such an important part in delivering community services in this primarily rural country, a decision was made to sustain and strengthen them with centrally established curriculum guidelines and organizational standards. For example, the smallest school would have one teacher for grades 1-6, the next size school would have two teachers, where grades 1-3 would be taught by one

Table 1
Implications for Teaching in A Multigrade Classroom

Principals' Perceptions	Teachers' Perceptions
1. Teachers need methods for small group instruction.	1. Teachers must be well organized to teach.
2. Teachers must be trained to teach multigrade classrooms.	2. Teachers should be trained in cross-age tutoring.
3. Teachers must be prepared to use cross-age tutorial systems.	3. Social studies and science need special adaptations.
4. Experience must be developed in working with auxiliary personnel.	4. Teachers need awareness of individualized reading programs.

teacher and grades 4-6 taught by the second teacher. The next size school would employ three teachers, with every two grades combined (1-2, 3-4, and 5-6). Curriculum was standardized by grade level. This posed a major problem for teachers of combined grades. If you teach a combined grade of third and fourth graders, what grade level do you teach—the third or fourth level curriculum or both? Students transferring from one school to the next might find themselves studying the same material they had the previous year. To avert potential problems, different types of grouping strategies were piloted by the Ministry of Education. The most successful practices centered on flexible grouping that was based on student and situational needs across grades rather than by age/grade groups.

Teachers in Finland who teach in combined or multigrade classrooms believe there are many advantages to multigrade instruction: "The small size of combined grades compensates many instructional difficulties. Age-wise heterogeneous groups are natural bodies where the members educate each other. The older pupils in a combined grade may function as instructors to younger ones" (Pietila, 1978, p. 15). However, materials preparation for use with flexible grouping makes a great demand on teacher time because materials must be explicit, readable, unambiguous and coherent. Materials must "include the elements . . . [which] lead to critical thinking and develop an

evaluative approach in the pupil. Primary emphasis should be placed on the development of an internal evaluation system in the materials" (p. 21). With so many different levels of students to teach, the teacher must rely heavily on student self-direction and materials that lend themselves to independent study.

The complexity of multigrade instruction is even more pronounced in developing nations. In 1980, UNESCO held a conference with representatives from India, Korea, Maldives, Nepal, Thailand, Philippines, Sri Lanka, and Indonesia. The conference focused on innovative approaches to teaching disadvantaged groups and teaching in the multigrade classroom. The problems and learning difficulties created by multigrade instruction were nearly similar for each country. These differences are primarily related to financial, geographic and demographic variables.

Multigrade classes in these countries tend to have large numbers of students and few teachers. The most common pattern of organization is the two-grade combination class. However, three or more grades per classroom were common to all countries. Of the eight countries represented, none indicated they had schools with a range of more than four grades. For example, an individual teacher may have a classroom of 30 fourth graders and 27 fifth graders or a classroom of 35 students in grades 3 through 6. Teachers in these situations face a formidable teaching challenge.

During the conference, five general problem areas emerged:

1. Inadequately trained teachers.
2. Scarcity of varied levels and types of materials.
3. Lack of flexible and special types of curriculum organization for multigrade classes.
4. Inadequate school facilities.
5. Lack of incentives for teachers of multiple classes (UNESCO,1981).

Similar to preservice training in the United States, all countries participating in the conference reported that the teacher preparation for working in multigrade classrooms was identical to that provided for teachers of single-grade classrooms. In other words, individuals going into teaching were not prepared for teaching multigrade classrooms.

Ironically, the concerns and depiction of problems in these developing countries echo many of the concerns voiced in the United States and Canada by multigrade classroom teachers and rural educators. The most prominent similarity is the need for curriculum and program modification that reflect the culture of the local community and the needs of students within the demands created by multigrade organization. In this regard, two recommendations emerged from the conference.

First, curriculum needs to be restructured so that it is community based: "The environment in which the community lives, the history and culture, the utilization of skilled persons in the community for improving the quality of education should be emphasized" (UNESCO, 1981 p. 80; Wigginton, 1985).

Second, innovative programs have a difficult time because the existing educational system is traditional and this constrains perceptions of what may be possible: "The four walls of the classroom and the long periods demanded by programs in different countries somewhat inhibit and restrict the child's activities. Outdoor activities should be encouraged and experiences outside the classroom should be given a place in the curriculum" (UNESCO, 1981, p. 86).

Multigrade classroom instruction places greater demands on teachers than teaching in a single grade. To be effective, teachers need to spend more time in planning and preparation. This often means modifying existing grade level materials to ensure students will be successful. In addition, there are many demands that are simply conditions of rural life. Although rural living can have many rewards, these demands impact the rural teacher (Miller, 1988). When considered along with the requirements of the multigrade classroom, it is clear that the rural, multigrade classroom teacher has a demanding, but potentially very rewarding, job.

INSTRUCTION IN MULTIGRADE CLASSROOMS

Clearly, teaching a broad range of grade levels in the same classroom is complex and demanding. How can one teacher juggle all those grades with their wide levels of student maturity, ability and motivation? How can one teacher possibly prepare for the many curricular areas, meet individual student needs and have a time to eat lunch? There are many successful teachers and students who are living proof that mixed grade classes are a viable organizational structure for learning. Although empirical studies of these classrooms are quite scarce, enough descriptive literature exists to illustrate both the complexity and the rewards of the multigrade classroom.

Dodendorf (1983) conducted a study of a Midwestern rural two-room school, where 35 students spanning five grades, were taught. The classroom was organized into two rooms. The "lower" room contained students in grades K-4 while the "upper" room contained students in grades 5-8. All aspects of classroom life were carefully observed and their achievement test scores were compared with students from urban schools. Five positive environmental characteristics emerged from the observational data:

1. *School Routines*: These were structured so that children began the day, completed workbook assignments, met in small groups, went to the library, told stories, etc., with a minimum amount of noise and disruption. In part, this was due to a scheduling tree where each student's assignment was posted. It was also due to the highly predictable nature of class routines. For example, spelling tests were given all at once with the unique words for each grade given in turn.

2. *Group Learning*: Each grade met with the teacher twice a day. When non-grouped students needed help, they sought out an older student first and then waited at the teacher's station. Aides from the commu-

nity might have been helpful, but the teacher felt that confidentiality was a problem.

3. *Interdependence*: This area was found to be the most striking quality in the school. Younger children often approached older children for help. Mixing of ages and grades was seen both in the classroom and at recess.

4. *Independence*: Observed work habits of children indicated a high degree of self-discipline. They had specific assignments and timelines to meet. They passed out corrected workbooks without teacher prompting.

5. *Community Involvement*: Community members frequently visited the school. Mothers cooked hot lunch once a month and planned holiday parties. The board chairman stopped by to see if there were any needs. There did not appear to be a clear demarcation between the school and the community. Student attitudes toward new people entering the classroom were always hospitable and friendly. An example was the way kindergartners were welcomed into the classroom. Older students were warm and helped them, frequently explaining what was being worked on.

Results were favorable for the rural school. In terms of academics, students performed nearly the same as their urban counterparts. Only on a social studies subtest was there any significant difference. In terms of classroom climate and social relationships, the author noted that:

> Several advantages accrued for children and their parents in this rural school. The observed positive qualities far outweighed the disadvantages, and, more importantly, the values emphasized in the school reflected the community's values. This match of values is rarely achieved in heterogeneous urban schools. Value congruence between home and school certainly fostered a secure,

stable world for these children to grow up in (p. 103).

Clearly, Dodendorf's study suggests that the five-grade classroom can be a socially and academically effective learning environment for students. The implication, however, is that success depends on the ability of the teacher to organize and manage instruction so that cooperation, independence and a motivation to learn become environmental norms.

Embry (1981) describes the history of Utah's country schools since the early 1900s. Of particular interest is her description of two very small one- and two-room schools. Garrison School is less than 20 years old and consists of a small office, closet space and one large classroom that can be divided into two areas. In 1980, there were nine students covering a span of six grades. Students were given responsibility for a large share of housekeeping tasks on a rotating basis: keeping the room clean (janitor), taking care of paper and supplies (supply clerk), checking out books (librarian), ringing the bell, monitoring play equipment, organizing the calendar, leading flag salute, and sharpening pencils. Each week a student was honored by not having duties for the week. Developing self-reliance, responsibility and independence in students enabled the teacher to better meet individual student needs. It also developed a strong sense of community and cooperation within the classroom.

In order to meet the needs of all students at their respective instructional level, the teacher relied heavily on scheduling and cross-age tutoring. For example, the student who was the acting librarian that week read a daily story to younger children while the teacher worked with the older students. Students also worked together to complete tasks while the teacher met students individually. Reading, math, English and spelling were handled in this individualized manner. All other subjects were taught as a group, with each student working at their particular level; art, social studies, science, and music projects were frequently employed. The entire school also sang together, played recorders, had a marching band, and published a school newspaper. Because the school is so isolated, it serves as the center of the community. Parents provided help with track meets, field trips and special programs.

Park Valley, Utah, is a slightly larger school than Garrison, with two teachers serving grades K-10. Students were divided into a K-4 class and a 5-10 class. There was an aide in the lower level who taught kindergarten under the teacher's supervision. This freed the teacher to work with the older students. An additional aide came in several times a week and provided time for the teacher to work on academic subjects. On the aide's days off, the teacher worked on music, arts, crafts and physical education. A similar pattern of organization was followed with the upper level class. Because of the complexity of subject matter in the upper level class, three aides worked under the teacher's supervision.

In the lower level class, the teacher organized instruction around key concepts that could be introduced to all students and then individualized to the different levels in the class. For example, time was explained to all the students. The youngest ones drew hands on clocks while the teacher gave instruction on minutes to other students. Special activities also serve as a basis for total grouping activities: fire prevention week led to a play, Valentine's Day led to an all-school party, the Christmas program involved everyone. For Columbus Day and Thanksgiving, students all worked together on special projects. Students were also grouped by ability so that the talented second grader could work with the fourth grader or the slower student could work with younger students for special skills.

In both Garrison and Park Valley Schools, the teachers took full advantage of the flexibility afforded a multigrade classroom. The teachers used a two-phased approach to group instruction. In the first phase, they introduced a concept to the entire class (across all grade levels). This allowed for cross-grade interaction with the concurrent benefits of younger students learning from older ones. It also was a more efficient use of teacher time. In the second phase, the teacher had students engaged in closed-task activities at their respective ability levels. Students also can be easily moved from one ability level to another as needed without feeling the stigma that is usually associated with out-of-grade placements.

Special events such as holidays, field trips, or any activity that does not require strict grouping by ability (such as closed-task skills), were organized around total class participation. Every member of the class contributes and shares in the successes of everyone else. Students also learn to be responsible and self-directed, able to work independently, provide help to others, and receive help when needed. This independence is critically important because it enables the teacher to work individually with students.

Betsy Bryan's (1986) story is unique. She completed her teaching degree in 1980 from an eastern

college. While getting her teaching degree, she student taught in a small, rural, two-room school and became convinced that she wanted to teach in a similar situation. Unable to secure a position on the East Coast, she went to New Mexico and obtained a position as a K-1 teacher (so she was told by the school board). With difficulty, she found a house to live in and then school began. However, things had changed since her interview with the school board. She now had a class of 18 students ranging from ages five to nine:

> Developmentally, they ranged from kids who barely spoke and still wet their pants to children who were ready for third grade work. Some spoke Spanish and some didn't. There were child neglect cases and others who came from caring homes. A few had learning disabilities while most learned easily and delighted in it (p. 3).

To make matters even more formidable, she had no "professional direction or support, limited materials, and little experience" (p. 3). She was not supervised or expected to maintain grade level differences. However, she had student taught with two master rural teachers who provided examples upon which she could pattern her own teaching.

At first, in order to provide structure and order, she stuck to the basal reader and the other available materials. As the year progressed and she developed a relationship with her class, Bryan began developing her own materials, "scrounging through garage sales for children's books, and visiting a teacher center one hundred miles away to get ideas and supplies" (1986, p. 3). Unfortunately, Bryan does not provide sufficient detail to allow the reader to know how she managed instruction or curriculum. She does tell us that national test scores revealed her students were performing above the national average. Although positive about her first teaching experience, Bryan left after only one year.

Unlike the Dodendorf (1983) study or the description of the two rural Utah schools (Embry, 1981), Bryan found herself an outsider in an unknown teaching situation. She faced difficulty finding housing, a sudden change in her teaching assignment, feelings of isolation from other teachers and the community. One wonders: If Bryan had remained, would her experience have turned out more like that described by Dodendorf? From her own words, it seems as if conditions in the school and the community preempted that possibility:

. . . it appears that the district [I] taught in [was] full of conflict and lacked leaders who could solve these conflicts. The staffs . . . were from diverse backgrounds and had widely different motivations and philosophies. There were bound to be problems and yet neither the community nor the administration nor the teachers were able to resolve them. [The district] lacked a sense of direction and demonstrated little concern for their teachers. Other factors that influenced [my] decision to leave included living conditions and the loneliness [I] felt trying to fit into [a] rural close-knit communit[y] (p. 5).

Ann Hoffman's (1973) story is quite different from that of Betsy Bryan (1986). Hoffman's school was smaller than Bryan's, but her class size and range of students was similar. When Hoffman first began to teach in the Kingvale two-room school, she had 15 students in grades K-3 and no aide, but after three years her class grew to 27 students and an aide was hired. Hoffman says that when she first began teaching in Kingvale, "we had a wonderful time. In the past two years the class load has grown. We still have a wonderful time . . . but a lot noisier one!" (p. 42).

Hoffman (1973) described in detail how she organized her classroom to accommodate student needs. Clearly, her planning and organization were well in advance of instruction. Before school began, she reviewed science and social studies texts for upper-grade students and made a list of what must be covered, by week, for the entire year. Materials and films were ordered at this time. Advanced planning and preparation proved invaluable to Hoffman's success as a multigrade teacher.

Hoffman distinguished between those subjects that lend themselves to total class instruction and those that must be taught on a more individualized and/or graded basis. For example, health, storytime, literature, drama, and music can be taught to the total class. These subjects are also considered "elastic" in that they can be altered, combined or skipped depending on circumstances. Consistent time is scheduled for high priority, skill-based subjects such as reading and math. For example, reading and math were taught in the morning, with students working independently while the teacher holds conferences with and instructs other students. First grade was taught as a group, but the other grades are primarily individualized. Index cards were used to track individual progress. Reading was

taught for 70 minutes daily.

What is clear from Hoffman's account of her classroom is that she was well organized and had a clear structure for the way instructional events unfolded. Students knew what was expected and classroom routines were well established. There was also a sense of the novel and interesting. There were daily student oral presentations (across grades) of stories, poems, reports and current events. A learning center on magnets and a center with special books for students could be found. Friends dropped into the classroom and became part of a lesson. Hoffman says she tried to keep her room interesting. But she notes the multigrade environment is not all roses:

I can't pass a problem child on to another teacher the next year. I can't use the same old art ideas year after year. Science, social studies, music—every subject has to be completely revamped each year (p. 45).

Films are boring when seen for several years in a row and so have to be changed. Room decorations must be new and different. I can't get new ideas from the teachers next door. I have to be super-prepared or I'm in for a very hectic day (1973, p. 45).

Yet, despite these changes, the strengths far outweigh the disadvantages:

. . .[I]t is a most satisfying feeling to watch a kindergartner mature into a hard-working third-grader. A child can easily be placed ahead or back in areas in which he excels or is having trouble. Older children can work with the younger children . . . we have a ski program for physical education. The parents are friendly and helpful (1973, p. 45).

CONCLUSION

The multigrade classroom and one-room school are alive and well in rural America. Stories like Ann Hoffman's (1973) from Kingvale abound if someone is there to hear them. Unfortunately, the story told by Betsy Bryan (1986) is often heard instead. Problems of inadequate facilities, poor leadership, and limited resources have been used as evidence for seeking consolidation. Without question, teaching in a multigrade classroom with more than two grades is a demanding task requiring a special type of individual. It also requires training, community understanding and support.

As evidenced in the descriptions presented, the multigrade teacher must be well organized and put in much preparation time. Educators have much to learn from these teachers about classroom management and instructional organization. The multigrade classroom is an environment where routines are clearly understood and followed. Students learn to be self-directed learners, often working alone or in small groups. They must also be able to help others and serve as positive role models. A supportive, family-like atmosphere often must be developed, one in which cooperation and solidarity among all students predominates. Without these elements, a multigrade teacher could not manage the vast variability in student needs. Bruce Barker (1986) does an excellent job summarizing the characteristics and working conditions that the multigrade classroom teacher faces:

> She lives in a remote setting in either the Midwest or far West, enjoys teaching in a small school . . . she teaches an average of 11 students ranging in grades one through eight, works an average of about nine hours a day in tasks related to instruction, yet is also the school custodian and school secretary. She may even prepare the school lunch and drive the school bus . . . the assignment to teach in a one-teacher school may be the most demanding of all positions in the profession, but for those who love young people and enjoy teaching, it could well be the most rewarding (p. 150).

On face value, students in multigrade classrooms would appear to fare better than students in a single-grade classroom. However, the evidence suggests that from the point of view of school organizational norms and levels of teacher preparedness, the multigrade classroom generally serves as a temporary remedy to school enrollment and financial concerns.

In other words, most multigrade (especially combined grades) classrooms are viewed as temporary remedies to be endured for a year (or so) until things return to "normal." Lest we too quickly forget our educational heritage in the district school, there still are more than 1,000 one-room schools in the United States where three or more grades are taught together (Muse, Smith, & Barker, 1987). The tide of teacher and administrative opinion strongly favors organizing schools by grade level.

The skills needed to effectively teach the multi-

grade and the single-grade (multilevel) classroom appears to be quite similar. The differences between the two classrooms may be more a product of socialization and expectation than of fact. Clearly, students are harmed when the teacher fails to recognize and teach to the individual differences in a classroom. It also is apparent that teachers are harmed when they have not been adequately prepared to teach students with varying ages and abilities. Wragg (1984) provides an overview of these instructional implications when he describes the results of a large-scale study of teaching skills:

> There seemed to be much less confidence among teachers about how best to teach bright pupils and slow learners in mixed-ability classes than in any other aspect of professional work we studied during the project. Most mixed-ability teaching was to the whole class, and some schools made almost no use at all of cooperative groupwork . . . Even the teachers we studied who were regarded as successful found it very exacting to teach a mixed-ability class well, and were less sure about their teaching of bright pupils than about other aspects (p. 197).

What does the research tell us regarding the skills required of the multigrade teacher? Wragg's (1984) observation suggests that the skills needed of the single-grade, multiability classroom are similar to those of the multigrade teacher. With an increase in the number of grades taught in a single classroom, a greater demand is placed on teacher resources, both cognitive and emotional. Six key variables affecting successful multigrade teaching were identified from the research:

1. *Classroom organization*: arranging and organizing instructional resources and the physical environment in order to facilitate student learning, independence and interdependence.

2. *Classroom management and discipline*: developing and implementing classroom schedules and routines that promote clear, predictable instructional patterns, especially those that enhance student responsibility for their own learning. Developing independence and interdependence is also stressed.

3. *Instructional organization and curriculum:* planning, developing and implementing instructional strategies and routines that allow for a maximum of cooperative and self-directed student learning based on diagnosed student needs. This also includes the effective use of time.

4. *Instructional delivery and grouping:* instructional methods that will improve the quality of instruction, including strategies for organizing group learning activities across and within grade levels, especially those that develop interdependence and cooperation among students.

5. *Self-directed learning:* developing skills and strategies in students that allow for a high level of independence and efficiency in learning individually or in combination with other students.

6. *Peer tutoring:* developing skills and routines whereby students serve as "teachers" to other students within and across differing grade levels.

In the multigrade classroom, more time must be spent in organizing and planning for instruction. This is required if the teacher wants to meet the individual needs of students and to successfully monitor student progress. Extra materials and strategies must be developed so that students will be meaningfully engaged. This allows the teacher to meet with small groups or individuals.

Since the teacher cannot be everywhere or with every student at the same time, the teacher shares instructional responsibilities with students within a context of clear rules and routines. Students know what is expected. They know what assignments to work on, when they are due, how to get them graded, how to get extra help, and where to turn them in.

Students learn how to help one another and themselves. At an early age, students are expected to develop interdependence. The effective multigrade teacher establishes a climate to promote and develop this independence. For example, when kindergarten students enter the classroom for the first time, they receive help and guidance not only from the teacher, but from older students. Soon, they learn to be self-directed learners capable of solving many of their own needs. They become self-sufficient. Kindergartners see how other students behave and they learn what is expected of them. Because older students willingly help them, kindergartners also learn cooperation and that the teacher is not the only source of knowledge.

Instructional grouping practices also play an important role in the successful multigrade classroom. Grouping is a strategy for meeting teacher and student needs. The teacher emphasizes the similarities among the different grades and teaches to them, thus conserving valuable teacher time. For example, whole-class (across grades) instruction is often used since the teacher can have contact with more students. However, whole-class instruction in the effective multigrade classroom differs from what one generally finds in a single-grade class.

Multigrade teachers recognize that whole-class instruction must revolve around open task activities if all students are to be engaged. For example, a teacher can introduce a writing assignment through topic development where all students brainstorm for ideas. In this context, students from first through eighth grade can discuss and share their different perspectives. Students soon learn how to listen and respect the opinions of others. For the older students, first graders are not simply "those little kids from the primary grades down the hall." They are classmates. Learning cooperation is a survival skill—a necessary condition of life in the multigrade classroom. Everyone depends on each other and this interdependency extends beyond the walls of the school to include the community.

Teaching in the multigrade classroom also has many problems. It is more complex and demanding than the single-grade classroom. A teacher cannot ignore developmental differences in students nor be ill-prepared for a day's instruction. Demands on teacher time require well-developed organizational skills. Clearly, the multigrade classroom is not for the timid, inexperienced, or untrained teacher. The implications for teacher educators, rural school board members, administrators, teachers, and parents are far reaching.

Those seeking more information regarding teacher preparation, student performance and instructional strategies for the multigrade setting are referred to the complete text from which this paper has been abstracted: **The Multigrade Classroom: A Resource Handbook for Small, Rural Schools,** *available from Northwest Regional Educational Laboratory, 101 S.W. Main Street, Suite 500, Portland, OR 97204.*

REFERENCES

Bandy, J. & Gleadow, N. (1980). *The identification of skills and characteristics needed by country school teacher.* Victoria, BC: University of Victoria.

Barker, B. (1986). Teachers in the nation's surviving one-room schools. *Contemporary Education, 57*(3), 148-150.

Bryan, B. (1986). Rural teachers' experiences: Lessons for today. *The Rural Educator, 7*(3), 1-5.

Dodendorf, D. M. (1983). A unique rural school environment. *Psychology in the Schools, 20,* 99-104.

Embry, J. (1981). *Utah's country schools since 1896.* Provo, UT: Brigham Young University. (ERIC Document Reproduction Service No. ED 221 273)

Hoffman, A. (1973). A nice warm situation. *Teacher, 91,* 42-45.

Horn, J. G. (1983). Attempting to develop a program response to the needs of those preparing to teach in rural/small schools. (ERIC Document Reproduction Service No. ED 230 320)

Knight, E. E. (1983). A study of double grades in New Haven City schools. *Journal of Experimental Education, 7,* 11-18.

MacDonald, P.A. & Wurster, S. R. (1974). *Multiple grade primary versus segregated first grade: Effects on reading achievement.* Bethesda, MD. (ERIC Document Reproduction Service No. ED 094 336)

Miller, B. (1989). *The multigrade classroom: A resource handbook for small, rural schools.* Portland, OR: Northwest Regional Educational Laboratory.

Miller, B. (1988). *Teacher preparation for rural schools.* Portland, OR: Northwest Regional Educational Laboratory.

Muse, I., Smith, R. & Barker, B. (1987). *The one teacher school in the 1980s.* Las Cruces, NM: ERIC Clearinghouse on Rural Education and Small Schools.

Pietila, A. (Ed.). (1978). *Small schools and combined grades in Finland.* Helsinki, Finland. (ERIC Document Reproduction Service No. ED 161 564)

Pratt, C., & Treacy, K. (1986). *A study of student grouping practices in early childhood classes in western Australian government primary schools.* (Cooperative Research Series #9). Nedlands, Australia: Education Department of Western Australia.

UNESCO. (1981). *Education of disadvantaged groups and multiple class teaching: Studies and innovative approaches.* (Report of a Study Group Meeting). Jakarta.

Wigginton, E. (1985). *Sometimes a shining moment.* Garden City: Doubleday.

Wragg, E. C. (1984). Teaching skills. In E. C. Wragg (Ed.), *Classroom teaching skills* (pp. 1-20).

Research in Rural Education, Volume 3, Number 3, 1986

On the Merits of Multiage Classrooms

DAVID PRATT, PH.D.[1]

This paper brings together evidence from a variety of fields which throws light on the practice of age segregation in schools. Strict age segregation is essentially a phenomenon of the last century. Research studies show no consistent benefits to age segregation, and some affective and social advantages from multiage grouping. It is concluded that multiage and multigrade classrooms are socially and psychologically healthy environments.

A PERENNIAL DEBATE

Reflection on the quality of learning environments is a hallmark of the educational professional. Those professionals who work in small schools often wonder about the costs and benefits of the multiage and multigrade classrooms with which they are more familiar than their colleagues in larger schools. This interest is currently shared by the increasing number of teachers in medium-sized schools who find themselves teaching split grades. Proposals to close small schools often act as a catalyst for debate on this issue, with the intuition of parents and teachers frequently pitted against the efficiency rationale of district administrators. Such debates usually end with the execution or reprieve of the school in question, but with the educational issue unresolved.

In this paper, I shall attempt to summarize evidence that bears on the question of the merits of multiage classrooms. This includes not only the findings of experimental research, but also relevant evidence from ethology, anthropology, and history. The weight of this evidence strongly suggests that multiage classrooms have many benefits to children which cannot be as fully realized in age-segregated classrooms.

THE HISTORICAL CONTEXT OF AGE SEGREGATION

Most of us grew up in an age-segregated school system. So did our parents and grandparents, and this makes it easy to assume that such a school structure is both natural and universal. In fact, it is universal neither geographically nor historically. A quarter of Scotland's primary schools have fewer than fifty students; 80% of Portuguese children go to schools with no more than two classrooms; and there are 11,000 one-teacher rural schools in France [34]. Age segregation, as practised in most large schools, is a relatively recent phenomenon, and one which runs counter to the pattern of upbringing of the young which previously existed for millions of years.

Studies of primates show that almost all of the 193 living species of monkeys and apes grow up in societies characterized by diversity of age. According to Jolly [26], "the striking characteristic of young, socially living primates is their social play" (p. 261). The context in which the young primate moves from dependence on the mother to adulthood is the mixed-age play group, whose members range from infancy to adolescence. In the play group, the young primate learns social and gender roles, control of aggression, and survival and nurturing skills. In general, the higher the primate is on the evolutionary scale, the more heterogeneous is the age composition of the play group.

A very similar pattern is found in anthropological studies of the approximately 180 hunting/gathering societies which survived into the present century, such as the Inuit, the Australian aborigines, and the !Kung San people of the Kalahari desert. Such societies typically live in groups of 30 to 40. Births are spaced a minimum of three years apart, so that the mother never has more than one infant to care for. The infant joins the play group after about the age of 18 months, imitating and relying on older children, who take responsibility for younger ones. Draper [13] records that "a typical gang of children joined temporarily in some play in the village might include a 5-year-old boy, an 11-year-old girl, a 14-year-old boy, and a 2-year-old toddler hanging on the fringe of the action" (p. 202). Cross-cultural studies show that in simpler societies, children spend more time caretaking infants, and are more nurturant than in more complex cultures. In all societies, aggression is more frequent among age-mates than in mixed-age groups [50]. Konner [27] draws the following conclusions from the ethological and anthropological evidence:

> Infants are inept in relating to one another for the simple reason that they were never called on to do so during millions of years of evolution; consequently they could not have been selected for an ability to do this. They were selected instead for an ability to become integrated into a multiage group . . . The apes and protohominids went to considerable trouble to evolve for us a successful childhood in nonpeer play groups. Perhaps we should be a bit more cautious before we abandon the nonpeer pattern. (pp. 122-123)

The age-stratified culture in which we live is largely a product of the last two hundred years. In medieval Europe and in colonial America, children grew up surrounded by other children and adults of all different ages.

---

[1]Professor of Education, Duncan McArthur Hall, Queen's University, Kingston, Canada K7L 3N6.

Families were larger, and infant mortality and a high fertility rate resulted in a wide variance in sibling age. Schools and classrooms contained considerable age diversity. In the dedicated one-room school building that emerged in the eighteenth century, a full-time teacher would use individual and tutorial methods to instruct a group of 10 to 30 pupils ranging in age from 6 to 14 years [10].

The death-knell of the one-room school was sounded when Horace Mann [33], Secretary of the Massachusetts Board of Education, visited schools in Prussia in 1843 and reported that

the first element of superiority in a Prussian school . . . consists in the proper classification of the scholars. In all places where the numbers are sufficiently large to allow it, the children are divided according to ages and attainments, and a single teacher has the charge only of a single class . . . There is a no obstacle whatever . . . to the introduction at once of this mode of dividing and classifying scholars in all our large towns. (p. 84)

Within a decade, Mann's ideas were being widely accepted by administrators who saw in them a parallel with successful manufacturing practice [32]:

The principle of the division of labor holds good in schools, as in mechanical industry. One might as justly demand that all operations of carding, spinning and weaving be carried out in the same room, and by the same hands, as insist that children of different ages and attainments should go to the same school and be instructed by the same teacher.

Legislation followed standardizing age of entry and establishing sequential grade levels and curricula. Population concentration and improved transportation facilitated the development of large schools. The death of the one-room school in the United States and Canada was delayed by the Depression, the world wars, and the long struggle of rural communities to preserve it against the will of urban educational bureaucracies [8]. But by the 1950s, the standard environment of youth was the suburb, consisting largely of middle-aged parents and school-age children. By then, the "generation gap" was accepted as a fact of life, and the over-60s, perceived as socially and economically marginal, were segregated in high-rise apartments, retirement villages, and homes for the elderly.

By the mid-twentieth century, classrooms were more narrowly segregated by age than ever before. In 1918 the standard deviation of age in American Grade 9 classrooms was 14.1 months; in 1952 it was 8.6 months [29]. Ability grouping, which became popular after about 1920, further reduced the variety present in classrooms. It was not until 1959 that the first major challenge to age segregation in schools appeared, in the form of *The Nongraded School* by Goodlad and Anderson. In the 1963 edition [19], the authors documented the variability in the intellectual, emotional, and physical growth of children and adolescents:

Grouping children "homogeneously" on the basis of a single criterion does not produce a group that is homogeneous to the same degree judged by other criteria . . . Teachers who proceed as though their class of gifted or retarded pupils were homogeneous are fooling themselves and cheating their pupils. (p. 17)

The influence of the book was rapid. Within a few years, thousands of school districts were claiming that at least some of their schools were nongraded. But the movement turned out to be an archetypal case of fashionable rhetoric concealing educational inertia. The research on nongrading, which includes at least 50 doctoral theses, shows that although formal grade distinctions were often removed, the narrow age structure of classrooms usually remained intact. Goodlad [18] expressed his own disillusion in 1968:

My own view . . . is that there are, indeed, precious few nongraded schools . . . The concepts guiding nongrading are becoming part of the rambling rhetoric, the cant of current educational orthodoxy. (p. 4)

The nongraded school movement was not powerful enough to overcome organizational structures which were politically safe and administratively convenient. But one thing it did was to stimulate a great deal of empirical research into the effects of multiage and multigrade grouping. The body of this research points to some significant benefits to pupils who are placed in multiage settings.

CHILDREN'S FRIENDSHIPS

Children's friendships, both in classrooms and in naturalistic settings, have been one theme of the multiage research. The general picture that emerges from these studies is one of increased competition and aggression within same-age groups and increased harmony and nurturance within multiage groups [24; 48]. When children and adolescents find themselves in a mixed-age context, they associate and make friends across a relatively wide age range [43]. Rhoades [42] found that children in a nongraded elementary school chose friends from two years older to two years younger than themselves. In a study of adolescents outside school in Salt Lake City [15; 37], it was found that 31% of companions were other adolescents more than two years older or younger. Adolescent boys tended to associate with girls about 1½ years younger. While the average age difference among friendship groups in school was only 6 months, outside of school it was 14 months.

In the increasing number of high schools which are enrolling adults in regular classes, such friendships can cross generations. A student in one such class commented, "I would love to participate in a mixed-age class again. It is great the way the different age groups can work with each other." [46, p. 7]. In a classroom containing adolescents and senior citizens, a senior says, "I get along beautifully with the young students. I'm enjoying it all, even the homework" [4]; while a 17-year-old states, "I'm learning a great deal about life and living from them . . . I've learned that old age can be a wonderful thing." [5] The majority of older adults surveyed by Daum and Getzel [11] and by Spouse [45] expressed a preference for programs that allowed interactions with people of all ages.

It is a characteristic of young people that they imitate

and (both literally and figuratively) look up to children or adolescents who are older [3; 30] or whom they believe to be older [40]. One of the effects of this is that children receive maximum verbal stimulation and develop new vocabulary most rapidly when grouped with children slightly older than themselves [12; 20; 31; 49]. Studies of tutoring support these conclusions. Tutoring has a greater effect on the achievement of both tutor and tutee when the tutor is older than when both tutor and tutee are the same age [9]. This is consistent with Piagetian research which indicates that interaction between individuals at different levels of maturity will stimulate disequilibrium, equilibration, and cognitive growth in the less mature partner [6; 41]. For these reasons, multiage grouping appears particularly beneficial to the younger members of the group [23]. In conventional classrooms, younger members suffer a disproportionate incidence of failure and, even more alarmingly, of suicide [47]. In contrast to this, Milburn [35] noted that the youngest students in the multiage classrooms he studied consistently outperformed their peers in age-segregated classrooms.

Experimental studies in preschool settings confirm the positive effects of multiage grouping on social and emotional development. Hammack [21] found that three-, four-, and five-year-old children made more progress in self-concept in multiage than in single-age groups. Goldman [17] found three- and four-year-olds in mixed-age classes were more sociable than those in single-age classes. And in Israel, Bizman et al. [2] found that children in age-heterogeneous kindergartens were significantly more altruistic than children in age-homogeneous kindergartens.

It seems that, while age is a determinant of friendship, children and adolescents choose friends who are at an equivalent level in terms of development rather than chronological age [22]. In a multiage situation, children will more readily find friends at their own level. This is supported by evidence that fewer isolates are found in multiage than in age-segregated classrooms [1; 51]. Younger children are particularly helpful in reducing the isolation of socially withdrawn older children when assigned to them as playmates [16]. As childhood isolation is a significant predictor of later psychiatric disorder [14; 38], this must be counted a significant benefit of the multiage classroom.

EXPERIMENTAL STUDIES OF MULTIAGE CLASSROOMS

A major purpose of this review was to survey the results of the available experimental research in multiage grouping in classrooms. A total of thirty experimental studies were located, conducted between 1948 and 1983 in the United States and Canada. All examined the results of multiage grouping in elementary schools. All "multiage" classes contained a range of two or three years. Achievement variables were usually reading and mathematics scores on standardized tests. Social/emotional variables were commonly self-concept and attitude toward school. Many of the studies suffer from imperfect control of dif-

TABLE 1

Empirical Studies in Multiage Grouping
(30 Studies)

	Academic Achievement	Social/Emotional Development
Studies favoring conventional grouping	5	0
Inconclusive studies	13	6
Studies favoring multiage grouping	10	9

ferences between teachers and schools which elected or rejected multiage grouping. Too few of the studies reported sufficiently complete statistical data to allow more than a counting procedure for summation of the results.

Studies were classified as "favoring conventional grouping," "inconclusive," or "favoring multiage grouping," on the basis of the expressed judgment of their authors, which in all cases appeared to be justified by their findings. Table 1 shows the results for all 30 studies. Table 2 shows the results from those studies which were conducted as doctoral theses. Doctoral theses are in general likely to be relatively rigorous in their design, and meta-analyses have found theses more likely to report inconclusive results [44].

The findings summarized in Tables 1 and 2 suggest that multiage grouping has no consistent effect on academic achievement. Multiage grouping does, however, tend to be associated with better self-concept and attitude toward school. None of the 30 studies found a consistent negative relationship in this area. Similarly, in the one study located of a nongraded secondary school, academic achievement was unaffected, but the drop-out rate was significantly lower in the non-graded school [7]. Teacher attitudes appear to be determined by experience: teachers were generally found to approve of the structure with which they had become familiar [36].

Collectively, the empirical studies indicate that multiage grouping has no consistent effect on academic achievement, but has a generally benign effect on social and emotional development.

DIVERSITY AND UNIFORMITY

District administrators often use two arguments to support the closing of small schools. One is that such schools

TABLE 2

Empirical Studies in Multiage Grouping
(10 Doctoral Studies)

	Academic Achievement	Social/Emotional Development
Studies favoring conventional grouping	1	0
Inconclusive studies	5	4
Studies favoring multiage grouping	2	3

are financially inefficient; another is that their multiage classrooms are educationally undesirable. The first argument is fallible; recent research [34] shows that financial savings from such closings are often illusory, as they are subsequently eaten up by costs of transporting students. The research reviewed in this paper indicates that the second argument is also ill-founded. Multiage classrooms appear to convey a number of benefits, and no disadvantages, to their pupils.

Age-segregated classrooms are particularly difficult for children whose development differs from the norm. In conventional schools, the child of exceptional intellectual gifts is sometimes allowed or encouraged to "skip" a grade, which, although usually successful [28], is socially problematic and a poor substitute for genuine acceleration. The child whose development is slower than the norm faces the unmitigated disaster of grade repetition [25]. Even the least radical multiage structure, the split-grade classroom, can deal much more flexibly with both faster and slower learners. Some jurisdictions are now beginning to take note of these factors. In Canada, the Province of Ontario recently proposed for discussion a policy of flexible entry, multiage integration, and continuous progress in the primary division [39].

The social environment of young people during their formative years is a matter of considerable importance to educators and to parents. Conventional structures, though sanctioned by a century of familiarity, must be questioned if they stimulate rivalry, aggression, and isolation, for no apparent advantage. Environments that include a range of ages must be considered if they promise greater cooperation, nurturance, and friendship, for no apparent cost. The evidence on multiage grouping appears to confirm the basic principle that diversity enriches and uniformity impoverishes.

Conventional schools and classrooms could reap some of the benefits of diversity by developing programs of cross-age tutoring, by encouraging adults and senior citizens to participate in schools as students and volunteers, by organizing extracurricular activities that cut across grade and age lines, and by welcoming rather than resisting split grades. In small schools and multiage classrooms, teachers live with the daily challenge of working in environments that depart from the general norm. The creativity and inventiveness required exacts a toll in time and energy. But such educators may take encouragement from the fact that the mass of evidence indicates that, for their pupils, these environments are socially and psychologically healthy places.

REFERENCES

1. Adams, J.J. Achievement and social adjustment of pupils in combination classes enrolling pupils of more than one grade level. *Journal of Educational Research,* 1953, *47,* 151-155.

2. Bizman, A., Yinon, Y., Mivitzari, E., & Shavit, R. Effects of the age structure of the kindergarten on altruistic behavior. *Journal of School Psychology,* 1978, *16,* 154-160.

3. Blythe, D.A., Hill, J.P., & Smyth, C.K. The influence of older adolescents on younger adolescents: Do grade-level arrangements make a difference in behaviors, attitudes, and experiences? *Journal of Early Adolescence,* 1981, *1,* 85-110.

4. Bowering, C. LC students, old people walk hand-in-hand down a two-way street. Kingston *Whig-Standard,* 28 November 1978, p. 14.

5. Bowering, C. The young and old "bridge the gap" at a Kingston school. Kingston *Whig-Standard,* 7 November 1978, p. 16.

6. Bunting, J.R. Egocentrism: The effects of social interactions through multi-age grouping. (Doctoral dissertation, State University of New York at Buffalo, 1974). *Dissertation Abstracts International,* 1965, *35,* 6356A.

7. Chalfant, L.S. A three-year comparative study between students in a graded and nongraded secondary school (Doctoral dissertation, Utah State University, 1972). *Dissertation Abstracts International,* 1973, *33,* 3178A.

8. Cochrane, J. *The one-room School in Canada.* Toronto: Fitzhenry and Whiteside, 1981.

9. Cohen, P.A., Kulik, J.A., & Kulik, C.C. Educational outcomes of tutoring: A meta-analysis of findings. *American Educational Research Journal,* 1982, *19,* 237-248.

10. Cremin, L.A. *The transformation of the school: Progressivism in American education 1867-1957.* New York: Vintage Books, 1961.

11. Daum, M., & Getzel, G.S. Preference for age-homogeneous versus age-heterogeneous social interaction. Paper presented at the annual meeting of the Gerontological Society, San Diego, November 1980. (ERIC Document Reproduction Service No. ED 200 854).

12. Day, B., & Hunt, G.H. Multiage classrooms: An analysis of verbal communication. *Elementary School Journal,* 1974, *75,* 458-464.

13. Draper, N. Social and economic constraints on child life among the !Kung. In R.B. Lee & I. De Vore (Eds.), *Kalahari hunter-gatherers: Studies of the !Kung San and their neighbors.* Cambridge, MA: Harvard University Press, 1976, pp. 199-217.

14. Duck, S. *Friends for life.* Brighton, U.K.: Harvester Press, 1983.

15. Ellis, S., Rogoff, B., & Cromer, C.C. Age segregation in children's social interactions. *Developmental Psychology,* 1981, *17*(4), 399-407.

16. Furman, W., Rahe, D.F., & Hartup, W.W. Rehabilitation of socially withdrawn preschool children through mixed-age and same-age socialization. *Child Development,* 1979, *50,* 915-922.

17. Goldman, J.A. Social participation of preschool children in same- versus mixed-age groups. *Child Development,* 1981, *52,* 644-650.

18. Goodlad, J.I. Editorial: The non-graded school. In *National Elementary Principal, the Nongraded School.* Washington, DC: NEA, 1968, pp. 4-5.

19. Goodlad, J.I., & Anderson, R.H. *The nongraded elementary school* (Rev.ed.). New York: Harcourt, Brace, and World, 1963.

20. Graziano, W., French, D., Brownell, C.A., & Hartup, W.W. Peer interaction in same- and mixed-age triads in relation to chronological age and incentive condition. *Child Development,* 1976, *47,* 707-714.

21. Hammack, B.G. Self-concept: Evaluation of preschool children in single and multi-age classroom settings (Doctoral dissertation, Texas Women's University, 1974). *Dissertation Abstracts International,* 1975, *35,* 6572-6573.

22. Hartup, W.W. Cross-age versus same-age peer interaction: Ethological and cross-cultural perspectives. In V.L. Allen (Ed.), *Children as teachers: Theory and research on tutoring.* New York: Academic Press, 1976, pp. 41-55.

23. Hartup, W.W. Developmental implications and interactions in same- and mixed-age situations. *Young Children.* March 1977, 4-13.

24. Hartup, W.W. The social worlds of childhood. *American Psychologist,* 1979, *34,* 944-950.

25. Holmes, C.T., & Matthews, K.M. The effects of non-promotion on elementary and junior high school pupils: A meta-analysis. *Review of Educational Research,* 1984, *54*(2), 225-236.

26. Jolly, A. *The evolution of primate behavior.* New York: Macmillan, 1972.

27. Konner, M. Relations among infants and juveniles in comparative perspective. In M. Lewis & L.A. Rosenblum (Eds.), *Friendship and peer relations.* New York: Wiley, 1975, pp. 99-129.

28. Kulik, J., & Kulik, C-L.C. Effects of accelerated instruction on students. *Review of Educational Research,* 1984, *54,* 409-425.

29. Lennon, R.T., & Mitchell, B.C. Trends in age-grade relationship: A 35-year review. *School Society,* 1955, *82,* 123-125.

30. Lewis, M., Young, G., Brooks, J., & Michaelson, L. The beginnings of friendship. In M. Lewis & L.A. Rosenblum (Eds.), *Friendship and peer relations.* New York: Wiley, 1975, pp. 27-66.

31. Lougee, M.D., Grueneich, R., & Hartup, W.W. Social interaction in same- and mixed-age dyads of preschool children. *Child Development,* 1977, *48,* 1353-1361.

32. *Lowell School Committee Report of 1852.* Cited in D. Bruck, The schools of Lowell, 1824-1861: A case study in the origins of modern public education in America. Unpublished doctoral dissertation, Harvard University, 1970.

33. Mann, H. Seventh report to the Massachusetts Board of Education, 1843. Cited in E.P. Cubberley, *Readings in public education in the United States.* Westport, CT: Greenwood Press, 1970, 287-288.

34. Marshall, D.G. Closing small schools: Or when is small too small? *Education Canada,* 1985, *25*(3), 10-16.

35. Milburn, D. A study of multi-age or family-grouped classrooms. *Phi Delta Kappan,* 1981, *62,* 513-514.

36. Moodie, A.G. *A survey of teachers' opinions regarding multi-age classes.* Vancouver: Board of School Trustees, Department of Planning and Evaluation, 1971.

37. Montemayor, R., & Van Komen, R. Age segregation of adolescents in and out of school. *Journal of Youth and Adolescence,* 1980, *9,* 371-381.

38. Oden, S. A child's social isolation: Origins, prevention, intervention. In G. Cartledge & J.F. Milburn (Eds.), *Teaching social skills to children: Innovative approaches.* New York: Pergamon Press, 1980, pp. 179-202.

39. Ontario Ministry of Education. *Report of the early primary education project.* Toronto: Ontario Ministry of Education, 1985.

40. Peifer, M.R. *The effects of varying age-grade status of models on the imitative behavior of six-year-old boys.* Newark, DE: The University of Delaware, 1971.

41. Piaget, J. *The psychology of intelligence.* London: Routledge & Kegan Paul, 1950.

42. Rhoades, W.M. Erasing grade lines. *The Elementary School Journal,* 1966, *67,* 140-145.

43. Roopnarine, J.L., & Johnson, J.E. Socialization in a mixed-age experimental program. *Developmental Psychology,* 1984, *20*(5), 828-832.

44. Smith, M.L. Publication bias and meta-analysis. *Evaluation in Education: An International Review Series,* 1980, *4*(1), 22-24.

45. Spouse, B.M. *Participation motivation of older adult learners.* Paper presented at the annual meeting of the Association for Gerontology in Higher Education, Cincinnati, March 1981. (ERIC Document Reproduction Service No. ED 199 404).

46. Steurer, S.J. Findings about mixed-age learning. Paper presented at the annual meeting of the American Educational Research Association, Toronto, March 1978.

47. Uphoff, J.K., & Gilmore, J. Pupil age at school entrance: How many are ready for success? *Educational Leadership,* 1985, *43* (Sept.), 86-90.

48. Wakefield, A.P. Multi-age grouping in day care. *Children Today,* 1979, May-June, 26-28.

49. Way, J.W. Verbal interaction in multiage classrooms. *Elementary School Journal,* 1979, *79*(3), 178-186.

50. Whiting, B.B., & Whiting, J.W.M. *Children of six cultures: A psychocultural analysis.* Cambridge, MA: Harvard University Press, 1975.

51. Zerby, J.R. A comparison of academic achievement and social adjustment of primary school children in the graded and ungraded school programs (Doctoral dissertation, Penn State University, 1960). *Dissertation Abstracts International,* 1961, *21,* 2644.

Ungraded Classrooms — Fail-Safe Schools?

Policy Briefs: A Publication of the Appalachia Educational Laboratory
State Policy Program • 1991

Too many students are not succeeding in school, and education reformers want to eliminate practices that, they believe, cause kids to fail. Some say doing away with grade levels, especially for young children, is one way to do that.

Advocates of ungraded classes argue that eliminating grade levels can help "curb ability tracking and grade retention, two factors that a growing number of educators identify as the detrimental precursors to failure for some young children."[1] Also, ungraded classes are a way "to steer schools away from competitive and overly academic instruction in the early grades and toward methods grounded in hands-on learning, play, and exploration"[1] — practices that research tells us are developmentally appropriate for 5- to 8-year-olds. Finally, ungraded primary programs eliminate the need to screen children to see if they are ready for school — a practice that flies in the face of what is known about the uneven and varied ways children develop.[2]

California and New York have appointed task forces to recommend changes in the early grades, but Kentucky is the only state to mandate the ungraded primary statewide. Part of the Kentucky Education Reform Act of 1990, the mandate was a response to an "overwhelming demand to re-examine our educational practices," says Linda Hargan of the Kentucky Department of Education and head of a task force charged with designing the implementation of the new primary school program.

Hargan added: "The way we are doing it now is not getting the job done. Somewhere between 20 and 30 percent of our children are being retained in kindergarten, first, and second grade, and we know there is a high correlation between children who are retained and those who drop out of school."[3]

Defining Terms

The terms ungraded, nongraded, mixed-age, multigrade, or combined classes are used interchangeably. This results in a lot of confusion about just what the terms mean.

An ungraded or nongraded school is a school that abandons grade levels. (This is not to be confused with schools that eliminate the use of letter "grades" to report student progress.) In ungraded programs, children of different ages and abilities "work together in an environment conducive both to individual and group progress without reference to precise grade-level standards or norms."[4] Teachers help children progress as far and as fast as they can. That's why Goodlad and Anderson also call such programs "continuous progress."[5] Ungraded schools grow out of a philosophical belief that schools should meet children where they are in their growth process and provide a developmentally appropriate program for them, a program in which they can learn and not fail.

In contrast, terms such as multiage, multigrade, split-grade, or combined classes refer to classrooms that contain students from more than one grade level and where students continue to be identified by their grade level. Student groupings that follow this pattern grow out of economic and geographic necessity, particularly in rural areas.

Although teachers in multigrade, split-grade, or combined-grade classes can group their students across age, grade, or ability levels, they seldom do. Instead, they tend to group students by grade and teach each grade separately.[6,7] While research shows that students in these multigrade classes benefit from being with children of different ages, maintaining separate grade levels results in an unnecessary burden for teachers. Yet, these teaching practices persist because of a "strong organizational expectation that student grade-level identities be maintained."[6] For example, state curriculum regulations require certain material to be taught at specific grade levels, students are tested on grade-level material, state reporting procedures require information by grade level, and promotion and retention policies remain in place.

Essential Ingredients of Ungraded Programs

Since ungraded classrooms are child-centered, they will not all look alike. But they can be expected to have at least six essential ingredients in common.

Goals of schooling. In ungraded schools, people think of the primary years as a developmental period when some children will move more rapidly than others. They need to see each child as a whole person who needs help to grow socially, emotionally, physically, aesthetically, and intellectually.[5,8,9,10]

Curriculum. Ungraded schools structure the curriculum to focus on learning to learn — concepts and methods of inquiry — not specific content. Ungraded curriculum is integrated, not compartmentalized; it is age-appropriate and individual-appropriate.[5,7,10]

Teaching. Teachers' roles change dramatically in ungraded settings. They prepare the environment for children to learn, work with each other to plan the curriculum, and put kids in groups so they learn from each other.[8,10]

Materials. Ungraded classrooms

have a wide variety of books and manipulative materials for a wide range of interests, ages, learning styles, and reading abilities. Grade-level textbooks are stumbling blocks to change, but some materials for whole language reading, mathematics manipulatives, and technology-based writing are suitable for the ungraded, mixed-age approach.[6,10]

Assessment. Children's progress in ungraded programs is measured not in terms of each child's past individual performance. Assessment is continuous and comprehensive — taking into consideration all aspects of growth.[10,11]

Grouping patterns. Children in ungraded settings work in small groups with flexible age boundaries. Those groups provide opportunities for children to have frequent contact with other children of different personalities, backgrounds, abilities, and interests, as well as different ages. They come in contact with as many sensory, concrete experiences as possible.[10,11]

That's what Kentucky wants. The state ungraded the K-3 "to allow the 5-, 6-, and 7-year-olds to see what 8-year-olds can do and to learn from that," says Jack Foster, Kentucky Secretary for Education and the Humanities. "It replicates real life in the classroom because every one of those kids goes out there not to learn what other kids their same age can do, but to be like the big kids."[12]

Nationwide Interest

Interest in ungraded programs may be the result of several related groups urging a more developmentally sound way to teach young children. For example, the National Governors' Association challenges schools to allow "more varied grouping arrangements that promote student interaction and cooperative efforts but are not limited to conventional age-grading practices."[13]

The Council of Chief State School Officers observes that ability grouping in elementary classrooms results in considerably different learning environments among groups, while heterogeneous grouping can make these inequitable learning environments less

likely.[14]

The National Association of State Boards of Education supports new primary units that provide developmentally paced learning for 4- to 8-year-olds.[15]

The National Association for the Education of Young Children (NAEYC), which stops short of promoting ungraded primary schools, identifies ungradedness as one aspect of developmentally appropriate practice.[16]

Overwhelming Research

While we don't have a lot of research on ungraded programs, "we've made remarkable breakthroughs in understanding the development of children, the development of learning, and the climate that enhances that," says Ernest Boyer of The Carnegie Foundation for the Advancement of Teaching. Kentucky's Hargan concurs; "We have a sound research base about how young children learn. What we lack now is a change in our practices to match what we know."[3]

How children learn. Young children learn best through active, hands-on teaching methods like games and dramatic play. "What looks like play to adults is actually the work of childhood, developing an understanding of the world."[1] The most effective way to teach young children is to capitalize on their natural inclination to learn through play.

Data on attitudes and peer relations have "tended overwhelmingly to favor" classes with students of mixed ages — graded or ungraded. But comparisons of student performance in graded and ungraded schools are inconclusive, partly because researchers failed to establish clear distinctions between the graded and ungraded settings they were comparing. Researchers agree, however, that students in ungraded classrooms do not fall behind and that they are more likely to enter the fourth grade with their classmates. Also, minority students, boys, underachievers, and low-income students benefit most from ungraded classrooms, but all students attending ungraded schools are more likely to

have good mental health and positive attitudes toward school. Further, the likelihood of positive attitudes and better academic achievement improves the longer students are in an ungraded program.[5]

Classroom practices. Ungraded programs in the 1960s were associated with a lack of structure.[17] Since that time the NAEYC and the National Association of Early Childhood Specialists in State Departments of Education have researched developmentally appropriate practices and clearly articulated the necessary structure on which to build a good program.[11]

In addition peer tutoring — encouraging children to learn from one another — is a practice especially compatible with ungraded classrooms. More important, it is likely to have a positive effect on student learning. Research shows that organized and focused tutoring benefits tutors and learners. Further, students who are tutored outperform students who have not been tutored.[6]

Cooperative learning — small student groups that permit every student to participate in the completion of a clearly assigned task — is another practice that, research shows, can result in significant increases in student achievement, interpersonal relations, motivation to learn, and student self-esteem. For these groups to be effective, students need to be trained in cooperative work behaviors, and teachers must orchestrate the implementation of group work.[6]

What States Can Do

What is best for young children and their education is well known, but putting all of those principles into practice is not easy. To improve the chances of success for ungraded programs, states can encourage the use of new developments, as well as tried-and-true strategies. Some of these strategies are discussed below.

Put computers in the classroom. Computers facilitate learning, information gathering, and management activities in the classroom. With computers, students can learn independently, retrieve information from computer databases, and use the computer word processor to organize that information. Teachers can use the computer not only as a teaching tool, but also as a convenient way to document the work children do and how they do it.[6]

Permit site-based decision making. Site-based decision making — the shifting of authority for certain education decisions from state and district offices to school building staff — gives teachers the latitude to design the most appropriate education program for that school's students. This not only strengthens the implementation of ungraded programs, it also permits diversity from one school to another.

Provide for teacher training and involvement. Reaching children at their individual level of development requires sophisticated, skillful teaching — the most critical variable in the effectiveness of ungraded, multiage grouping.[6] Some teachers have difficulty implementing this kind of approach. The reason? "Our teachers are not all trained for it," says Sharon Kagan, Yale University.[17] Not only do teachers need training, they also need to be involved.

Schools that have instituted an ungraded program find that teachers adjust better when they're involved in the planning and decision making.

Encourage parent education and involvement. Parent acceptance of ungraded programs is essential. When parents of students in ungraded classrooms see that their children like school, get along with other children, and learn to be good thinkers, "they become convinced."[17]

Provide for ungraded materials. Teachers need access to and information about appropriate materials for a variety of age and developmental levels. Teaching in an ungraded classroom can seem overwhelming when all the standard classroom materials are geared to single grades.

Summary

Moving to ungraded programs — a developmentally appropriate practice for 5-through 8-year-olds — is a fundamental change. Kentucky's Hargan sums it up this way: "It's a change from conformity to diversity; from sequential, step-by-step approaches to self-paced and developmentally paced approaches; from age and ability grouping to multiage, multiability grouping. It means moving from the notion that the child should fit the school to a notion that the school should fit the child, from segregating special programs to integrating special programs, from competition to cooperation, and from failure-oriented to success-oriented schools."[2]

References

1. Cohen, D. L. (1989, December 6). First stirrings of a new trend: Multiage classrooms gain favor. *Education Week*, pp. 1,13-15.
2. Shepard, L. A. & Smith, M. L. (1986). Synthesis of research on school readiness and kindergarten retention. *Educational Leadership*, pp.78-86.
3. Hargan, L. (personal communication, March 15, 1991).
4. Yates, A. (Ed.) (1966). *Grouping in education: A report sponsored by the Unesco Institute for Education*, Hamburg. New York: John Wiley and Sons.
5. Goodlad, J. I. & Anderson, R. H. (1987). *The nongraded elementary school.* New York: Teachers College, Columbia University.
6. Miller, B. A. (1989, September). *The multigrade classroom: A resource book of small, rural schools.* Portland, OR: Northwest Regional Educational Laboratory.
7. Galluzzo, G., Cook, C. R., Minx, N. A., & Neel, J. H. (1990, October). *The organization and management of split grade classrooms* (AEL Mini-grant Report Series No. 19). Charleston, WV: Appalachia Educational Laboratory.
8. National Association for the Education of Young Children. (1986, September). Position statement on developmentally appropriate practice in early childhood programs serving children from birth through age 8. *Young children*, 41(9), 4-17.
9. Katz, L. G. (1988). *Early childhood education: What research tells us.* (Phi Delta Kappa Fastback). Bloomington, IN: Phi Delta Kappa Educational Foundation.
10. Appalachia Educational Laboratory & Kentucky Education Association. (1991, April). *Ungraded primary programs: Steps toward developmentally appropriate instruction.* Charleston, WV: Author.
11. National Association for the Education of Young Children. (1991, March). Guidelines for appropriate curriculum content and assessment in programs serving children ages 3 through 8: A position statement of the National Association for the Education of Young Children and the National Association of Early Childhood Specialists in State Departments of Education. *Young Children*, 46(3), 21-38.
12. Foster, J. (1990, October). *Reflections on the legislation and its underlying considerations.* Presentation at the Regional Laboratory Symposium on Kentucky Education Reform. Lexington, KY.
13. David, J. L., Purkey, S. & White, P. (1989). *Restructuring in progress: Lessons from pioneering districts.* Washington, DC: Center for Policy Research, National Governors' Association:
14. Harris, C. (1989, November). *Success for all in a new century: A report by the Council of Chief State School Officers on Restructuring Education.* Washington, DC: Council of Chief State School Officers.
15. The National Association of State Boards of Education. (1988, October). *Right from the Start: The report of the NASBE Task Force on Early Childhood Education.* Alexandria, VA: Author.
16. National Association for the Education of Young Children. (1988, January). NAEYC Position Statement on Developmentally Appropriate Practice in the Primary Grades, Serving 5-Through 8-Year-Olds. *Young Children*, 43(2), 64-68.
17. Krantrowitz, B. & Wingert, P. (1989, April 17). How kids learn. *Newsweek*, p. 50-56.

Moving to ungraded programs means moving from the notion that the child should fit the school to a notion that the school should fit the child, from segregating special programs to integrating special programs, from competition to cooperation, and from from failure-oriented to success-oriented schools.

Teaching Combined Grade Classes: Real Problems and Promising Practices

A Joint Study by the Virginia Education Association and Appalachia Educational Laboratory

The concept of the multigrade class — also known as grade combination, split level, mixed grade, multiage, ungraded, non-graded, vertical, and family grouping — is not new. It has its roots in the one-room school of the early days of education in the United States. Multigrade classes are defined here as the assignment of two or more grade levels of students as one teacher's instructional responsibility. Since the term multi-grade class is the one most frequently discussed in the literature, it will be used throughout this rationale.

Current trends in demographics and economics, such as decreasing student population and rising costs of building construction and maintenance, have motivated educators to consider school reorganization and consolidation to deal with the problems of uneven student distribution, limited instructional resources, and inadequate facilities. Multigrade classes are often a result of such reorganization.

Recent research findings support multigrade grouping, indicating it can provide both cognitive and social benefits for students (e.g., Pratt & Treacy, 1986; Rule, 1983; Milburn, 1981) In response to the demands of changing demographics, particularly a decreasing and shifting student population, as well as to recent research, several state legislatures — including Kentucky, Mississippi, Florida, and Louisiana — have called for implementation of multigrade programs. For example, the Kentucky State Legislature, in its Education Reform Act of 1990, mandated the implementation of ungraded primary programs (K-3) by September 1992; and the Mississippi State Legislature in 1990 mandated mixed-aged classrooms in elementary schools to be phased in over the next few years.

Although multigrade classes are an educational reality, and the literature reveals positive effects from this type of instructional organization, little research exists on teacher strategies for delivering instruction to two or more grades of students at one time.

"Throughout its history the concept of 'non-gradedness' has been presented as an ideal to which schools may aspire rather than as a specific program which they may implement" (Slavin, 1986, p. 47). Consequently, efforts to capture the ideal have been largely unsuccessful (Miller, 1989).

Effects of Multigrade Classes

Research indicates no negative effects on social relationships and attitudes for students in multigrade classes. In fact, in terms of affective responses, multigrade students outperform single-grade students in more than 75 percent of the measure used (Miller, 1989, pp. 4-13). Results from several studies reviewed by Miller show positive effects of multigrade classes when measures of student attitude toward self, school, or peers are compared across a range of schools and geographic areas (Pratt & Treacy, 1986; Milburn, 1981; Schrankler, 1976; Schroeder & Nott, 1974). For example, Milburn (1981) found that children of all ages in the multigrade school had a more positive attitude toward school than did their counterparts in traditional grade-level groups. Schrankler (1976) and Milburn (1981) found multigrade students have significantly higher self-concept scores than students in single grades. A trend toward more positive social relations is indicated also (Sherman, 1984; Mycock, 1966; Chace, 1961). Sherman (1984) found that multigrade students felt closer to their multiage classmates than did single-grade students. Chace (1961) and Mycock (1966) determined that multigrade students had significantly better teacher-child relationships and better social development than single-grade students. These studies indicated that students in multigrade classes tend to have significantly more positive attitudes toward themselves, their peers, and school.

In terms of academic achievement, the data clearly support the multigrade class as a viable, effective organizational alternative to single-grade instruction (Miller, 1989, p. 113). Little or no difference in

Studies indicated that students in multigrade classes tend to have significantly more positive attitudes toward themselves, their peers, and school.

student achievement in the single or multigrade class was found in the studies. In a study conducted in 1983, Rule found in general that multigrade students scored higher on standardized achievement tests in reading than did single-grade students. Milburn (1981) found little difference in basic skills achievement levels between students in multigrade and grade-level groups, but multigrade classes did score significantly higher on the vocabulary sections of the reading test administered. To account for this, Milburn concluded that teachers in multigrade classes may have placed greater emphasis on oral language, or that teachers working in multigrade settings may tend to speak at a level geared to the comprehensive abilities of the older children. In all cases in Milburn's study, children in the youngest age group in the multigrade class scored higher on basic skills tests than their age-mates in single grade classes. The findings of Milburn's study suggest that multigrade classes may be of special benefit to slow learners. Such children may profit from the tendency to emulate older students. Also, if they are in the same classroom with the same teacher for more than one year, slow learners have more time to assimilate learning in a familiar environment. Furthermore, multigrade grouping enable youngsters to work at different developmental levels without obvious remediation — a situation that can cause emotional, social, or intellectual damage — and without special arrangements for acceleration (Milburn, 1981, pp. 513-514).

A number of other studies indicate that multigrade grouping can provide remedial benefits for at-risk children. For example, it has been established that children are more likely to exhibit prosocial behaviors (Whiting, 1983) and offer instruction (Ludeke

& Hartup, 1983) to younger peers than to age-mates. Brown and Palinscar (1986) make the point that the cognitive growth stemming from interaction with peers of different levels of cognitive maturity is not simply a result of the less-informed child imitating the more knowledgeable one. The interaction between children leads the less-informed member to internalize new understandings. Along the same lines, Vygotsky (1978) maintains that internalization of new concepts takes place when children interact within the "zone of proximal development, the distance between the actual developmental level and the potential developmental level as determined through problem solving under adult guidance or in collaboration with more capable peers." Slavin (1987) suggests that the discrepancy between what an individual can do with and without assistance can be the basis for cooperative peer efforts that result in cognitive gains, and that children model in collaborating groups behaviors more advanced than those they could perform as individuals. Brown and Reeve (1985) maintain that instruction aimed at a wide range of abilities allows novices to learn at their own rate and to manage various cognitive challenges in the presence of "experts."

Obstacles to Multigrade Instructional Organization

In view of the advantages to multigrade instruction cited in the literature, the reader may wonder why more schools have not been organized into multigrade classes. One response is *tradition*. Although schools of the 1800s were nongraded, with the beginning of the industrial revolution and large scale urban growth, the practice of graded schools was established as the norm

for organizing and classifying students. Educators found it easier to manage increased numbers of students by organizing them into grades or age divisions. Other factors, such as the advent of graded textbooks, state supported education, and the demand for trained teachers, have further solidified graded school organization. The graded school system was largely a response to a need for managing large numbers of students rather than an effort to meet individual student needs (Goodlad & Anderson, 1963).

Although the graded school developed as a result of demographics and economics, it has become the predominant way educators and parents think about schools. Ironically, changes in demographics and economics are now necessitating different school organizational patterns. However, the expectations created by the norm of graded schools have created a handicap for anyone seeking to operate a multigrade school (Miller, 1989). Also, most teachers receive training for teaching single-grade classes organized around whole-class instruction and/or small ability-grouped instruction, which are characterized by low student diversity. Different and more complex skills in classroom management and discipline, classroom organization, instructional organization and curriculum, instructional delivery and grouping, self-directed learning, and peer tutoring are needed to deliver instruction successfully in a multigrade class (Miller, 1989). Lack of attention to these skills in teacher education programs is a problem to teachers who are assigned multigrade classes (Miller, 1988; Horn, 1983; Jones, 1987; Bandy & Gleadow, 1980). Too frequently, the teacher skill deficit and the need to develop community understanding and support of multigrade instruction are overlooked by administrators or policymakers when decisions to implement multigrade classes are made and teacher assignments to these classes are given.

Teaching Strategies

The Northwest Regional Educational Laboratory's (NWREL) Rural Education Program recognized the need for material to assist the multigrade teacher in 1987 when concerns were raised about the availability of research and training materials to help rural, multigrade teachers improve their skills. As a result, the Rural Education Program developed a handbook which contains a comprehensive review of the research on multigrade instruction, key issues teachers face in a multigrade setting, and resource guides to assist multigrade teachers in improving the quality of instruction. Twenty-one multigrade teachers reviewed a draft of this handbook and provided feedback, strategies, and ideas which were incorporated into the final version completed in September 1989. *The Multigrade Teacher: A Resource Handbook for Small, Rural Schools* by Bruce A. Miller has been of benefit to the VEA-AEL Study Group in preparing its study. Particularly helpful were the bibliographies and the overview of current research on the effects of multigrade instruction on student and teacher performance.

Teaching a multigrade class is a demanding task requiring a special type of individual. It also requires training, communication with parents and community members, and support. *Teaching Combined Grade Classes; Real Problems and Promising Practices* suggests types of training, resources, and support that facilitate multigrade instruction; effective strategies and practices employed by teachers experienced in multigrade class instruction; and state and local policy initiatives that can support and assist teachers in multigrade class settings. The teachers who prepared this study, as well as those who responded to the study group's survey, have experience teaching multigrade classes. Their suggestions can be valuable to novice teachers in the multigrade approach, to administrators who are reorganizing schools, to those who plan professional development activities, and to those who recommend or initiate educational policy.

Perceived Advantages and Difficulties of Grade Combination Teaching

In addition to identifying experience characteristics of grade combination teachers, the survey was designed to assess respondent perceptions of grade combination teaching. Perceived advantages and difficulties were recorded in response to questions 15 and 16 of the survey. Following the questions is a description of respondent data.

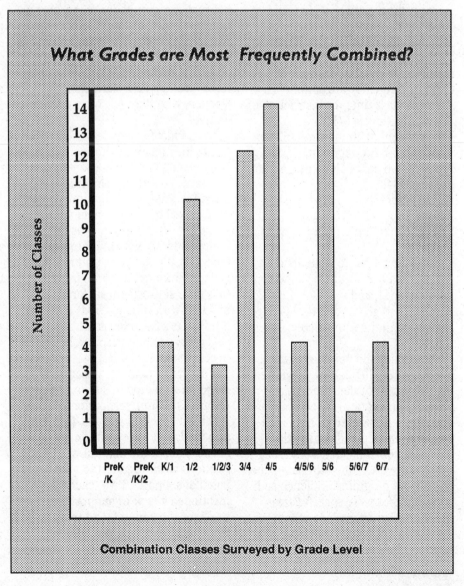

What Grades are Most Frequently Combined?

Number of Classes

PreK/K PreK/K/2 K/1 1/2 1/2/3 3/4 4/5 4/5/6 5/6 5/6/7 6/7

Combination Classes Surveyed by Grade Level

15. Please describe any difficulties you have experienced in teaching curricula of two grade levels.
16. Please describe advantages you perceive to teaching grade combination classes.

Difficulties

The consensus on difficulties experienced by 83 percent of the respondents can be capsulated in the response "*double* planning, *double* teaching, *double* grading, and *double* record keeping." These teachers cited specific difficulties indicating, as one teacher stated, "The time factor is most critical — in terms of covering materials with students." The individual difficulties reported by teachers that relate to the "time factor" in daily class instruction in order of frequency are as follows:
- lack of class time for instruction of two grade levels (71%);
- insufficient planning time (62%);
- not enough time for teachers to master two curricula in preparation to teach (48%);
- insufficient time to effectively cover two sets of curricula (45%);
- never caught up on written work (38%);
- insufficient time to remediate or work on a one-to-one basis with a child (24%); and
- inability to go beyond basics (e.g., not enough time for science experiments) (7%).

After time, the next most frequently cited difficulties, identified by 38 percent of the respondents, were fragmentation, scheduling, and grouping. Several responses illustrate these perceived difficulties. Two teachers indicated scheduling problems were related to the number of pull-out programs. Science and social studies were specific areas mentioned as difficult to schedule. Two teachers noted that in subjects such as family life, health, and sex

education, the curriculum for one grade is not appropriate for the other grade. Therefore, teachers must "farm out" children before they can teach certain lessons. Three other teachers said they could not arrange field trips because the subject would not be appropriate for both grade levels.

The third most frequently experienced difficulty in teaching curricula of two grade levels was the inability of one group of children to work independently while the teacher instructed the other group (20 percent). For example, one teacher stated there was constant competition between the groups for the teacher's time, and another described problems with children who fit in no group. However, three teachers identified problems related to scheduling for team teaching and working with teachers who they felt were uncooperative.

Respondents also identified difficulties related to how children were placed in combination classes. Concerns about how children were placed in grade combination classes were raised by six teachers who specified that class size was too large; children were inappropriately added during the year; children felt isolated from others in their grade, thus their self-esteem suffered; and children with special needs such as English as a Second Language students were inappropriately placed in combination classes.

Finally, 11 teachers described difficulties related to supports and resources. Three respondents specified a lack of support from their principal, and four mentioned concern about the amount of public relations work required to gain parental support. Two teachers mentioned a lack of support and assistance in general, and two responses described insufficient resources and materials to teach and

to integrate two curriculum levels.

Advantages

In describing advantages to teaching grade combination classes, the consensus of 26 percent of the 69 teachers who responded to this question was that peer tutoring is the greatest benefit. In contrast to a perceived disadvantage mentioned by one teacher, 14 percent of the teachers who responded to this question stated that having the children two consecutive years allowed them the advantages of knowing the children's strengths and weaknesses and of being able to group ahead of time. One teacher responded, "Keeping students for a second year is great — no lost time!"

Integration of language arts and other curricula was identified as an advantage by 14 percent of the teachers. Six of these 10 responses specified the particular benefit combination classes had to integrating the reading curricula.

Respondents perceived a wide variety of other advantages. However, each was mentioned by only one or two persons. These advantages are categorized below under the headings of grouping, academic, behavioral, and resource and support advantages.

Grouping advantages:
- Children are always taught in small groups.
- Gifted and talented programs, differentiation, and general grouping are no problem.
- Class size is always smaller.
- You get the top notch students academically and no behavior problems.
- All children can read.

Academic advantages:
- Upper grade can review what is taught to the lower grade.

- One group motivates the other group.
- Children in the lower grade get enrichment by listening to what is taught to the upper group.
- Children in the lower grade are better prepared for the next year.

Behavioral advantages:
- Different ages learn to socialize.
- Teacher can observe nine- and 10-year olds interacting.
- More independent work habits are developed.
- Upper grade children act as role models for lower grade children.

Resource and support advantages:
- I received an extra computer for my room.
- Help from an aide was provided.

Although 24 percent of the 69 teachers who answered this question responded negatively with "no advantages," one teacher noted, "Kids learn from kids. I use students to help other students with word recognition, spelling, math, etc." However, this teacher went on to say, "This isn't really an advantage because this could be done in a one-grade class." Another respondent stated, "After 12 years of teaching combination grades, I can see no advantages. Because of time limitations, you cannot reach all students and meet their needs. They become angry and 'turned off.' Teachers are left frustrated and emotionally and physically drained."

In summary, a diversity of difficulties and advantages to grade combination classes were perceived by survey respondents. Difficulties identified by respondents in teaching curricula of two grade levels fall into five categories; time, scheduling/grouping, children's inability to work independently, student placement, and supports/resources. Teachers cited specific difficulties, most notably lack of planning and instructional time, relating to the most frequently identified problem — time. In contrast, a number of advantages to grade combination classes were identified, most frequently peer tutoring. Moreover, problems cited by some respondents were perceived as advantages by others, although there was greater consensus on specific difficulties. For example, 83 percent of the respondents identified "double planning, teaching, grading, and record keeping" as a difficulty, while 14 percent identified curriculum integration as an advantage. Also, some teachers indicated grouping was a problem, while others perceived grouping as an advantage to grade combination classes. Although they also may have identified difficulties, a majority of the respondents perceived some advantages to teaching grade combination classes.

Bibliography

Brown, A.L., & Palinscar, A. (1986). *Guided Cooperative Learning and Individual Knowledge Acquisition* (Technical Report No. 372). Champaign, IL: Center for the Study of Reading.

Brown, A.L., & Reeve, R.A. (1985). *Bandwiths of Competence: The Role of Supportive Contexts in Learning and Development* (Technical Report No. 336). Champaign, IL: Center for the Study of Reading.

Chase, E.S. (1961). *An Analysis of Some Effects of Multiple-Grade Grouping in an Elementary School.* Unpublished doctoral dissertation, University of Tennessee.

Ludeke, R.J., & Hartup, W.W. (1983). Teaching Behavior of 9 and 11 year-old Girls in Mixed-age and Same-age Dyads. *Journal of Educational Psychology,* 75(6), 908-914.

Milburn, D. (1981). A Study of Multiage or Family-Grouped Classrooms. *Phi Delta Kappan,* 64, 306-319.

Miller, B.A. (1989). The Multigrade Classroom: A Resource Handbook for Small, Rural Schools. (Contract No. 400-86-0006). Portland, OR: Northwest Regional Educational Laboratory.

Mycock, M.A. (1966). A Comparison of Vertical Grouping and Horizontal Grouping in the Infant School. *British Journal of Educational Psychology,* 37, 133-135.

Pratt, C., & Treacy, K. (1986). *A Study of Student Grouping Practices in Early Childhood Classes in Western Australia Government Primary Schools.* (Coopera-tive Research Series No. 9). Nedlands, Australia: Education Department of Western Australia.

Rule, G. (1983). Effects of Multigrade Grouping on Elementary Student Achievement in Reading and Mathematics (Doctoral dissertation. Northern Arizona University). *Dissertation Information Service* No. 8315672.

Schrankler, W.J. (1976). Family Grouping and the affective Domain. *Elementary School Journal,* 76, 432-439.

Schroeder, R. & Nott, R.E. (19974). Multiage Grouping — It Works! *Catalyst for Change,* 3, 15-18.

Sherman, L.W. (1984). Social Distance Perceptions of Elementary School Children in Age-Heterogeneous and Homogeneous Classroom Settings. *Perceptual and Motor Skills,* 58, 395-409.

Slavin, R.E. (1986). *Using Student Team Learning.* Third edition. Baltimore, MD: John Hopkins University.

Slavin, R.E. (19887). Developmental and Motivational Perspectives on Cooperative Learning: A Reconciliation. *Child Development,* 58, 1161-1167.

Vygotsky, L.S. (1978). *Mind in Society: The Development of Higher Psychological Processes.* Edited by M. Cole, V. John-Steiner, S. Scribner, and E. Souberman. Cambridge, MA: Harvard University Press.

Whiting, B.B. (1983). The Genesis of Prosocial Behavior. In D. Bridgeman (Ed.), *The Nature of Prosocial Development.* New York: Academic Press.

An excerpt from Teaching Combined Grade Classes: Real Problems and Promising Practices, September 1990, by the Virginia Education Association and Appalachia Educational Laboratory. Reprinted with permission of AEL.

VOLUME 9, NUMBER 1

FALL 1992

Research ROUNDUP

NATIONAL ASSOCIATION OF ELEMENTARY SCHOOL PRINCIPALS

Nongraded Primary Education

Joan Gaustad

Nongraded education is the practice of teaching children of different ages and ability levels together, without dividing them into groups labeled by grade designations. Although nongraded education can be used with all ages, it is particularly appropriate during the primary years, when developmental differences are greatest. Children move from easier to more difficult material at their own varying rates of speed, making continuous progress rather than being promoted once per year. Curriculum and teaching practices are developmentally appropriate, and an integrated curriculum seeks to foster children's physical, social, and emotional growth along with their intellectual growth.

Flexible grouping is a key element of nongraded education. Students are grouped homogeneously by achievement for some subjects, such as math and reading. For other subjects, children usually learn in heterogenous groups. At different times they may work independently, in pairs, or in groups formed for specific purposes and then disbanded. Various names have been used to describe this approach, including *mixed-age grouping* and *heterogenous grouping*.

Many experimental nongraded programs and closely related *open education* programs were tried in the sixties and early seventies. However, most of these failed due to inadequate understanding, lack of administrative and community support, and poorly planned implementation.

Now, as the year 2000 approaches and schools are being re-evaluated in light of changing social and economic conditions, nongradedness is the focus of renewed interest. Nongraded primary education, supported by decades of research and refined by the study of successful programs, has been mandated in British Columbia and Kentucky, is under consideration in Oregon, and is being explored in many schools and districts—although alternate terminology is sometimes used to avoid negative associations with earlier, unsuccessful programs. It is certainly an appropriate time to review the research literature on the subject.

John I. Goodlad and Robert H. Anderson stimulated extensive research and the implementation of thousands of nongraded programs across the nation as co-authors of *The Nongraded Elementary School,* first published in 1959. Reissued with a new introduction in 1987, the book remains the classic work defining nongraded primary education and arguing for its superiority over graded education.

The National Association for the Education of Young Children summarizes current knowledge of child development and describes appropriate teaching practices for primary-age children in its 1987 position statement, edited by Sue Bredekamp. Its list of recommended developmentally appropriate practices closely matches the components of nongraded education.

Lilian G. Katz, director of the ERIC Clearinghouse on Elementary and Early Childhood Education, is a tireless promoter of mixed-age grouping. In a comprehensive review of relevant research, she and her colleagues establish the social and cognitive benefits of mixed-age grouping for both older and younger children.

The Ministry of Education of British Columbia,

Joan Gaustad is a research analyst and writer for the ERIC Clearinghouse on Educational Management at the University of Oregon.

in a resource document for teachers and parents, explains assessment and evaluation practices used in the province's new nongraded primary program, and reviews the supporting research on child development and learning.

Joan Gaustad, in a two-part series for the Oregon School Study Council, defines nongraded education, reviews its research base, describes how a nongraded primary classroom functions, and explores the process of transition between graded and nongraded organization at the local and state level.

Goodlad, John I., and Anderson, Robert H. **The Nongraded Elementary School**, Revised Edition. New York: Teachers College Press, Columbia University, 1987. 248 pages.

Goodlad and Anderson present achievement data demonstrating that children entering first grade can vary in mental age by up to four years, that the amount of variation increases as students progress through subsequent grades, and that achievement patterns of individual children differ greatly among subject areas. They argue against "procrustean" attempts to force all children of the same chronological age to fit narrowly defined grade norms.

Questioning the effectiveness of nonpromotion in reducing achievement discrepancies, they present evidence showing that this policy affects most children even more negatively than the unsatisfactory alternative of social promotion.

Age-graded instruction originated in the mid-1800s, when the new idea of mass public education created the need for an efficient, economical system capable of handling large numbers of students. Goodlad and Anderson place grading and nongrading in a historical perspective and discuss the evolution of the modern nongraded model, including its relationship to modern theories of curriculum development.

About ERIC

The Educational Resources Information Center (ERIC) is a national information system operated by the Office of Educational Research and Improvement (OERI). The ERIC Clearinghouse on Educational Management, one of 16 such units in the system, was established at the University of Oregon in 1966.

This publication was prepared by the Clearinghouse with funding from OERI, U.S. Department of Education, under contract no. OERI-R-188062004. No federal funds were used in the printing of this publication.

ERIC® Clearinghouse on Educational Management University of Oregon, 1787 Agate St., Eugene, Oregon 97403.

They describe the operation of nongraded schools, devoting an entire chapter to the reporting of student progress, and discuss the emotional consequences of graded and nongraded expectations.

The book's final chapters examine the process of establishing a nongraded school and the factors that commonly impede or facilitate the process. The authors draw on the reports of program participants to cite the problems and rewards of nongrading. Goodlad and Anderson also analyze the underlying causes of common implementation problems and suggest directions for further research and development.

The introduction to the revised edition reviews historical and theoretical developments in nongrading since the publication of the first edition, and presents a set of 36 principles of nongradedness developed by fellow researcher Barbara Pavan. These principles explicitly state the assumptions on which nongrading is based, and describe the educational goals, the administrative-organizational framework, and the operational elements, including materials, curriculum, teaching methods, and evaluation.

A new book by Anderson and Pavan, *Nongradedness: Helping It to Happen*, is scheduled for publication by Technomic Press this year.

National Association for the Education of Young Children. **Developmentally Appropriate Practice in Early Childhood Programs Serving Children from Birth through Age 8**. Sue Bredekamp, editor. Washington, D.C.: The Association, 1987. 92 pages.

Concerned about the use of instructional practices which are inappropriate and harmful to young children, the NAEYC prepared this document as a decision-making guide for educators and parents.

Research has established that children aged 5-8 are cognitively unready to learn abstractly. While they are beginning to use symbols, they still need concrete reference points. They "construct" knowledge from personal experience and absorb information in meaningful contexts more easily than they learn unconnected facts. Young children need to practice developing physical skills, and they actually become more fatigued by long periods of sitting than by running and jumping.

Children's physical, social, emotional, and cognitive development are interrelated. Successful peer interaction, physical coordination, emotional self-control, and following rules are goals as important for young children to master as reading, writing, and calculating. Normal children are eager to master new skills, and confident that they can do so. But even normal children vary enormously in learning style, personality, and rate of development. When rigid expectations exceed their current capabilities, failure may damage both their self-esteem and their motivation to learn.

The NAEYC emphasizes that teachers must teach the "whole child," supporting intellectual, social, emotional, and moral growth. A wide variety of teaching methods and materials should be used to accommodate individual differences as well as those resulting from varied cultural and family backgrounds. Expectations of when specific goals should be mastered must be flexible.

The NAEYC strongly recommends curriculum integration, with lessons that actively involve children both physically and cognitively. While participating in interesting group projects, children can simultaneously learn factual information, writing, and calculating as they practice physical, social, and communication skills.

A lengthy chart describes and compares specific examples of appropriate and inappropriate instructional practices for primary-age children. The chart addresses such components as curriculum goals, teaching strategies, integrated curriculums, guidance of social and emotional development, and program evaluation.

Katz, Lilian G., and others. **The Case for Mixed-Age Grouping in Early Education**. Washington, D.C.: National Association for the Education of Young Children, 1990. 59 pages.

Mixed-age grouping, defined here as "placing children who are at least a year apart in age into the same classroom groups," recreates a pattern common throughout human history, in which children of diverse ages learn together and from one another in family, village, and neighborhood settings.

Research has found that, even though children tend to spontaneously form mixed-age play groups, adults in our society typically segregate children by age. Trends toward smaller families, and increased reliance on preschools and childcare centers, further reduce opportunities for cross-age interaction.

Cooperation is fostered in mixed-age groups by the different expectations children have of those older and younger than themselves. Younger children are perceived as needing assistance, older children as sources of help and leadership. As a result, cooperative and prosocial behaviors increase in mixed-age groups, while discipline problems decrease.

Mixed-age grouping offers social and emotional benefits for both older and younger children. Older children practice leadership skills while taking a greater role in directing and organizing play. Younger

children, in addition to being able to join in more complex play than they could initiate themselves, grow socially by interacting with more mature playmates. At the same time, insecure older children may improve their social skills by interacting with younger, less threatening classmates.

Mixed-age grouping also offers less advanced students opportunities to learn from more advanced classmates as well as from the teacher. Studies show that younger children master more advanced problem-solving skills when grouped with older children. Peer-tutoring research finds that both tutors and the tutored benefit academically from their interaction, and that the tutors' self-confidence and attitudes toward school improve.

Katz and her colleagues note the need for further research to establish the optimum age range, the best ratio of older to younger children, and the best proportion of school time to be spent in mixed-age grouping. An appendix suggests specific teaching strategies to support and encourage social, emotional, and intellectual development in mixed-age classes.

Ministry of Education, Province of British Columbia. **Supporting Learning: Understanding and Assessing the Progress of Children in the Primary Program. A Resource for Parents and Teachers.** Victoria, British Columbia, Canada: The Ministry, 1991. 62 pages.

Written as a resource for British Columbia's new nongraded primary program, this document emphasizes that reporting student progress is not a one-way process, school to home. Teachers and parents are partners in educating children, and information needs to be shared in both directions.

To provide a context for assessment, the ministry summarizes knowledge about human development and learning, then describes and explains the evaluation and reporting practices to be used.

The three sources of information about children's progress are listed as *Observation of Process, Observation of Product*, and *Conversations and Conferences*. Teachers are asked to regularly record their observations of children in action, to collect samples of children's work, and to have frequent informal conferences with children in order to discover how they feel about their progress and any problems they may be having. Teachers periodically share their observations with parents in telephone conversations and during formal conferences.

To give teachers and parents a frame of reference in which to judge student progress, the ministry lists *Widely Held Expectations* for development in physical, social, emotional, intellectual, and artistic areas, as well as in the specific curriculum areas of mathematics and reading. Charts describe the behaviors, skills, and concepts children usually master within certain age ranges, rather than listing specific achievements expected at specific ages.

The document concludes by suggesting specific actions and activities parents can use at home to support their children's learning in each of the listed areas.

Gaustad, Joan. **Nongraded Education: Mixed-age, Integrated, and Developmentally Appropriate Education for Primary Children.** *Oregon School Study Council Bulletin* 35:7 (March 1992). 38 pages.
Making the Transition to Nongraded Primary Education. *Oregon School Study Council Bulletin* 35:8 (April 1992). 41 pages.

Gaustad begins this two-part series by surveying the history of graded and nongraded education in the United States, and discussing the reasons why the "first wave" of nongrading failed. She then reviews research supporting nongraded primary education, and describes its components in practice.

The second bulletin summarizes the elements of successful change. Shirley M. Hord and others find that innovations often fail because policy makers underestimate how long change will take, and the amount of training and support teachers will require. Realistically, full implementation of a major innovation requires several years.

Studies of nongraded programs show that understanding and support by teachers and parents are crucial to success, and that both groups are more likely to support nongrading when they are involved in decision making. In addition, teachers need practical training, including opportunities to observe effective models. Nongrading also requires more ongoing planning time than graded education.

Gaustad next examines the transition process as it is currently occurring in British Columbia, Kentucky, and Oregon. Educators who were interviewed agreed that individual schools—and individual teachers—should be allowed considerable flexibility as to when and how to implement nongrading.

Like their students, teachers differ in their rates and patterns of learning. Changing from graded to nongraded education not only involves multiple innovations, but requires a basic change in educational philosophy that often clashes with deeply ingrained expectations. Fortunately, components of nongrading can be effectively combined in many ways to suit individual teaching styles, and introducing components one at a time is easier than attempting to change everything at once.

The series concludes with a discussion of ways by which school boards can support and encourage nongrading. □

From *Research Roundup*, Vol. 9, Number 1, Fall 1992. Reprinted by permission of the National Association of Elementary School Principals.

Voices

The child who creeps at an early age is not superior to the child who takes his own sweet time. Children are born when they are ready. They creep when they are ready. They walk when they are ready. They talk when they are ready. They teethe when they are ready. But they go to school . . . ready or not, when they are five.

Jim Grant
I Hate School

Reprinted with permission of Programs for Education, Rosemont, NJ. ISBN 0-935493-04-2

The Multiage, Nongraded
Continuous Progress Classroom
Bibliography

Compiled by SDE Presenters: Jim Grant, Bob Johnson, Elizabeth Lolli, and Mary Garamella
Titles marked (CSB) are available through Crystal Springs Books, 1-800-321-0401

American Association of School Administrators. *The Nongraded Primary: Making Schools Fit Children.* Arlington, VA: Author, 1992. (CSB)

Anderson, Robert H., and Pavan, Barbara N. *Nongradedness: Helping it to Happen.* Lancaster, PA: Technomic Press, 1992. (CSB)

Appalachia Educational Laboratory. *Ungraded Primary Programs: Steps Toward Developmentally Appropriate Instruction.* Charleston, WV: Author, 1991. (CSB)

Boyer, Ernest L. *Ready to Learn: A Mandate for the Nation.* Princeton NJ: Carnegie Foundation for the Advancement of Learning, 1991.

Bredekamp, Sue, ed. *Developmentally Appropriate Practice in Early Childhood Programs Serving Children From Birth Through Age 8.* Washington DC: (NAEYC) National Association for the Education of Young Children, 1987. (CSB)

Ellis, Susan, & Whalen, Susan F. *Cooperative Learning: Getting Started.* New York Scholastic Professional Books, 1990. (CSB)

Fogarty, Robin. *The Mindful School: How to Integrate the Curricula.* Palatine, IL: Skylight Publishing, Inc, 1991.

Gardner, Howard. *Frames of Mind: The Theory of Multiple Intelligences.* New York: Basic Books, Inc., 1983.

Gayfer, Margaret, Ed. *The Multi-Grade Classroom Myth and Reality: A Canadian Study.* Toronto, Ontario, Canada: Canadian Education Association, 1991. (CSB)

Gaustad, Joan. *Making the Transition from Graded to Nongraded Primary Education.* Oregon School Study Council Bulletin, Vol. 35, Issue (8). Eugene, OR: Oregon School Study Council, 1992. (CSB)

_____. *Nongraded Education: Mixed-Age, Integrated and Developmentally Appropriate Education for Primary Children.* Oregon School Study Council Bulletin, Vol. 35, Issue 7. Eugene, OR: Oregon School Study Council, 1992. (CSB)

George, Paul. *How to Untrack Your School.* Alexandria, VA: Association for Supervision and Curriculum Development, 1992. (CSB)

Goodlad, John I., and Anderson, Robert H. *The Nongraded Elementary School.* New York: Teachers College Press, rev. 1987. (CSB)

Grant, Jim. *I Hate School! Some Commonsense Answers for Parents Who Wonder Why.* Rosemont, NJ: Programs For Education, 1986. (CSB)

_____. *Worth Repeating: Giving Children a Second Chance at School Success.* Rosemont, NJ: Modern Learning Press/Programs for Education, 1989. (CSB)

_____. *Developmental Education in the 1990's.* Rosemont, NJ: Modern Learning Press, 1991. (CSB)

Gutierrez, Roberto, and Slavin, Robert E. *Achievement Effects of the Nongraded Elementary School: A Retrospective Review.* Baltimore, MD: Center for Research on Effective Schooling for Disadvantaged Students, 1992.

Hunter, Madeline. *How to Change to a Nongraded School*. Alexandria, VA: Association for Supervision and Curriculum Development, 1992. (CSB)

Katz, Lilian G.; Evangelou, Demetra; and Hartman, Jeanette Allison. *The Case for Mixed-age Grouping in Early Education*. Washington DC: (NAEYC) National Association for the Education of Young Children, 1990. (CSB)

Kentucky Department of Education. *Kentucky's Primary School: The Wonder Years*. Frankfort, KY: Author.

Kentucky Education Association and Appalachia Educational Laboratory. *Ungraded Primary Programs: Steps Toward Developmentally Appropriate Instruction*. Washington DC: Office of Educational Research and Improvement, US Department of Education, 1990. (CSB)

Kohn, Alfie. *No Contest: The Case Against Competition*. Boston: Houghton Mifflin Company, 1986.

Lamb, Beth, and Logsdon, Phyllis. *Positively Kindergarten*. Rosemont, NJ: Modern Learning Press, 1991. (CSB)

Manitoba Department of Education. *Language Arts Handbook for Primary Teachers in Multigrade Classrooms*. Winnipeg, Manitoba, Canada: Author, 1988.

Miller, Bruce A. *The Multigrade Classroom: A Resource Handbook for the Small, Rural Schools*. Portland, OR: Northwest Regional Educational Laboratory, 1989.

_____. *Training Guide for the Multigrade Classroom: A Resource Handbook for Small, Rural Schools*. Portland, OR: Northwest Regional Educational Laboratory,1990.

National Association of State Boards of Education. *Right From the Start: The Report of the NASBE Task Force on Early Childhood Education*. Alexandria, VA: Author, 1988.

National Association of Elementary School Principals. *Standards for Quality Elementary and Middle Schools: Kindergarten through Eighth Grade*. Alexandria, VA: Author, rev. 1990.

_____. *Early Childhood Education and the Elementary School Principal*. Alexandria, VA: Author, 1990.

Oakes, Jeannie. *Keeping Track: How Schools Structure Equality*. New Haven: Yale University Press, 1985.

Province of British Columbia Ministry of Education. *Foundation*. Victoria, British Columbia, Canada: Author, 1990.

Province of British Columbia Ministry of Education. *Our Primary Program: Taking the Pulse*. Victoria, British Columbia, Canada: Author, 1990.

Province of British Columbia Ministry of Education. *Primary Program Foundation Document*. Victoria, British Columbia, Canada: Author, 1990.

Province of British Columbia Ministry of Education. *Primary Program Resource*. Victoria, British Columbia, Canada: Author, 1990.

Province of British Columbia Ministry of Education. *Resource*. Victoria, British Columbia, Canada: Author, 1990.

Society For Developmental Education. *Into Teachers' Hands* (5th Ed. SDE Sourcebook). Peterborough, NH: Author, 1992. (CSB)

_____. *The Multiage, Ungraded Continuous Progress School: The Lake George Model*. Peterborough, NH: Author, 1992. (CSB)

Virginia Education Association and Appalachia Educational Laboratory. *Teaching Combined Grade Classes: Real Problems and Promising Practices*. Washington DC: Office of Educational Research and Improvement, US Department of Education, 1990. (CSB)

Audio/Video Resources

Anderson, Robert H., and Pavan, Barbara N. *The Nongraded School*. Videocassette. Bloomington, IN: Phi Delta Kappa, Agency for Instructional Technology.

Association of Supervision and Curriculum Development. *Tracking: Road to Success or Dead End?* Audio cassette. Alexandria, VA: Association for Supervision and Curriculum Development.

Oakes, Jeannie, and Lipton, Martin. *On Tracking and Ability Grouping*. Videocassette. Bloomington, IN: Phi Delta Kappa, Agency for Instructional Technology.

Province of British Columbia Ministry of Education. *A Time of Wonder: Children in the Primary Years*. Videocassette. Victoria, British Columbia, Canada: Crown Publications.

Characteristics of the Nongraded Primary

A nongraded primary is:

➤ Developmentally appropriate curricula for primary-age children.
➤ A heterogeneous community of learners as related to age and ability.
➤ Supportive of continuous learning.
➤ Committed to honoring the development of the whole child.
➤ Conducive to active student involvement — hands-on activities, classroom discussions and projects, concrete experiences related to real-life examples, discovery, and student-initiated learning.
➤ A teacher operating as the classroom facilitator — modeling, monitoring, observing, and giving guided instruction.
➤ An emphasis on the process of learning.
➤ A provider of an integrated curriculum across many subject areas so that children learn concepts and processes in a meaningful context.
➤ Free of rigid instructional structures that impede learning, such as fixed ability grouping, grade levels, retention, and promotion.
➤ Evaluated continuously using multiple data sources such as portfolios, anecdotal records, and samples of student work, as well as formal evaluation measures.

A nongraded primary is not:

➤ An excuse for using the "back-to-basics" movement to narrow the curriculum and adopt instructional approaches that are incompatible with current knowledge about how young children learn and develop.
➤ Based on rigid ability groups or age/grade groupings.
➤ A static, lock-step learning system with little regard for a child's interest or motivation to move vertically (advancing upward into a higher grade level) and horizontally as he or she is interested in new knowledge.
➤ An emphasis on learning based solely on the intellectual domain defined as discrete, technical, academic skills.
➤ Work time where children are expected to work silently and alone on worksheets or with teacher-directed groups where a lecture or "Round Robin" reading in a circle occurs.
➤ The teacher at the front of the room all day as the "sage on the stage."
➤ An isolated learning of subjects with worksheets to support teaching and little relationship of concepts among subject areas, with the day divided into individual time segments for each subject area, and learning not seen as a part of the whole.
➤ A system that considers grades are the motivator for children to do work.

Contributors:

The Chance School
4200 Lime Kiln Lane
Louisville, KY 40222
Elizabeth Rightmyer, Director

Dixie Elementary School
1940 Eastland Parkway
Lexington, KY 40505
Linda Keller, Principal

Essex Elementary School
Brown's River Road
Essex, VT 05452
Robbe Brook, Principal

Lake George Elementary
Sun Valley Drive
Lake George, NY 12845
Bob Ross, Principal

Mast Landing School
116 Bow St.
Freeport, ME 04032
Irv Richardson, Principal

Miller Grade School
Box C
Waldoboro, ME 04572
Kay Sproul / Beth Ogden, Teachers

Milwaukee Public Schools'
Ungraded Program
P.O. Drawer 10K
5225 West Vliet St.
Milwaukee, WI 53201-8210
**Dr. Milly Hoffman,
Curriculum Specialist**

New Suncook School
Box H
Lovell, ME 04051
Karen Johnson / Lauren Potter

Norridgewock Central Grade School
P.O. Box 98, Rt. 2, Mercer Road
Norridgewock, ME 04957
Sharon Bottesch, Teacher

Saffell Street Elementary
210 Saffell St.
Lawrenceburg, KY 40342
Max Workman, Principal

Union Elementary School
1 Park Ave.
Montpelier, VT 05602
Mary Garamella, Principal

Creating

Multiage

Programs

to Meet

Student and

Community

Needs

MULTIAGE M·O·D·E·L·S

The Chance School
4200 Limekiln Lane
Louisville, KY 40222

PHILOSOPHY

Strong self-esteem is vital to developing positive attitudes about learning and living together in a democratic society. Self-esteem must be nurtured daily as it emerges within a child's cognitive, emotional, physical, social, and moral development.

In all the span of life, the early years of childhood — two through eight years — are the fastest time of growing, learning and development. Children advance through successive stages of development and each child progresses in his/her own special way.

Chance School provides an environment which fosters a child's confidence in his/her whole being. Day by day, children have the opportunity to discover knowledge through first hand experiences that challenge and stimulate learning, thinking, creativity, and social interaction. We recognize that, in the early years, children learn much through their play and sensory experiences.

At Chance School, we value and respect individual differences among all children. Positive developmental guidance from nurturing adults, both parents and teachers, helps to create a community of learning and discovery.

I hear, and I forget.
I see, and I remember.
I do, and I understand.   Chinese proverb

What Makes Chance Unique?

PROGRAM
- We are a school of early childhood education which specializes in the teaching of young children and their parents.
- Each child is challenged at his/her developmental level, regardless of chronological age.
- Learning experiences are structured to encourage children to learn by doing, not by passively listening.
- The school's atmosphere is warm, loving and supportive.
- Teachers plan experiences that strengthen the whole child; intellectual, physical, social, and emotional growth are all valued.

STAFF
- Each class has two facilitators: a lead teacher and an assistant.
- Lead teachers are chosen for their understanding of child development, their ability to provide varied, developmentally appropriate learning experiences and their impact as a positive role model in the classroom.
- The executive director, trained in early childhood and elementary curriculum, coordinates the educational, financial, and emotional health of the school.
- Staff training is provided weekly both from within the school and drawing upon resources from outside the school.

PARENTS
- We welcome visits at any time.
- Every parent participates in the life of the school by volunteering time, talent, and job related skills.
- Parent education programs are offered throughout the year.

When adults understand the early childhood stages of growth and development and respect individual needs and differences, they can help children develop self-esteem.

- Parent-teacher conferences are scheduled three times a year.
- Carpools are arranged for parents' convenience.

NUTRITION
- Parents take turns providing nutritious snacks.
- The school provides orange juice and milk for children who eat lunch at school.

FACILITIES
- Our historic building and huge gymnasium are specially equipped for young children.
- Classrooms are organized into interesting learning center activities which stimulate exploration and discovery, problem solving, and cooperation.
- Our outdoor playground is in a natural, wooded setting with developmentally appropriate play structures.

Sample Schedule Primary

8:50 Homeroom. Children turn in their homework, hang up coats and bookbags, and prepare for work.

9:00 Math. Students work in individual math folders toward weekly goals. Using a unique, self-pacing program (Miquon Math Lab Materials), the children discover and learn to apply math concepts by using a variety of manipulative materials: cuisenaire rods, pattern blocks, chips, weights and measures, geoboards and many others. Students work as independently as possible, and teachers move from student to student asking and answering questions and teaching new ideas.

Centers. As children complete their math goals they move into other learning centers. Creative art or craft projects, handwriting practice, science and cooking experiments, board games, mapping and measuring activities, as well as explorations with books and blocks, and the computer are available for the children to select. Through working and playing together in centers, the children put to use their cognitive, emotional, social, and physical skills in a completely natural way.

A nutritious snack, provided by parents, is offered during center time.

10:15 Recess. The children have a half hour to stretch and exercise their developing muscles. Outside on the playground or in the Funroom, the children run, climb, jump, skate, and slide on developmental equipment. Primary children often organize their own games and clubs during the recess period.

10:45 Big Group. The children and teachers come together to talk about the day's special activities and share important events from life at home.

11:00 Writing. The children write and draw letters, stories, essays, lists and poetry in their journals, choosing their own topics and creating rough drafts. One day a week, the children "have a go" at correcting words they know are misspelled. When a child wants to publish a story she/he works at the editing table to perfect the selected work.

11:30 Literature. Teachers read aloud to children, children read to each other or work on book reports in small groups, teachers conduct mini lessons on English and reading skills, or children sit in the authors' chairs and read their original stories to the group. One day a week each class travels to the central library to explore the world of books.

12:00 Lunch. The children bring a lunch from home; the school provides milk and 100% orange juice.

12:30 Recreational Reading. Children select books or magazines from the classroom library and read silently. Teachers listen to selected students read orally, and ask questions to check interest, readability, and comprehension. Students learn that reading is an enjoyable and interesting activity — an end in itself.

1:00 Recess/Physical Education. The group has a second recess; three days a week the group works with a physical education specialist in soccer, bowling, sportsmanship, and small ball skills.

1:45 Big Group. The group reassembles to share ideas and deal with the business of the class. The teacher may read aloud from a book or introduce a topic for discussion. The healthy give and take that occurs at group time leads to self-assurance, group awareness, and individual self-discipline.

Science and Social Studies Projects. The children work on projects derived from the thematic unit for the semester. Projects are designed to actively engage the children, such as building a submarine, researching the whale, planting a terrarium, creating masks of paper mache, or conducting science experiments.

Music. One day a week, the class sings with a music specialist. Music is an effective medium for learning language, group cooperation, and project development and completion.

2:30 Clean-up. Learning to clean up creates in children a sense of ownership in the classroom and a sense of responsibility in planning future activities. The primary children are also responsible for collecting their own homework, clothing, and other possessions.

2:50 Dismissal.

8:50 Arrival. Children sign in, hang up coats and book bags, and write and draw in their files. Students learn to portray their experiences first by drawing pictures and later by labeling their pictures and adding phrases and sentences to their books.

9:15 Grouptime. Each class meets in a small group to do opening exercises (calendar, choose the leader, etc.) sing songs, do directed reading and math activities, play games and read a story. Once a week the children go to the library or music room for a special class.

9:45 Playtime. Outside on the playground or inside in the Fun Room, children run, climb, jump, and exercise on developmental equipment.

10:15 Big Group. Teachers and children share items of interest and demonstrate the learning centers for the day.

10:30 Learning Centers. The heart of the kindergarten program, learning centers are carefully planned to attract and hold a five-year-old's interest and provide appropriate challenges. These activities supply the vehicle through which the children learn concepts in math, science, language arts, and writing. Being able to choose their own work is a natural motivator for children: everyone is busy doing an activity that is full of teaching possibilities. Teachers move from center to center encouraging, questioning, and observing children's progress. It is by carefully watching what children can do today that forms the teacher's plans for tomorrow.

Children learn to report their choices on a weekly contract to follow through on the self-initiated activities and to work with and among others in a cooperative way. Children work and play in several areas: blocks, pretend, woodworking, language, math, science, creative arts, library, listening, computer, sandbox, and other centers as appropriate.

11:30 Clean-up. Learning to clean up creates in children a sense of ownership in the classroom and a sense of responsibility in planning future activities.

11:40 Half-day dismissal. Students in the half-day class meet for a moment to gather their belongings and discuss their day.

Full-day lunch. Full-day kindergarten students eat the lunch they brought from home; school provides milk and orange juice.

12:30 Recess and P.E. Three times a week the children play games with a physical education specialist.

1:00 Rest. Children listen to music, read or write in their files, and rest for the afternoon activities.

1:30 Projects. Paper mache, mural-making, puppet design, musical instruments, cooking, science experiments, language experience stories, field trips, and a variety of enriching activities are offered in the afternoon session. Each project period concludes with the children choosing or inventing games to play with friends.

2:50 Dismissal.

Voices

Schools can't possibly teach students all the factual knowledge they will need to know in their lives. Workers and citizens need to know how to learn, how to think critically, how to communicate effectively, how to solve new problems as they arise. Teaching those skills must become a primary goal of education.

Joan Gaustad
Nongraded Education: Mixed-Age, Integrated, and Developmentally Appropriate Education for Primary Children

Reprinted with permission of the Oregon School Study Council.

MULTIAGE MODELS

Individually Prescribed Education

FEATURES

Prescribed Education which allows for plans and objectives to be developed, taking into account the physical, social, emotional and academic development of each child.

Personalization which values each child as a unique individual that differs from others in her or his capabilities, interests, and rate of physical, mental, emotional and social growth.

Individual Assessment to determine appropriate placement in a curriculum and systematic monitoring of a child's progress.

Parental Involvement which is essential to a well-planned educational program for each child.

Continuous Progress which allows each child to progress from one level to another at her or his own rate.

Development of Independence which gives students responsibilities, choices and opportunities to use self-discipline within a controlled environment.

Variety of Instructional and Curricula Approaches to accommodate the different learning styles of children.

Team Teaching which offers children the benefit of working with a group of educators with complementary abilities, skills and talents.

*Montessori Materials and Methods to encourage a "hands on" approach to learning.

*Nongraded Approach which allows each child to work at a level suited to her or his ability level regardless of age or year in school.

*Multiage Grouping which de-emphasizes grade and age labels and encourages children to learn from and appreciate roles and abilities of others.

*A.L.E.M. Adaptive Learning Environments Model which emphasizes adapting the classroom environment to meet the varied needs of children including special education, remedial and gifted education.
(Dixie serves as Kentucky's model site)

> *Multiage grouping de-emphasizes grade and age labels and encourages children to learn from and appreciate roles and abilities of others.*

While many of the features described may be found in other Fayette County Public Schools, *these components are unique to Dixie Elementary School.

CRITERIA FOR ADMISSION

1. Must be a resident of Fayette County eligible to attend an elementary school for the 1990-91 school year.
2. Must exhibit a level of independence and self-discipline required for the program.
3. Parents must indicate an understanding and support for the philosophy of the program.
4. Parents must agree to participate in the planning of their child's program and be involved in school activities.

NOTE: An admissions committee will review all applications to insure a balance of age, race, and achievement level. In the event more applications are received than spaces available, the committee will take into account the admissions criteria and will give priority to the date of the application. In the event the admissions committee has questions regarding the application, an interview with the parents and student may be requested. **For further information contact Dr. Anita Jones, Special Pupil Services, (606) 281-0175.**

OBJECTIVES

- To develop a positive attitude toward learning in each child.
- To foster self-esteem and self-reliance through academic accomplishment.
- To provide for each child an individualized, educational program suited to her or his needs.
- To provide for each child the opportunity to progress at her or his own pace.
- To encourage the development of the total child which includes the social, emotional, physical and academic development.
- To foster the development of independence and self-discipline in each child.
- To develop a classroom environment conducive to learning for each child.
- To provide successful school experiences for each child.
- To provide opportunities for parents to be involved with their child's educational program.
- To provide trained staff prepared to implement a variety of instructional approaches and curricula.

MULTIAGE M·O·D·E·L·S

Providing Multiage Options

*Excerpt from parent handbook, **Information for Parents**, 1992–93*

Essex Elementary School has an enrollment of approximately 430 students in kindergarten through grade 2. In addition, we have an Essential Early Education (EEE) and Hearing Impaired Program in our school, bringing our total enrollment to 450 students.

In keeping with *The Essex Design for Learning* and its philosophy of teaching every child based on individual needs, our school offers both single grade and multiage classrooms, with two options for kindergarten.

The kindergarten options are: a morning half-day session, or K-1 and K-2 multiage, and all-day programs for kindergarten students.

Students in grade 1 and grade 2 may be placed in single-grade classes or K-1, K-2, or 1-2 multiage classes.

Seven of twenty-two classes are currently multiage. The aspects unique to a multiage classroom environment are the consistency of a two or three year program and the opportunity for children to interact with individuals of different ages. Placement in all programs is based on parent input and request.

Regardless of which program children are in, all classrooms adhere to the same Essex Town School District philosophy and curriculum.

School Philosophy

The staff of the Essex Town School District recognizes that children develop at independent rates. We continually encourage growth by guiding each child emotionally, socially, physically, and intellectually. We adapt instruction to meet the abilities, needs, and interests of each child.

School Principles
1. We respect ourselves.
2. We respect each other's feelings.
3. We respect each other's bodies, space, and belongings.

These school principles reflect our school attitudes towards student expectations and behavior. Individual classrooms may have additional rules that are an extension of these principles.

The Goals of the Essex Town School District
(from The Essex Design for Learning)

1. Learning for each child should be a meaningful experience.
2. Each individual should progress at his or her own rate of learning.
3. Each individual should feel successful in the development of the learning process.
4. Each individual should be encouraged to utilize the inherent desire to learn from all experiences.

The overall aim of early childhood education is the development of each child socially, emotionally, physically, and intellectually. It is a time for each child to discover the excitement and joy of learning.

5. Each child should have the opportunity to combine subject matter studies in a unit approach to learning.
6. Each individual should be encouraged to relate knowledge to new situations in order to solve problems.
7. Individuals should be encouraged to develop a sense of responsibility.
8. Each individual should be guided toward the development of a set of personal guidelines which will enable him or her to meet the challenges of life both now and in the future.

Curricula

The Essex Town School District has written curriculum for all curricular areas. The curricula include goals, objectives, teaching methodology, and assessments based on goals. They are available in the school Learning Center for parents to view or borrow.

K-2 Curriculum

The Essex Town School District views curriculum as an individualized, sequential educational plan with common concepts, skills, and values developed across subject areas and throughout all grade levels.

The curriculum is child-centered in that the teacher bases instructional decisions upon the needs, interests, and abilities of each child.

The curriculum is sequential in that concepts, skills, and values are introduced, reinforced, and extended according to child development theory, and according to the individual development of each child.

The overall aim of early childhood education is the development of each child socially, emotionally, physically, and intellectually. It is a time for each child to discover the excitement and joy of learning.

Social and Emotional Development

One of the goals of early childhood education is to help children develop a high sense of self-esteem. This is facilitated in part by helping children develop the components of self-esteem: a sense of one's own identity, a sense of recognizing and respecting one's uniqueness, and a sense of self through using the power of self-definition.

Children are encouraged to identify and express their emotions so they can learn to live with them, eventually becoming the master of their emotions rather than being controlled by their emotions.

Children will begin to develop many skills as they learn to interact with adults and children other than family members.

Essex Primary Unit

by Elizabeth Dreibelbis and Jane Meyers
Excerpt from information shared with parents during Parent Night

The Primary Unit contains two multiage classrooms, with grades 1 and 2 combined, that will work closely together in small and large group situations. The teachers will team teach and coordinate planning. This approach will provide children with small and large group activities, integrate subject areas, allow each child to progress at his own speed, and have peers at a similar level in both classrooms. As in single-graded classrooms, the multiage classes will have children with a wide range of abilities and needs.

Alternatives in education are an integral part of The Essex Design. This combination of grades 1 and 2 offers an optional environment in which children can learn.

Our program offers each child the opportunity to benefit from an ungraded learning situation in which learning is emphasized, not the grade. The grade-by-grade structure arbitrarily imposes an expected rate of progress on all students, which is not consistent with current research findings in the areas of cognitive and affective development. Consequently, a graded system distorts each student's perception of his/her own rate of progress and emphasizes a grade-by-grade progression instead of basic skill acquisition.

Even more important in a multiage class is the feeling of a caring family that develops over the two years each child is in the classroom. The teacher gets to know the child and his/her family well, and a feeling of trust develops and continues for that two-year span. The "August anxiety" and the "getting to know you" time usually lost in September are unnecessary as the teacher and half the students are old friends.

Personalized and cooperative learning make school a challenging, fun, and safe place where children can think and take risks when solving problems and learning.

Benefits
1. The consistency of the same team of teachers for two years provides stability for the children. Time is not lost "getting to know each other."
2. Inter-classroom grouping provides more flexibility, both academically and socially, to work with peers.
3. Peer tutoring and contact with two classrooms offer more opportunities for children to learn with and from each other.
4. Thematic units can be established and the curriculum integrated over a two-year span.
5. A pair of teachers will be able to teach, observe children's growth and plan the best path for each child's success over a two-year span.

What Is Whole Language? Or Will My Child Get Phonics?
The term whole language is heard over and over in school systems throughout Vermont. This approach for teaching reading and writing is fast replacing basal series in many classrooms. Whole language is a controversial topic which has caused many debates among teachers, parents, and administrators.

We have taught reading from a basal in the past but have been incorporating the whole language process into our classrooms more and more each year. Here are some of our reasons:

On a basic level, whole language can be defined as a child-centered approach to language instruction which recognizes that language and literacy development are best facilitated when the subskills (reading, writing, talking) are interrelated. In whole language classrooms there is a blurring of language subskills and subject disciplines. Reading, writing, and talking emerge as logical developments of every lesson, and as a result, it is difficult to distinguish a writing lesson per se from a reading lesson. Whole language teachers use certain strategies and teaching techniques that are consistent with psycholinguistic research.

What Whole Language Is
1. **Language kept whole.** Reading, writing, talking, viewing are natural parts of every lesson.
2. **Child-centered.** Language lessons are geared to meet individual interests and needs. The curriculum is organized around broad themes within which each child can explore his/her own interests.
3. **Literature-based.** In order to come to literacy naturally, children need exposure to high-impact reading material. This material is read to, by, and with the children in a variety of ways.
4. **Context-rich.** Specific reading skills are taught within the context of rewarding material. This way children can access four cueing systems: graphophonic, syntactic, semantic, and pragmatic.
5. **Writing-rich.** From the beginning, children are encouraged to write. The writing helps establish links to the graphophonic cueing system and enables children to practice being authors. They pretend their way into writing and, in so doing, learn the way writing works.
6. **Talk-focused.** Because whole language teachers know that children need to talk to facilitate thinking, reading, and writing, they provide many opportunities for verbal interaction. Children talk about what they are doing, and the teacher listens.
7. **Activity-based.** Children learn best when they are actively involved in structuring their own learning. When you do, you learn.
8. **Parent-involved.** Whole language teachers know that parents can be their strongest allies and try to involve parents in the classrooms. Newsletters feature children's writing,

class news, parent information, and professional articles.

9. **Self-esteem building.** Children in whole language classrooms feel that they are capable. The program focus is on the individual child's strengths. When a child does not seem to be functioning effectively, the teacher examines the program, teaching, and materials and makes accommodations that will enable the child to learn.

10. **Corporate, small group, and individual teaching/learning situations.** No single teaching methodology suits all children. Whole language teachers use all of their knowledge and strategies with every class.

11. **Fun!** What a marvelous way to teach and to learn. We are too busy to be bored, and the children are flying with enthusiasm.

12. **Hard work!!** Teachers put in more hours teaching whole language. We need to know each child. We vary our teaching style and methods. But it is worth the effort!

What Whole Language Is Not
1. Phonics taught is isolation
2. Teacher-centered
3. Vocabulary-controlled, syntax-controlled texts
4. Context-deprived
5. A focus on form over content
6. Quiet
7. Work sheets
8. Isolated from the community
9. Self-esteem damaging
10. Every class taught in the same way every day
11. Boring
12. Easy

Why We Use Manipulatives to Teach Primary Math
Children best develop understanding and insight of the patterns of math through the use of concrete materials. The activities we use are designed to help young children see relationships and interconnections in math and to enable them to deal flexibly with mathematical ideas and concepts.

Children need to touch and to manipulate math concepts. We provide them with the materials and guidance to do this. They use material for free exploration, patterning, sorting and classifying, counting, comparing, graphing, numbers, place value, and other concepts. We use beans, unifix cubes, and all kinds of counters (from spiders at Halloween to buttons and tiles). Pentominoes and tangrams help the child learn to problem solve and to think.

We use the math text and various paper/pencil activities at the symbolic and abstract levels when the child is developmentally ready for them.

This way of approaching math — a hands-on, concrete approach — may seem to go slowly at first, but it lays a firm, broad-based foundation on which more complex math concepts can be added in the upper grades.

This multi-faceted math program helps create, not a class of rote learners, but a class of thinking, problem-solving math students who understand the concepts as well as the answers.

Voices

T*he successful nongraded classroom isn't unstructured — it's just differently structured.*
Joan Gaustad
Nongraded Education

Reprinted with permission of the Oregon School Study Council.

MULTIAGE M·O·D·E·L·S

Letting Children's Needs Lead the Way
by Robert J. Ross, Principal

The basic strength of Lake George Elementary School, Lake George, New York, is our commitment to excellence and our belief that schools exist for students. Students, parents, teachers, and administrators working cooperatively provide the extra effort necessary to make the elementary school the most productive place possible for student learning. We are not in awe of accountability; we welcome it.

> "This is the first school I have seen that is actually *doing* something *different*. Many talk, point to one or two 'showcase' classrooms, but children are still at the mercy of whatever teacher or individual philosophy he/she holds. Lake George is consistent in its philosophy, willing to take political risk to keep that uniformity. What I see is the way I've always thought primary education should be — teaching how to learn."
> Comment from 1990-91 visitor.

We are not in awe of account-ability; we welcome it.

Lake George is located in the eastern Adirondack Mountains and is widely known as a resort community. Located halfway between Montreal and New York City, it combines the quiet and beauty of the mountains and lakes and is easily accessible to major metropolitan centers.

While our community would be classified as above average socially and economically, in recent years we have experienced an increase in student mobility, students with learning problems, and students involved in single parent homes. This has led to an increase in counseling time, the addition of a social worker, and an increase in our remedial/special needs staff.

To facilitate our learning process in a child-centered way, we take advantage of three important educational concepts: continuous progress education, team teaching, and multiage/family grouping. These educational concepts are incorporated in our 1968 open-plan building with portable partitioning to accommodate various instructional groupings.

Promoting Child-Centered Learning

Continuous progress/nongraded education is based on the premise that children learn most successfully when they are working at their own levels of ability. Whenever possible, students move through our continuum without regard to age or grade barriers. Students do not compete with, and are not compared to, other students, but do compete and are compared against their own measured abilities and achievements.

Our teachers work in teaching teams to determine students' progress, to develop the best approaches for solving the instructional problems of individual students, and to divide teaching assignments according to ability, interest, and strength of each member of the teaching teams. Teams vary from 40 to 60 students and contain two or three teachers. Most students spend two years with each teaching team. An additional year might be required of some students, while a few might spend a single year with a teaching team. While students are generally assigned to teaching teams randomly, a student may be assigned to a team or cluster by parental choice.

Our multiage grouping is a procedure that results in most classrooms containing students of various ages rather than the traditional one age group or grade. Family grouping refers to our procedure of housing students varying in ages from 6 to 13 in each of three clusters, color coded green, yellow, and red. Within each cluster, students are grouped for instruction by teaching teams containing 6-8 year-olds, 8-10 year-olds, and 11-13 year-olds. Kindergartners are housed in Orange Cluster where five teachers team with a ratio of approximately 17 students per teacher. Ratios of our other teams vary from 20 to 25 students per teacher. Our total school body varies from 520 to 550 students.

Advantages of Multiage

Some of the advantages of our multiage grouping are:

1. Teachers have the average student for a two-year period rather than for one year. This allows the teacher to do a more effective job of pacing the student's education and providing a much greater understanding of each child's style of learning. It is important that teachers vary their teaching style to be congruent with the child's learning style rather than to assume that 6, 7, and 8 year-olds have the necessary understanding to accommodate the various teachers with different teaching styles.

2. Stereotyping of students is reduced. For example: the tallest, shortest, fastest, or slowest does not necessarily remain in this position year after year. In the first year in the classroom a child may be the smallest, but the next year there may be younger "newcomers" who are smaller. The same is true in math or any subject. The first year the students may be working at a lower level relative to others in the groups, but at the second year some of the newcomers will be at levels lower than they are.

3. Parents and teachers get to know each other better!

4. Students learn positive modeling from their older associates, develop more independent study skills, and more self-reliance. As parents and teachers, we sometimes focus on the bad examples youngsters acquire from older youngsters and take for granted the day-to-day positive examples exhibited by older students. We must recognize and reinforce each and every one of these positive examples.

5. Older youngsters learn about responsibility and caring through their association with the younger students.

6. At the beginning of the school year the older youngsters are more familiar with the instructional procedures than the younger ones. Therefore, less teacher time is needed to start the class and teach appropriate classroom behavior, and there is more time to devote to the younger children who need the most help.

Some of the advantages of our family plan of grouping are:

1. It provides common agreement, expectation, and sharing of educational priorities, objectives, and practices among a team of seven or eight teachers for a six-year period. Students are managed in very consistent patterns.

2. The students' and parents' anxieties of who their teacher will be in September is greatly reduced.

3. It provides for effective transfer of student information from teaching team to teaching team.

4. It assists in the accommodation of students working at various instructional levels regardless of the student's age.

Measuring Success

In 1979 parents of the Lake George Elementary School indicated on our annual parent survey that 88% of their children were receiving a quality education. Today that figure reads 97%.

We measure success of our program in many ways: progress of individual students, results of our state and standardized testing, parent and student reactions to our parent survey and student questionnaire, feedback from visitors, and the accomplishment of our stated objectives. There are many factors which contribute to the success of our school.

Those factors I consider most unique to our school are:

1. Removal of traditional letter grades which allows *all* students to experience success, eliminates the comparison of students, and allows students to compete with themselves rather than with their associates.

2. Shared, not advisory, staff decision making. Decisions made at the cabinet level are made from the "bottom up" and are approved by the majority and binding to all, unless someone can suggest a better decision/solution.

3. Staff attitude that *we* are responsible and in control of student behaviors, not what the student or parent needs to do or change, but what *we* must do to create positive behavior on the part of individual students. The attitude that modeling of teachers is just as important as the modeling of students. If we do not want students to "put down" other students, as staff members and adults, we must not "put down" students. We are not so much concerned with what is happening at home and what type of home the student comes from as we are about creating the right options so the child will be successful during the time spent with us at school.

4. We teach self-discipline, self-concept, and independent learning skills. We do not assume that as children increase in age they become better disciplined, grow in self-concept, or acquire independent learning skills.

Other significant contributing factors to our plan: a well-designed inservice program which at times makes use of instruction from some of our own staff members; PTA and parental involvement and support; administrative leadership; student support teams; supportive school board and superintendent; evaluation that allows teachers to develop their own methods of evaluation for the purpose of self-improvement; practical use of school-wide goals and objectives; a model process writing program beginning in kindergarten; the integration of art, music, health education, and physical education programs with the classroom instruction; a late bus one hour after school closing allowing an extension of the school day for the purpose of including art, music, gifted and talented, computer, and sport activities.

While the basic strength of the Lake George Elementary School is our commitment to excellence, of equal value is our attitude that change is always occurring, that we have never arrived, but are always *almost* getting there.

Voices

I n an ungraded, multiage or combined-grade program, children are expected and encouraged to learn at different rates and levels. This greatly reduces the pressure on young learners and makes academic failure far less likely to occur. It also creates an environment in which discipline problems and the formation of negative attitudes are far less prevalent, because students are accepted and supported at their current stage of development.

Jim Grant
Developmental Education in the 1990's

Reprinted with permission of Programs for Education, Rosemont, NJ.

Mast Landing School
116 Bow Street
Freeport, ME 04032

Letting Parents Choose
by Irving Richardson, Principal

Freeport, Maine is a small town located on the coast of southern Maine. It is probably best known as home of the well-known sporting goods store, L.L. Bean. The large number of outlet stores that have opened in Freeport over the past decade have made the town into one of the Northeast's shopping meccas. Freeport residents are a combination of people whose families have lived in town for a long time and people who are relatively new and who appreciate its coastal location and proximity to Portland, the largest city in Maine.

About 1,100 students attend public schools in Freeport; over 600 are elementary-age students. Since 1971, parents of elementary-age students have had a choice about which school their children would attend. Prior to 1985, the choice was between a nongraded open school and a more traditional classroom program. In 1985, a combination of a small class graduating from the open school along with a large number of parents requesting the program created a large waiting list for the nongraded program. The superintendent of schools convened a study group to recommend solutions. Among the recommendations were creation of a third alternative program and organization of the building committee to work toward a single facility for upper elementary-age students in Freeport. The Multi-level Program was created to meet the parental demand for another nongraded elementary program.

Staffed with teachers who volunteered to leave the traditional classroom program and begin the new program, the Multi-level program opened in the fall of 1986 with 88 students. Since that year, district parents have continued to have their choice of three elementary education programs for students ages 8-12.

Over the past seven years, the program has experimented with different structures and techniques and has evolved into the structure reported here.

Before school opens in the fall, the staff examines assessments that provide information about a student's instructional needs for math and language arts. Social/emotional factors are also considered as the initial instructional groupings are determined. The year begins with each student assigned to a home math group and a reading group. Students may or may not have the same teacher for these groupings. Students may also switch groups during the year if the staff determines a student's instructional needs are better met in another instructional group.

STRUCTURE AND PHILOSOPHY

Teachers working in the program are committed to meeting individual student needs while working on group social skills. The program's mission is to "create an environment that meets the social, emotional, and academic needs of the students." Staff members put in very long hours as they strive to meet the program's mission.

To meet individual student needs and to allow students to make continuous academic progress, the daily schedule has been arranged so that teachers have congruent schedules. During the day, every teacher teaches math, language arts, and science/social studies. Times for the subjects are blocked out so that students can move between rooms for instruction in the different subjects. Congruent scheduling also creates blocks of cooperative planning time for staff members. The schedule is as follows:

The Multi-level Program was created to meet the parental demand for another nongraded elementary program.

Morning	Opening	Afternoon	Language Arts
	Math		Science /
	Recess/Snack		Social Studies
	Language Arts		
	Lunch/Recess		

The program is administered by a half-time teaching principal who teaches in the morning and has release time in the afternoon to perform administrative duties.

DEMOGRAPHICS

About 120 students from ages 8 to 12 are enrolled in the Multi-level Program, which is designed to serve students traditionally enrolled in grades 3 through 5. There are six full-time teaching positions for the program along with a half-time special education teacher and two Chapter I aides. About 16% of the student population has identified special needs, and about 20% of the student population receives Chapter I services.

Students with identified special needs are served in regular classrooms unless their needs require a different environment. Teachers modify the curricula and expectations for students with special needs with the help of the special education teacher.

Students who are eligible for Chapter I services are clustered in two rooms, and each room is assigned a Chapter I aide. Students are given informal reading inventories and then a plan is implemented to improve each child's reading skills.

CURRICULUM

Math – For mathematics instruction, the Multi-level Program uses the Conceptually Oriented Math Program (C.O.M.P.). This program divides K-8 math instruction into levels. Each level has specific skills and concepts which must be mastered. Although the skills and concepts are identified, the methods are left to the teacher. Concepts like multiplication and division can thus be taught through a variety of lessons and materials. Each teacher assumes teaching responsibility for two small instructional groups that are at different C.O.M.P. levels. Students receive instruction at their "level" until they demonstrate mastery and proceed to the next level. Students who achieve mastery more quickly than others can be placed with another math teacher who is teaching the next highest level.

Language Arts – Students receive instruction in reading, writing, and spelling in language arts groups. Reading is taught through a whole language process approach which encourages students to read and discuss a variety of types of literature. Writing is taught through a process approach which encourages students to write successive drafts as they refine their thoughts.

Reading and writing instruction occurs in small "needs-based" groups, through individual conferences with students, and through whole group presentations. Teachers use a variety of approaches to teach spelling. Each classroom teacher develops a program to meet the needs of students in each group.

Students attend art and music once a week, and physical education twice a week. They attend these classes in their language arts groups.

Science/Social Studies – The last hour of each day is reserved for teaching science and social studies.

The teaching staff determines themes for the coming year before the opening of school. A week prior to each theme, descriptions of the upcoming units are sent home to parents. Students sign up for the unit of their choice. The district's science and social studies outcomes are taught through these different units. By offering science/social studies instruction in this way, students select their course of study by interest. Staff members work hard at developing units that actively involve students in their learning. (See chart.)

SPECIAL FEATURES AND EVENTS

A few days before school opens, students and their families are invited to a picnic on the school grounds. This allows students entering the program to visit their classrooms and to spend some informal time with their new teachers. It also allows students already attending the program to see friends and orient themselves to another year of school.

To keep students working as an entire program, all students and faculty meet once a week for about 30 minutes. This offers students a chance to voice opinions and offers the faculty the chance to bring up issues with students. It also offers an opportunity to share and celebrate student learning.

The Multi-level Program has a constitution that is modeled after the three different branches of government. Students are the legislative branch, teachers are the executive branch, and the principal is the judicial branch. Students write bills which are debated and voted upon at large group meetings.

After January's science units, students present their science projects and what they've learned at a science fair. Parents and community members are invited to this evening event which highlights students' work.

Each February, the program holds a writing festival. During the festival, the afternoon science and social studies units focus on different aspects of writing. Parent and community volunteers offer instruction in different genres of writing. At the end of the writing festival, parents are invited to an Authors' Tea during which students read their pieces of writing. In addition, each child selects a piece of writing to be entered in an anthology, which is published with the help of parents. Each student receives a copy of the anthology.

Toward the end of the year, students who will enter the middle school in the fall participate in a unit designed to bring them together as a group. This group works on an environmental project that culminates in an overnight at a nearby state park.

FUTURE ISSUES

Like all public schools, the Multi-level Program is striving to meet demands placed upon it while receiving fewer resources to meet those demands. The program will continue to evolve with assessment of educational outcomes being a major focus of staff development work in the immediate future.

Dates	Theme/Topic	Mrs. Southard	Mrs. Arsenault	Mr. Donaldson	Mr. LaPierre	Mrs. K-Chesley	Mrs. Winship
Sept. 3–Sept. 25 3 weeks	Government	Metropolitan Community	Government	Citizenship	Council	Government	Community
Sept. 28–Oct. 23 4 weeks	Explorers	Pond Water	They Crossed The Atlantic	Leonardo	Dig	Columbus' Journey	Pioneers
Oct. 26–Nov. 24 4 weeks	Science	Mystery Powders Colored Solutions	Sharks	Computers	Nature Trail	Economics	Mammals Endangered Species
Nov. 30–Dec. 23 3+ weeks	Global Neighbors	Canada	China	Spain	Maine and Canada	Central America	Iceland
Jan. 4–Jan. 29 4 weeks	Science Exp.	Individual Projects	Scientific Method	Chemistry	Individual Projects	Prove It	Individual Projects
Feb. 1–Feb. 11 2 weeks	Writing Festival	Fairy Tales	Book Making	Fiction	Short Stories	Autobiographies	Poetry
Feb. 22–Mar. 19 4 weeks	Simulations	Pioneers	Caravans	Flight	Merchant	Heritage	Native Americans
Mar. 22–Apr. 15 4 weeks	Science	Rocks and Minerals	Simple Machines	Structures	Electricity	Woods in Winter	Land Forms
Apr. 26–May 14 3 weeks	Human Devel.	Anatomy	Drugs, Alcohol, & Tobacco	Mechanics of the Human Body	First Aid and Safety	Human Growth and Development	Exercise and Nutrition
May 17–June 5 weeks	Environment	Trash to Energy	Ecosystems	The Sky	Fifth Grade Unit	Fifth Grade Unit	Plants Environment

Project Key — Opening Doors for Young Children

Excerpt from Project Key Information Brochure

Project Key is a multiage classroom for children between the ages of six and nine. It is based on a continuous progress model where individual patterns of growth among children are acknowledged. These are accounted for by providing flexible time to meet standards without emphasis on comparisons to grade levels. An important feature of the program is that the single grades of first and second are not separated; children enter the program following kindergarten and remain for two years. This feature alleviates the threat of retention between the two grades, which can damage self-esteem.

Through this model, more advanced students learn together in mixed-age groups and less developed students are given the time they need to master skills at their own pace. At other times, children are put into groups of differing levels of ability to learn from each other. By staying with the same teachers for more than one year, adjustment time in the fall is minimal and, academically, children can pick up from where they were in the spring. The younger students of the previous year take on the roles of older students, which benefit members of both groups.

HOW DO CHILDREN SPEND THEIR DAY?

Children spend their time engaged in a variety of activities and experiences which foster growth in the physical, social, emotional, aesthetic, and cognitive domains. The activities and experiences offered are based on "developmental appropriateness." The National Association for the Education of Young Children describes developmental appropriateness as using what is known about child development and the particular needs and interests of each child to plan programs and prepare the classroom environment.

When planning the curriculum and preparing the environment, Project Key takes into consideration the following characteristics of young learners:
- Young children are innately curious and will strive to learn
- Playful activity is a natural way of learning
- Young children learn by imitating, talking, and interacting with each other as well as with adults
- Learning occurs at different rates
- Real life experiences related to the interests of children promote learning
- Experiencing success builds a sense of security and self-confidence

Therefore, to be congruent with characteristics of young learners, Project Key offers these components in the classroom:
- Integrated curriculum
- Flexible grouping
- Opportunities for small group, large group, and individual instruction, and conferences
- Literature-based reading
- Process writing
- Learning centers
- Discovery math, science, and social studies

More advanced students learn together in mixed-age groups and less developed students are given the time they need to master skills at their own pace.

- Opportunities to experience and respond to their world through art, movement, and music
- Varied instructional strategies
- Child-initiated and teacher-directed activities
- Parental support and involvement
- Authentic assessment

HOW IS LEARNING MEASURED?

The focus of assessment in Project Key is based on the individual child's performance.

Information is gathered using a variety of assessment strategies to determine what a child's abilities and attitudes are upon entering the classroom. Assessment begins in the fall and progress is recorded continually throughout the two years. This information is then reported to parents, teachers, and administrators and can be used to make appropriate changes in the program to better meet each child's needs.

The following is a list of the most commonly used strategies in the Key Program:
- Informal observations
- Anecdotal records
- Developmental checklists
- Portfolios (samples of students' work)
- Reading miscue analyses
- Conferences
- District tests

The following article, written by 6–8-year-old students in Miller School's multiage class, offers a look at the classroom through the children's eyes. The program is based on a continuous progress model and is designed to be developmentally appropriate. Kay Sproul and Beth Ogden team teach the program, which is currently in its fourth year.

> *"Although humans are not usually born in litters, we seem to insist that they be educated in them."*
>
> — Lilian Katz
> Former Vice-President,
> National Association for the
> Education of Young Children

MORNING LETTER

We come to school at 8:30 a.m., do lunch count, and read the morning letter. Then, we check for work to finish from the day before. Next, we do the morning activity. It might be math, spelling, a crossword puzzle, or something to write about. It always has something to do with whatever theme we are working on. After we finish and get our work checked by a teacher, we can choose and go to a center.

CALENDAR

Every morning two kids do the calendar. They add a number on for each day. At calendar time, we use straws to keep track of the number of days in the school year. There are three boxes for the straws — one for the one's place, ten's place, and the hundred's place. A weather chart tells us what kind of weather we are having. A birthday cake shows who has birthdays in the month we're in. We do lots of counting and other stuff with numbers at calendar time.

MATH WORKSHOPS

After we finish the calendar, we have math workshops. We work in groups of four to do math activities that have something to do with our theme. When we did fruit, we guessed how many seeds were in a piece of watermelon. Then we had to count them and use the correct number in number sentences. During presidents, we had an election and graphed the results. We practiced telling time when we did dinosaurs by scheduling a paleontologist's day. Sometimes we do math packets.

QUIET READING

Quiet reading is when we read books. We use quiet voices with our reading partners. Sometimes we get to choose our partners and sometimes the teachers choose them. We have "book bags" to keep our books in. After we read our "practicing books," we can go to the classroom library to choose other books. Our teachers read with one kid at a time. Parents come in and read with us, too.

CENTERS

There are eight centers in our classroom. Each center has an activity that has to do with our theme. We work in groups during center time. We go to four centers the first week and the other four the second week of our theme. On Fridays we have free choice centers.

Math Center — In the Math Center there are lots of materials to use. We have clocks, blocks, dominoes, beans, scales, rulers, counters, dice, flashcards, money, math games, an abacus, and more. Now we are studying dinosaurs so we are measuring strings that are as long as the dinosaurs. We ate food and filled in a graph when we studied the five senses. We made butter once, too. During Halloween we measured and weighed pumpkins. We do adding and subtracting, too.

Games Center — There are lots of things to do in the Games Center. We have puzzles, blocks, letter games, Bingo, Lincoln Logs, Pictionary, and card games. We will name things that we have done. When we studied about insects, we played "The Ladybug Game." We had fly swatters and we slapped the ladybug that had the correct answer to math facts. During dinosaurs we had lots of models of different dinosaurs to play with at our sand table. We also had a dinosaur card game that Evan brought in.

Discovery Center — In the Discovery Center we usually do things that have to do with science or social studies. Once we made flashlights with batteries, bulbs, and wires. When we were studying transportation, we made birch bark canoes. We had a tub of water to test them in. During our unit on fruit, we wrote secret messages on paper with orange and lemon juice. We let them dry, then ironed the paper, and the messages appeared. When we studied about early Waldoboro there were some old things there. We had to guess what the things were and what they were used for.

Art Center — In the Art Center we have markers and crayons to draw pictures with. We have brushes, paints, and easels to paint with. We have lots of paper, glue, and scissors. We also have a closet full of other supplies. This week we are making dinosaurs out of pipe cleaners. There are models there to help us. In October, we made Mr. Macaroni Skeletoni. We used special crayons to make a class quilt and Mrs. Lackoff sewed it together for us. We made a still life using chalk and black paper during our fruit unit.

Writing Center — We have writing folders, paper, crayons, chalk, chalkboards, staplers, dictionaries, clipboards, pencils, erasers, and bookmarks in the Writing Center. When we studied dinosaurs, we copied riddles in our best handwriting and took a guess at the answers. Another week we put nine dinosaurs in categories according to what they ate. Then we listed the dinosaurs under "herbivores" and "carnivores." During Halloween, we wrote the steps on how to make a jack-o-lantern. When we studied insects, we listed things that really "bug us." During our study about early Waldoboro, we listed things that settler children would and would not have seen.

Computer Center — We have a Macintosh and an Apple IIc in our Computer Center. Four people can be in the center at a time. Miss Pinkham helps us with the computer games. Some of the games help us learn about money, spelling, addition, subtraction, weather, and counting. Other games are just plain fun! Some of our favorites are Oregon Trail and Kid's Math. Miss Pinkham publishes stories with us sometimes.

Language Center — We have crossword puzzles and other word games in this center. We also have a flannel board. We use it to tell stories like *The Three Little Pigs*. Last week we used the letters in "paleontologist" to make words. This week we are playing word scrabble with our spelling words. During transportation, we had a real bike to label. Once we put the lines to *Solomon Grundy* in order. In October, we labeled the bones on a skeleton.

Listening Center — In the Listening Center we have a tape player, headphones, lots of tapes, and books. We usually listen to a tape and read along. Last week we listened to a nonfiction tape about dinosaurs. Then we listed facts about them on chart paper. When we listened to *The Ox-Cart Man*, we wrote and drew what the family would do next. After listening to *There Was an Old Lady Who Swallowed a Fly*, we put the animals that she swallowed in order. Sometimes we write about the problem and solution of a story. Sometimes we write and draw about the characters.

SPELLING AND JOURNALS

We do spelling two times a week and journals three times a week. Our spelling words all belong to families like **ent, us, one,** and so on. We copy our words and take them home to study. Sometimes — we put them in ABC order, make sentences and pictures to go with them, or have spelling bees and other games. Every other Friday we have a test on our spelling words.

When it's time for journals, we write in a little blue book. We're supposed to write and not talk so that we can get all of our thoughts on paper. We write about things that happen at home and at school. Sometimes we write about how we're feeling. Usually we share our journals with the class. Miss Sproul and Miss Ogden read our journals and write us notes.

SHARING / READ ALOUD

After recess we come in and sit on the rug. Then we share things that we bring from home and have something to do with our themes.

We also listen to the teachers read stories. They usually read one fiction and one nonfiction book.

WRITING WORKSHOP

We have writing workshop almost every afternoon. We start off having a "Status of the Class" meeting. That means the teachers ask us what we will be working on that day. Then we start writing. Some people write, publish, edit, illustrate, have a conference, or are thinking about a new story. We can work alone or with a friend. We can choose our own topic. At the end of writing time, we get to share our stories.

VOLUNTEERS

Volunteers help out in our classroom. They read with us, publish our stories on the computers, and help out with centers. They also go on field trips with us. Sometimes we have visitors like Dr. Lackoff, who came in to talk about bones at Halloween. (He brought a skeleton with him.) Dr. Beaudoin talked about teeth. Mr. and Mrs. Scott helped us make Christmas wreaths. Mrs. Lackoff talked about Hanukkah and made doughnuts with us. Mr. Cartwright talked about newspapers. It is good to have volunteers. We like them a lot.

Celebrating the Success of Project Key

by Mary B. Dauderdale, Curriculum Coordinator
MSAD #40, Waldoboro, Maine

Change, restructuring, school improvement — the specific term doesn't matter. What matters is ensuring that all students succeed in school. Miller Grade School's Project Key is meeting this challenging standard. What can be learned from Project Key's success?

A collaborative culture exists not only at the building level but at the district level as well. The two teachers who team teach in Project Key have been involved since the inception of the project through participatory leadership. This sharing of authority in decision making has linked the classroom teachers, school principal, and central office (superintendent and curriculum coordinator) as a supportive team with a common vision.

At the heart of this program's success are the two teachers, Kay Sproul and Beth Ogden. These teachers have high expectations for all students and utilize a variety of instructional methods to help students succeed.

In addition, the principal has facilitated an environment where change has been encouraged and supported.

There are many ways to celebrate. This article celebrates the vision, dedication, professionalism, and plain hard work that has sustained Project Key. Waldoboro, Maine is a great place to view change in action.

At the heart of this program's success are the two teachers . . . . These teachers have high expectations for all students and utilize a variety of instructional methods to help students succeed.

Project Key students and teachers celebrate Octoberfest, 1992.

Milwaukee Public School
PO Drawer 10K
Milwaukee, WI 53201-8210

Milwaukee Public Schools' Ungraded Program
by Milly Hoffman, Curriculum Specialist

The Milwaukee Public Schools' Ungraded Program is an educational design for young children that is organized in a creative, flexible manner based on each individual's developmental needs and learning styles. The learning environment includes developmentally appropriate practices and instructional materials to encourage active learning and appreciation of cultural diversity. No grade level designations are attached to placement. Children progress at their own pace through an integrated, child-centered curriculum.

PHILOSOPHY

The Ungraded Program is rooted in the following five research-based principles:
1. We match educational practices to the way children learn.
2. We create a classroom environment that encourages exploration and facilitates learning and development.
3. We view the developmental range as a continuum of development rather than as discrete grade levels.
4. We consider parent involvement a critical and essential element in the Ungraded Program.
5. As educators, we are researchers and we use our data for decision making and curriculum development.

CURRICULUM

The ungraded curriculum is consistent with the MPS K-12 Curriculum. The ten K-12 Teaching and Learning Goals are the standards for guiding teaching and learning in all classrooms. The K-12 Teaching and Learning Goals are:
1. Students will project anti-racist, anti-biased attitudes through their participation in a multilingual, multiethnic, culturally diverse curriculum.
2. Students will participate and gain knowledge in all the arts (visual arts, dance, theatre, literature, music), developing personal vehicles for self-expression reinforced in an integrated curriculum.
3. Students will demonstrate positive attitudes towards life, living, and learning through an understanding and respect of self and others.
4. Students will make responsible decisions, solve problems, and think critically.
5. Students will demonstrate responsible citizenship and an understanding of global interdependence.
6. Students will use technological resources capably, actively, and responsibly.
7. Students will think logically and abstractly, applying mathematical and scientific principles of inquiry to solve problems, create new solutions, and communicate new ideas and relationships to real world experiences.
8. Students will communicate knowledge, ideas, thoughts, feelings, concepts, opinions, and needs effectively and creatively using varied modes of expression.
9. Students will learn strategies to cope with the challenges of daily living and will establish practices which promote health, fitness, and safety.

As educators, we are researchers and we use our data for decision making and curriculum development.

125

10. Students will set short- and long-term goals, will develop an awareness of career opportunities, and will be motivated to actualize their potential.

The Ungraded Council has developed the following Developmental Learning Goals:
The child will:
1. experience success in learning activities.
2. view himself/herself as a positive contributing member of various multicultural communities including the home, school, neighborhood, and the world.
3. use listening skills to acquire knowledge, follow directions, and interact with peers.
4. speak articulately, fluently, and with understanding.
5. respond to various types of literature.
6. use strategic reading skills when reading narrative and expository texts.
7. compose, edit, and publish based on his/her background experiences.
8. develop the ability to communicate, understand, and compute using his/her working knowledge of numbers.
9. participate in fine arts and humanities activities.
10. develop and apply strategies to solve a wide variety of problems.

INSTRUCTION

Instruction in ungraded classrooms is child-centered, which means it is based on the interests and needs of the students. Flexible grouping is used including the integration of exceptional education and regular education students. All learning styles are accommodated and active learning is expected. Learning centers, discovery learning, and a process approach are practiced.

Heterogeneous grouping is encouraged including paired learning, cooperative learning, whole class instruction, direct instruction, modeling, guided practice, and independent practice.

The language arts (reading, writing, speaking, and listening) are taught in an integrated manner. Science and mathematics are taught using manipulatives and concrete objects. Thematic units are used to integrate the curriculum. Students' background knowledge is used as a foundation for further learning.

LEARNER CHARACTERISTICS

Learners develop at different rates and exhibit a wide range of capabilities within their chronological development. The learner:
1. pursues topics of interest.
2. focuses on self-evaluation.
3. works in cooperative groups.
4. gives peer support.
5. uses thinking skills to solve problems.
6. works at own pace.
7. makes good choices about own learning.
8. helps maintain a nonjudgmental, safe classroom environment.
9. uses practical, manipulable objects.

ENVIRONMENT (MATERIALS, RESOURCES, ORGANIZATION)

The ungraded classroom should include a variety of interest centers, such as a science center, writing center, listening center, manipulative center, etc. Movable furniture, carpeting, and storage "bins" for instructional materials and individual student materials should be available. Materials, such as maps, globes, manipulatives, art materials, audio-visual aids, science experiment materials, computers and software, and a variety of literature are essential. Students' work should be prominently displayed.

The heterogeneous organization of classes should be a cooperative effort of staff and principals to reflect the ungraded concept.

Classroom labeling should not include grade level designations.

ASSESSMENT

Authentic assessment measures are being developed which will be consistent with the learning objectives and goals. A portfolio approach to assessment is currently practiced in some of the schools.

The report card must be consistent with the philosophy and practices of the Ungraded Program. Each school will develop its own report card(s) within the following guidelines:
1. No letter or number grades
2. Narrative comments following an outline of topics, curricular areas, themes, or content areas
3. Reflects individual's growth and progress rather than grade level standards
4. No promotion/retention statements

FAMILY INVOLVEMENT
Family involvement is a critical component of a student's success in the Ungraded Program. Parents are expected to volunteer and be active participants in their children's education. Communication with family is achieved through meetings, newsletters, conferences, and mailings. The school parent group is encouraged to participate in the program implementation.

ACTION RESEARCH (STAFF DEVELOPMENT)
Staff development has been essential for the implementation of the Ungraded Program. This has included participation in workshops, inservices, and conferences. Local school planning is ongoing and has included staff development activities such as:
1. Viewing of the *Discovering the Future: The Business of Paradigms* videotape.
2. Discussion of the following professional articles:
   • NAEYC Position Statement on "Developmentally Appropriate Practice in the Primary Grades, Serving 5- Through 8-Year-Olds"
   • NAEYC Position Statement on "Guidelines for Appropriate Curriculum Content and Assessment in Programs Serving Children Ages 3 Through 8"
   • *The Whys and Hows of the Multiage Primary Classroom*
3. Discussion of the Ungraded Position Paper.
4. Local school planning for implementation.

SCHOOLS WITH AN UNGRADED PROGRAM
Clement Avenue School
Emerson Elementary School
Gaensien School
Green Bay Avenue Elementary School
Honey Creek School
Kluge Elementary School
Frances Starms Early Childhood Center
Thirty-eighth Street Elementary School
Thirty-seventh Street Elementary School
Thurston Woods Campus
Townsend School
Victory Elementary School

UNGRADED COUNCIL
The goals of the Ungraded Council are to review the literature for background knowledge and maintain the Milwaukee Public Schools' philosophy. In addition, the council sets priorities and guidelines relative to the following: curriculum, instruction, resources, materials development, staff development, assessment/evaluation, communication to parents, family involvement, and budget. The council also provides support and coordination for school implementation.

The Ungraded Council includes one or two representatives from each of the implementing schools. The council meets monthly during the school day.

MULTIAGE MODELS

New Suncook School
Box H
Lovell, ME 04051

Adapting the Learning Environment to Meet Students' Developmental Needs

by Karen Johnson and Lauren Potter

Over the past several years, New Suncook School in Lovell, Maine has been involved in the restructuring process. This process has included the creation of multiage classes of five- to seven-year-old children. The following assumptions undergird the program:

1. Children operate on variable biological and psychological time and not on uniform physical time.
2. Each child is unique with his or her own individual pattern of growth, personality, learning style, and family background.
3. All aspects of children's development are integrated — physical, social, emotional, cognitive, and aesthetic.
4. Children's learning is also integrated. They do not distinguish learning by subject area.
5. Primary-aged children learn best through active, rather than passive activities. Learning activities and materials need to be concrete, real, and relevant to the lives of young children.
6. Opportunities to make choices help children gain independence in thinking, decision making, and problem solving.

The multiage classes allow children to grow and develop at their own pace in an environment that encompasses a wide range of developmental levels. The curriculum is designed to be integrated, meaningful, and relevant to children's lives. Classrooms contain learning centers, and children have many opportunities to choose their learning activities.

Instructional practices were carefully considered so children could experience an active, integrated learning environment. Through a theme-based curriculum, children incorporate reading, writing, and math skills to explore a theme at their own developmental levels. Instructional practices such as whole language, Math Their Way, the writing process, cooperative learning, and process science facilitate children's explorations.

To examine how well these practices were being implemented, we conducted an evaluation of the multiage classes. Through a classroom-based innovative grant, multiage class activities were documented for a school year. An observer followed nine children in different multiage classes and recorded their daily activities. The data collected was then evaluated using qualitative research methods.

The study found that indeed children were experiencing an active, integrated learning environment that allowed for individual developmental differences and opportunities for children to make choices and to gain independence in thinking, decision making, and problem solving.

PROGRAM DESCRIPTION

Five teachers teach this multiage, multiability K-2 program that includes handicapped children who are fully mainstreamed into the program. This primary program enables children to grow and develop at their own pace without leaving

> *The study found that indeed children were experiencing an active, integrated learning environment that allowed for individual developmental differences and opportunities for children to make choices and to gain independence in thinking, decision making, and problem solving.*

their peer group or familiar school setting.

In 1989, in an effort to better accommodate the developmental needs of young children, two teachers combined and team taught their respective kindergarten and first grade classes while another teacher worked with special education students in the program. This initial multiage program was expanded in the fall of 1990 to include the second grade level and all primary composite resource room special needs students. The program has currently grown so that all primary children who attend New Suncook School are in one of the five multiage classrooms. The teachers plan together in order to make the best use of all available resources.

The curriculum is integrated and encompasses a wide range of developmental levels. Children may spend three to four years in the program depending on their development. The classrooms contain learning centers centered around science, social studies, literacy, math, and other areas. The children have many opportunities to make choices about their learning materials.

SAMPLE DAY

8:00 — Meeting time including attendance, lunch count, calendar, share circle

8:15 — Read aloud and shared reading using big books, picture books, and charts (theme related)

8:30 — Cooperative group theme-based activities

9:15 — Math Their Way tubbing activities

9:45 — Centers — a moveable wall between two classrooms opens and students have the opportunity to choose from twenty different learning centers that focus on classroom themes

10:45 — Kindergarten children go outside for recess and dismissal.
Full-day children work on math computation and problem solving.

11:35 — Lunch

12:00 — Recess

12:25 — Read aloud chapter book that relates to our theme.

12:45 — Individualized literacy work

1:30 — Continuation of cooperative group and theme-based activities.

2:10 — Dismissal

THE NEED FOR INNOVATIVE ASSESSMENT

As these instructional practices developed it became apparent that traditional forms of assessment did not reflect the growth of individual children. Traditional assessment methods previously used assumed that all children developed at the same rate and did not take into account children's thinking, decision making, and problem-solving skills. New assessment tools were considered that would most accurately reflect a child's progress based on the assumptions of the primary classes. Alternative forms of assessment were discussed with educators from other primary programs through the University of Southern Maine's Partnership, an extension of John Goodlad's Network of Renewing Schools.

After much discussion and field testing, the following methods were put into practice in New Suncook's primary multiage classes:

Observation — Children are observed in whole group, small group, and individual settings. Anecdotal records are kept for each child. Teachers now have documentation of how students naturally approach learning tasks.

Portfolios — Samples of children's work based on assumptions of the multiage classes are collected on a regular basis. New Suncook has now established a uniform list of yearly samples to be kept in a child's permanent portfolio. This list includes a taped reading conference, a self-portrait, a self-selected journal entry, a cumulative math assessment, a reading log, a research project, and writing samples.

SHARING WITH PARENTS

As assessment practices have changed it has also become necessary to change the way children's progress and learning are reported to parents. Parents were accustomed to letter grades in specific subject areas. Teachers found that this type of reporting method did not fully reflect children's progress in the multiage classes. The following methods of reporting to parents have evolved:

Magic Moments Books were based on books we learned of during a Southern Maine Partnership meeting. A teacher writes in the book about a proud moment the child has had in school. The child takes the book home and the parent writes about a proud moment the child has had at home. The teacher writes in this book as soon as possible when it is returned from home.

Weekly News is a dictated reporting of daily activities by children and is sent home once a week. A member of our staff developed the idea as a way of reviewing the activities of that day.

New Suncook Newsletter evolved from a staff development need to communicate with parents schoolwide. Teachers take turns contributing to the newsletter with information about activities in their classes. The newsletter often includes an article about parenting or education that might be of specific interest to parents.

Of Primary Importance is published and sent home bi-monthly. It includes a detailed description of activities occuring in the primary classrooms, upcoming events and an article about a different curriculum area each time.

To adapt this learning environment to meet the individual developmental needs of every student, we strive to challenge each at his or her appropriate level and to provide each child with the tools necessary to help him or her to explore individual curiosities about the world.

Quarterly Progress Reports record a child's progress on a K-2 continuum. This continuum includes the developmental stages of literacy and mathematical growth. These stages of development on the progress reports match up with those stages used when assessing children with our performanced-based tools for reading, writing, and math.

Conferences occur twice a year or more frequently if requested by a parent or teacher.

There are several outcomes of this reporting process. With information about what school is like today, parents are more supportive and more involved in their child's education. Parents are better able to understand what is happening and to partake in the "joy" occuring in the classroom on a daily basis. For the most part, parents have been very positive and appreciative of the time and effort they realize it takes to make the reporting process so individualized.

SUMMARY

As educational facilitators, we feel a commitment to provide our students with an enriching and meaningul environment that enables them to explore new experiences and expand understanding of their world. To adapt this learning environment to meet the individual developmental needs of every student, we strive to challenge each at his or her appropriate level and to provide each child with the tools necessary to enable him or her to explore individual curiosities about the world. We are also committed to help children begin to understand their roles and responsibilities in keeping our world healthy and safe.

This report is an attempt to give you a knowledge of your child's learning achievements, strengths, and educational needs. It is our hope that strong communication between parent and teacher will be a major part of your child's development.

The progress of your child is reflected by the following:
1. Consistently **2.** Most of the time **3.** With teacher assistance **4.** Not at this time
A blank space indicates a skill not introduced.

Student _____

Teacher _____

School _____

Grade _____ Year _____

Grade placement for September 19_____

ATTENDANCE RECORD:				
Report Quarter	I	II	III	IV
Number of Days in Quarter				
Days Absent				
Times Tardy				
Times Dismissed				

LITERACY

I	II	III	IV

A. INTEREST/BOOK KNOWLEDGE

1. Looks to books for enjoyment to satisfy curiosity and to gain information.

2. Shows interest in listening to stories from texts, peers, and teacher and is able to listen to stories for an appropriate length of time.

3. Begins to ask about print (e.g. how to print or read a letter, word, or phrase).

4. Demonstrates print awareness, i.e., understands print has a message and reads top to bottom, left to right.

5. Can identify and use book terms: page, author, illustrator, title, page numbers, title page, and table of contents.

B. COMPREHENSION

1. Can tell a story from a set of sequential pictures.

2. Participates in language experience activities.

3. When reading aloud, uses voice intonation to enhance meaning.

4. Responds to simple comprehension questions.

5. Begins to discuss inferences, predict outcomes, show cause and effect, and make comparisons.

6. Understands various aspects of story such as fact/fantasy, setting, plot and characters, main idea, and climax.

7. Begins to make a personal evaluation of material read.

C. READING STRATEGIES

1. Can reproduce from memory short sentences or part of familiar stories.

2. Demonstrates one to one matching:

    a. can point to each word as it is spoken and/or

    b. matches words or phrases on a chart story.

3. Acquires sight words by seeing those words often.

4. When reading unknown words in a story:

    a. uses context clues

    b. uses phonetic knowledge

    c. substitutes a word

    d. skips the word and reads on

5. Self-corrects when something does not make sense.

6. Begins to recognize base words, endings, compound words, and contractions.

7. When reading silently, comprehends what is read.

D. CONCEPTS ABOUT PRINT AND DEVELOPMENT OF WRITING STRATEGIES

1. Can dictate a simple story.

2. Uses recognizable letter shapes when writing.

3. Demonstrates that print is written left to right.

4. Reproduces print from environment.

5. Demonstrates sound-symbol connection in writing.

6. Composes simple sentences using invented spelling.

7. Leaves spaces between words when composing.

8. Spells commonly used words with increasing accuracy.

9. Attempts to use spelling generalizations (possessives, plurals, phonetic rules).

10. Writes stories showing an understanding of story structure by establishing an opening and one or more events.

11. Writes stories developed beyond simple events with a defined ending.

12. Identifies characters and setting.

13. Shows strong sentence sense through capitalization and punctuation.

14. Produces simple, coherent, non-chronological writing (reports, summaries, descriptions).

15. Revises in consultation with teacher or other children in the class, attending to meaning and clarity.

16. Demonstrates evidence of editing for correct spelling, capitalization, and punctuation.

MATHEMATICS

A. PATTERNS

1. Recognizes patterns.

2. Creates patterns.

3. Analyzes patterns.

4. Extends patterns.

B. NUMBERS

1. Counts by ones to:

2. Skip counts by 2's, 5's, and 10's to 100.

3. Shows 1 to 1 correspondence to 20.

4. Identifies numbers to:

5. Writes numbers to:

6. Orders numbers to:

I	II	III	IV

	I	II	III	IV

C. ARITHMETIC

ADDITION:

1. Understands concept.

2. Applies concept.

3. Mastery of facts to:

4. Adds 2 digit numbers without regrouping.

5. Adds 2 digit numbers with regrouping.

SUBTRACTION:

1. Understands concept.

2. Applies concept.

3. Mastery of facts to:

4. Subtracts 2 digit numbers without regrouping.

5. Subtracts 2 digit numbers with regrouping.

D. FRACTIONS

1. Identifies fractions.

2. Writes fractions.

3. Compares fractions.

E. GEOMETRY

1. Identifies shapes.

2. Reproduces shapes.

3. Describes shapes.

F. MEASUREMENT

1. Identifies 1¢, 5¢, 10¢, 25¢.

2. Gives value of 1¢, 5¢, 10¢, 25¢.

3. Counts coins to $1.00.

4. Tells time to hour, ½ hour, 5 minutes.

5. Measures in standard and metric units.

6. PROBLEM SOLVNG

1. Creates graphs.

2. Analyzes graphs.

3. Is developing estimating strategies.

4. Analyzes word problems.

5. Solves word problems.

6. Applies problem-solving skills in daily situations.

SOCIAL STUDIES

A. Expresses interest.

B. Shows understanding of concepts.

SCIENCE

A. Expresses interest.

B. Shows understanding of concepts.

C. Demonstrates skills in:

    1. Observing

    2. Classifying

    3. Recording

    4. Predicting

FINE MOTOR

A. MATERIALS

    1. Uses scissors with ease.

    2. Uses writing tools with ease.

B. HANDWRITING

    1. Uses neat handwriting in practice.

    2. Uses neat handwriting in daily work.

PERSONAL AND SOCIAL GROWTH

• Exhibits positive self-image.

• Demonstrates a positive attitude.

• Complies with school rules.

• Is growing in knowledge of consequences of personal actions.

• Makes responsible choices.

• Respects material and work of others.

• Cares for personal belongings.

• Claims only fair share of attention.

• Demonstrates sensitivity to and respects the feelings of others.

• Plays well with others.

• Works well alone.

• Works cooperatively in small groups.

• Participates in large group activities

• Initiates own learning.

• Seeks help when appropriate.

• Demonstrates good listening habits.

• Focuses on task/topic at hand.

• Finishes required tasks.

I	II	III	IV

134

MULTIAGE MODELS

Norridgewock Central Grade School
PO Box 98, Rt. 2 Mercer Road, Norridgewock, ME 04957

The MAP Class: A Multiage Primary Program
by Sharon Bottesch, Teacher

This fall, six-year-old Anthony (who recognized ten letters) was working with seven-year-old Thomas (who was reading *Charlotte's Web*). They were making a wall map of the world showing major routes in the discovery of America. Each child was contributing equally to the project. Each recognized and valued the work of the other.

The MAP class is a regular classroom of 20 to 24 students ages five to nine, with a teacher and an aide. The class population reflects the school population in academic ability, gender, and number of special needs students.

The program blends the first and second grade curriculum into thematic units with subjects integrated and skills sequenced over a two-year time period. Children work at their own level and rate. Grade levels are disregarded even for specials such as art, music, and physical education.

Assessments are maintained in individual reading and writing portfolios. Periodic screening in math provides a record of each student's growth in understanding.

Thematic units usually culminate in a student-designed project for display to parents and other classes. These have included museums, art shows, dramatic productions, video newscasts, and celebrations with food, games, music, and dance.

> *The program blends the first and second grade curriculum into thematic units with subjects integrated and skills sequenced over a two-year time period.*

Daily Schedule

MORNING

Approximate time Minutes	Activity
15	**Prep Time** Students responsible for caring for belongings, lunch count, snack, materials ready for the day, including pencils sharpened
15	**Morning Meeting** (at circle area) Songs, announcements, oral sharing by students Discussion of theme
	Literacy Component
	Writing Process Workshop
15	Mini-lesson (still at circle) Activity focused on a single aspect of writing Teacher takes a quick check of individual work
30	All students write (students' choice of location in room) Students write on topics of students' or teacher's choice Read work to peers for response Edit with teacher

Approximate time Minutes

Writing Process Workshop (continued)
Publish best work at publishing center and illustrate

15 Author's Chair
- Once-a-week reading of finished, published work
- Annual Authors' Tea with parents

10-15 **Reading Workshop**

Whole group (gathered at circle)
- Reads together poem or story from wall chart or big book, usually about theme for the week
- Discusses meaning, graphophonic or mechanical skills using poem or story

40 Interest Groups (4 or 5)
- Break into mostly self-selected interest groups focused on book choice from the theme
- Groups somewhat similar skill based due to reading level of books
- Book choices available cover ability levels from emergent to fluent
- Read together as a group or read individually
- Discuss book according to guide set up by teacher, based on learning objective
- Reread to partner, listen to partner, respond
- Record in reading journal
- Work on book response project to share with rest of class approximately once a week
- Project may include art work, puppets, drama, or written report
- Teacher meets with each small group while others work independently
- Teacher listens to readers, discusses work, also discusses phonics/spelling objectives for week as one of several reading/writing strategies

10 **Prep Time**
- Students put away materials, select silent reading books for afternoon, get ready for lunch and recess

Lunch / Recess

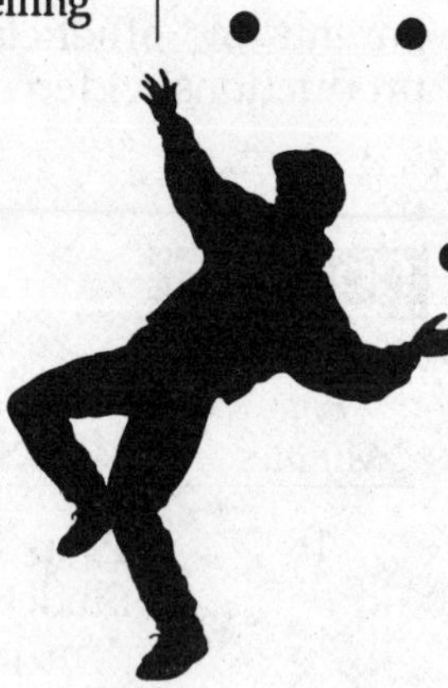

AFTERNOON

Aproximate time minutes	**Activity**
10	**Prep Time** Students take care of belongings, personal needs, sharpen pencils
10	**Story Time** Silent reading (students at location of choice) Students must have one book on reading level, others may be more challenging or old favorites
10-15	**Read Aloud by Teacher** (at circle area) Book choice usually relates to theme
	Discovery Component
	Math Workshop

Aproximate time minutes	**Math Workshop** (continued)
10	Math Their Way calendar and extension activities — (whole group still at circle)
30-40	Math Activity (heterogeneous cooperative groups at tables) Activity focuses on critical thinking, problem-solving skills using manipulatives or other materials
10-20	Math Groups (similar skill level groups at tables) Activity focuses on number concepts with manipulatives and, usually, paper response sheet
10	**Theme Project Time** – may include science or social studies related to theme Whole Group — Discussion, demonstration or planning time
40-60	**Activity Center** Students engaged in center or project of their choice Center choices include computer, listening, art, all math manipulatives, and science discovery table
10-15	**Prep Time** Students straighten room for next day, prepare for dismissal Discuss day's events

Voices

The vast majority of educators who have worked with nongrading are enthusiastic about it. Some of them speak of higher achievement among pupils in nongraded schools, a reduction of discipline problems, a greater challenge for the gifted, the removal of the non promotion stigma for the slow, a more positive classroom atmosphere, and so on. Negative reactions from teachers and administrators actually conducting nongraded schools are hard to find. Similarly, surveys report positive reactions from parents, 83 to 96 per cent responding favorably.

John I. Goodlad and Robert Anderson
The Nongraded Elementary School

Reprinted by permission of the publisher, Teachers College Press, Columbia University, New York. © 1987. All rights reserved. Excerpt from page 209.

Primary Education Faces Major Changes
by Max Workman, Principal

Educators across the nation are looking with great interest at the development of Kentucky primary schools.

The primary concept is based on conclusive evidence that shows primary-age children learn best by:
- being active
- having appropriate developmental learning
- learning from their own experiences

If we accept the above conclusions, we then must make changes in the way we provide learning experiences for primary students. Let me discuss each of these basic conclusions in detail.

ACTIVE LEARNING

If you had walked into most kindergarten, first, or second grade classrooms prior to the primary movement in Kentucky, they would have been much as they had been for the past 50 years; children sitting quietly in rows, the teacher in front of the classroom dispensing skills to be learned or students being drilled from textbooks, workbooks, and innumerable worksheets.

Research has repeatedly shown that primary children are not capable of sitting quietly for extended periods; yet we demanded that they sit quietly in rows for as long as six hours per day.

Children that could not sit still and learn were labeled as discipline problems or too immature for grade level. The most severe were labeled as behavior disordered or learning disabled.

The primary school of the future will have classrooms designed with activity centers, work areas, and quiet areas. There will be short blocks of time during the school day for teacher instruction and times for students to be active, discovering for themselves the desired learning.

The teacher will be changing her/his role to become a facilitator of learning by providing opportunities for students to learn in an active manner. This type classroom will be busy, a little noisy, very active, and require much more teacher preparation and involvement.

In summary, students are encouraged to move about the room and work in centers and work areas instead of sitting quietly in rows.

DEVELOPMENTALLY APPROPRIATE LEARNING

In the past, teachers were expected to teach textbooks that followed a basic skills progression for each grade level. The teacher usually taught to the average child. The very bright or the slower students had to adapt.

The teacher tried to meet the varied needs by grouping students according to their ability level. Some schools went so far as to group whole classrooms by ability level.

In the primary school of tomorrow, students will learn when they are developmentally ready and at a pace appropriate for them.

The learning experiences will be provided through centers, small group-teacher instruction and computers. Multiage grouping will also provide children the oppor-

Students are encouraged to move about the room and work in centers and work areas instead of sitting quietly in rows.

tunity to learn from other students.

Children will no longer be labeled failures because they have been asked to learn a particular skill before they were developmentally ready to be successful. Successful experiences will be building blocks for future success.

The nongraded primary school will not expect a student to complete a predetermined set of skills or be retained and go back over the same skills the next year, but will allow the student to start the new school year at his/her own learning rate and ready to experience success.

EXPERIENCED-BASED LEARNING

We have all heard four, five and six-year-olds tell stories about their grandparents, their pet, or some tall tale from their imagination. What better way for students to read or spell than to learn from their own vocabulary?

If the student sees frogs develop from tadpoles, learns to count by lining up lima beans or to multiply by grouping beans, learning will be more relevant and more lasting.

Memorization is one of the lowest levels of learning; yet the schools of the past were almost totally based on memorization — no wonder we had to continually reteach skills.

The primary school will use curriculum techniques that will provide students opportunities to discover and learn from their own experiences. Will this not make learning more relevant and more transferable to life?

In summary, the primary school is a change in the way we think children learn most effectively and a change in our curriculum.

Our curriculum must allow students to be active, provide developmentally appropriate learning experiences, and give students the opportunity to learn from their experiences.

Moving Toward a Nongraded Primary — Information for Parents

In our effort to implement the law concerning the primary school, let me illustrate the direction we should be moving.

Students sitting and working quietly in rows	➧ Actively working in groups
Students working exclusively in basal texts	➧ Working with various learning materials, computers, books, etc.
Students grouped with same ability levels	➧ Varied ability levels, even special needs children and gifted children together
Students of same grade together	➧ Varied age and ability groups working together
Students failing for lack of maturity	➧ Moving forward as developmentally ready and successful
Students having four or five workbooks, bringing home stacks of handout sheets	➧ Less emphasis on busy work and more on relevant active learning
Letter grades – A, B, C	➧ Parent conferences, narrative portfolios, and report cards
Homework	➧ Less emphasis on homework and more emphasis on active learning experiences while at school
Teacher lectures	➧ Teacher managing learning experiences and opportunities for students to discover

Classroom teacher, special education teacher, and librarian working in isolation	➡ Teaching as a team
State department of education mandating what and how long each student is taught per day	➡ Teachers making decisions based on their students' readiness to learn
Teachers teaching reading, social studies, and health separately	➡ Teaching lessons that incorporate more than one subject
Math and science taught from text	➡ Hands-on, active learning, (adding real objects, science experiments)

The following quote seems to summarize the future direction of primary schools:

> *"It is the responsibility of the school to be ready for the child. It is not the responsibility of the child to be ready for the school."*

It is our goal to move in this direction as teachers gain expertise and a comfort level in this approach to teaching.

The emphasis of the nongraded primary school should not be a new way of leveling or grouping children, but a different way of thinking about children's learning. No longer should the teacher be presenting a certain body of knowledge to your child, but will be providing opportunities for each child to learn by discovering when he/she is developmentally ready. To do this, the teacher will be drawing from varied materials and curriculums. This will provide an exciting atmosphere for your child's learning.

Although we are very excited about the opportunities and possibilities that are offered by the nongraded primary direction, we want to make the transition gradually to make sure that each child receives an excellent educational foundation in the primary years.

Voices

If children spontaneously form heterogeneous peer groups, why do adults typically segregate them by age? One reason might be that, as impressions we have gained from our own experience suggest, when children in a class are close in age, teachers and parents tend to expect them to be ready to learn the same things at the same time. Indeed, from a normative point of view, such an expectation is reasonable, but the effect can be to penalize children who don't happen to meet these expectations.
Lilian G. Katz, Demetra Evangelou, and Jeanette Allison Hartman
The Case for Mixed-Age Grouping in Early Education

Reprinted with permission of the National Association for the Education of Young Children.

"It is the responsibility of the school to be ready for the child. It is not the responsibility of the child to be ready for the school."

Multiage Classrooms: Creating Communities for Learning

by Mary Garamella, Principal

Schools have established multiage classrooms for years; however, only recently have a large number of practitioners and researchers considered the developmental appropriateness of such settings. Each year several of these practitioners and some of the researchers come to Union Elementary School in Montpelier, Vermont "to see it really happening in a regular school with all kinds of kids."

Eighteen years ago, four Union School teachers and a small group of parents approached the administration with their desire to start a multiage, three-year placement option for Montpelier primary students. This group saw the value of a multiyear placement including children of various ages and stages as a direction toward a better way of offering early education. Since that time, Union School has grown to include six 1-3 multiage classes, three 1-2 multiage classes, looping first and second grades, looping third and fourth grades, as well as some straight grade, single-year options.

Union School is the only publicly provided education for K-4 students in Vermont's state capital, Montpelier. Currently the school houses around 500 students. The philosophy of the program supports developmentally appropriate practices for all students in a fully inclusionary setting.

Over the years, visitors to Union School have asked many questions and caused us to focus on what a multiage, developmentally appropriate program looks like.

CREATING CLASSROOM COMMUNITIES

Our school is a community of children and adults who study and learn together. Each class, regardless of whether it is a three-year, two-year or one-year placement, includes students with different needs and abilities and who represent the various home and neighborhood cultures. All teachers are challenged to establish their classroom community by providing for the needs of the group while ensuring success for each individual.

The curriculum has been designed to be content flexible, allowing teachers and students to develop thematic topics. Curriculum expectations include the following:
- concept, skill and language development
- building understandings of patterns and relationships
- learning how to learn — gathering and organizing information and problem solving
- building positive learning attitudes
- increasing awareness and understanding of the tools of learning from blocks to books and from cuisinaire rods to computers

Teachers encourage and assess student growth on a continuing basis and record evidence of progress on skill continuums and in anecdotal records, reading logs, journals and portfolios of student work. Children and adults demonstrate and celebrate success each day as they perform real life tasks in real life situations. All members of the school community see each other as enablers of learning.

Teachers design lessons for whole group, small group, one-to-one interactions,

The philosophy of the program supports developmentally appropriate practices for all students in a fully inclusionary setting.

and encourage cooperative learning. Classroom teachers, specialists, parents, volunteers, administrators, aides and tutors work with children to enhance personal development within the areas of social, emotional, physical, aesthetic as well as cognitive growth for all members of the community. As we work together, we grow together.

Teachers have been trained in the philosophy and pedagogy of whole language, process writing, transitional spelling, manipulative math and thematic unit design. They have also received training in the philosophy and use of Dr. William Glasser's *Reality Therapy* and *Control Theory* as an approach for encouraging positive behavioral patterning. Also, national consultants have supported our understanding of learning styles, the hierarchies of knowing and the models of teaching. But the focus remains on the needs of each child as a member of a community of lifelong learners.

Multiage grouping has flourished at Union School because it established the foundations for our rooting ourselves in developmentally appropriate practices and because it represents a school structure that most closely replicates a community — that is, people of different ages and backgrounds, with different needs and abilities, coming together for the evolution of each individual as well as the whole.

Voices

The nongraded school provides for the irregular upward progression that is characteristic of almost every child . . . . Children do not advance evenly, a year of graded accomplishment for a year of living and schooling. They spurt and stop, regress and advance in both their general and their specific development. Classes in the nongraded school are set up to recognize and account for wide ranges of accomplishments so that even very long lags or very gross spurts on the part of pupils still fall within normal expectancies for the group.

John I. Goodlad and *Robert Anderson*
The Nongraded Elementary School

Reprinted by permission of the publisher, Teachers College Press, Columbia University., New York. © 1987. All rights reserved. Excerpt from page 220.

Why Multiage?

Pros:

- Multiyear, predictable placement, deeper understanding of child's learning needs and style

- Value of the significant adult

- Differentiated developmental stages

- Differentiated academic stages

- Extended family style, in-depth relationship with child & child's family, youngest, middle, oldest

- Must attend to individual needs

- Social, emotional and academic

- Patterns, rituals, traditions — time to build

- Established community that adds new students each year

- "Guide on the side" as well as the "sage on the stage"

- You and your family get to know your teacher very well

- Easier to see and follow progress

- Intersection is increased

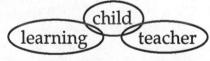

(The greater the intersection, the greater the success for the child.)

- Encourages cooperative grouping (so many levels and interests)

Mary Garamella

Cons:

- Everyone isn't ready

- Small peer group — leaving

Needs of the Child to Be Considered:

- Academic — accelerated, right on, struggling

- Social — assertive, shy, highly competitive, too hard on himself

- Developmental stage — young, very mature

- Family make up — only child, single parent, youngest

- Specific needs — handicapped, attention span

- Parents' feeling about the setting

Montpelier School District Placement Policy

It is the belief of the Montpelier School District that children receive the most benefit from their educational experience when in a balanced setting representative of the greater community in which they live. For this reason, the assignment of children to individual teachers takes into account several factors to assure that each class is organized in a way that best maximizes the intellectual, psychological and social development of each child.

Further it is the belief of the district that the professional staff members are most familiar with each child and the school resources and are in the best position to recommend individual student/teacher placements following review of the placement team which considers other information and parental input. The final decision regarding the placement of each child will rest with the building principal. The following procedures, having been approved by the Board of School Commissioners, will be followed in placement decisions.

Placement Policy Procedures

Grades K–6

1. A grade level professional placement team will, using the following criteria, make a recommendation to the building principal as to the placement of each child within that given grade level for the subsequent school year. The composition of each team will include the principal, the sending and receiving teachers of the grade level being placed, the school guidance counselor, the school nurse, a special educator and others as deemed appropriate and appointed by the principal.

   CRITERIA
   • The child's educational needs
   • The child's psychological and social needs
   • Parent input to placement teams
   • Distribution of special needs children across teachers
   • Approximate equal number of children by teacher
   • Representation of total community in each class

2. Parent input regarding the needs of the child will be given full consideration by the placement teams.

3. The building principal, using the recommendations of the placement teams, will make a final determination on the placement of each child in accordance with the established criteria and the unique needs of the child and/or the school organization which might be unknown to the placement teams.

Grades 7–12

While the selection of individual courses is at the discretion of the student and his/her parents, the placement of grade 7-12 students with individual teachers or teams of teachers will be at the discretion of the professional staff. While all courses offered within the district are open to all students, the school reserves the right to determine the grade level at which a student may take a course and, where grouping exists, in which group a student will be placed. When limited seating in a course precludes acceptance of all interested students, the final decision as to which students will be

Mary Garamella

145

Union Elementary School

1 PARK AVENUE, MONTPELIER, VERMONT 05602

Dear Parents or Guardians:

Our staff will be considering student placement recommendations for next fall during the month of May. Your involvement can be an important step in this process, and I encourage your participation. Therefore, I have enclosed a Placement Information Request Form with this letter. If you would like the staff and me to consider your information, you need to return the completed form to the school office by Friday, April 5, 1991. The information that you give will be considered by your child's teacher when he or she makes student placement recommendations, and also by me when I make the final placement decisions in early June.

It is important to realize that placement decisions are the responsibility of the Principal, and that the highest priority considered in making placement decisions is the academic need of the child as identified by his or her teacher. Also, it is important to remember that many other factors influence these decisions. These factors include: consideration for the social needs of the child, class size, the need to maintain a balanced group, and date of registration as well as parent preference.

Please be reminded that we are not accepting specific requests for next year's teacher, but we will appreciate any information that you share with us concerning your child's needs.

Thank you.

Sincerely,

Mary Garamella
Principal

Mary Garamella

Placement Procedure Information

What are the goals of placement procedures?

Through its placement procedures, the school seeks to: 1) consider individual needs of the students, 2) provide balanced classrooms, 3) ensure that all of our children are being given equal consideration in the placement process.

How do parents have input into the placement process?

This year we are seeking additional parent input to tell us about the kinds of things that have worked well for your child in the past, special strengths of your child, and what you would want next year's teacher to work toward with your child. This information from a parental viewpoint will be invaluable to the staff in matching your child with the best academic situation for next year.

How do the teachers know which classroom might match the needs of my child?

In addition to parent input, your child's teacher has been given the opportunity to visit and observe the next year's teachers. In this way, your child's teacher will be better informed in making placements for the next grade level. Professionally, teaching staff are trained to evaluate student needs and academic situations and know best how to match a child's needs with a positive and appropriate learning environment.

May I visit next year's classrooms?

Visitation for the purpose of placement is no longer happening. However, parents are always welcome and encouraged to visit their own child's current class. Parents are not expected to determine next year's placement for their child. It is not necessary for you to visit next year's classrooms in order for your child to be given fair consideration. We highly recommend, however, that you work with your child's current teacher to best communicate your child's needs and strengths.

How is placement going to be done?

Your child's current teacher will meet with next year's teachers, the guidance counselor, special education staff, Chapter I staff, the principal, and at least one support staff member (music, gym, library) in order to carefully consider your child's placement needs. These meetings will be completed by early June.

What do I do if my child's placement does not work out?

We realize that there are occasional mistakes made regarding placement. Concerns should be handled initially through a parent conference with the teacher. If, after a reasonable period of time, things cannot be worked out, a consultation can be arranged with the principal, the teacher, and the parents in order to seek ways to correct the situation.

It is our hope that these procedures will produce a fair and well-rounded approach to placement decisions. Staff see children in many ways throughout the school year and are in a unique position to match the child with the new teacher and with the new class composition.

Mary Garamella

Parental Placement Information

Name of student: _____

Name of student's parents and/or guardians:

_____

_____

Address: _____

_____

Home phone: _____ Mom's work phone: _____

Dad's work phone: _____

Name of child's teacher this year: _____

1. What methods, techniques or aspects of the learning environment have worked for your child this year? What haven't worked?: _____

_____

_____

2. What are your child's greatest academic, social and emotional strengths? _____

_____

_____

_____

3. What are your child's greatest academic, social and emotional needs? _____

_____

_____

_____

4. Is there a special goal you would like to see next year's teacher work toward for your child?

_____

_____

_____

5. Is there anything you would like to tell next year's teacher before the year begins?

_____

_____

_____

INITIAL PLACEMENT
Montpelier Elementary School

For September _____

Teacher _____ Grade _____

To be completed by the present teacher prior to _____

Student Name	Ret.	Read Level	Read Material (Series, etc.)	Math Level	Referrals — Circle Appropriate Areas									Possible Placements
					IEP	RR	RM	S/L	OT/PT/APE	T	G	C	Med	
					IEP	RR	RM	S/L	OT/PT/APE	T	G	C	Med	
					IEP	RR	RM	S/L	OT/PT/APE	T	G	C	Med	
					IEP	RR	RM	S/L	OT/PT/APE	T	G	C	Med	
					IEP	RR	RM	S/L	OT/PT/APE	T	G	C	Med	
					IEP	RR	RM	S/L	OT/PT/APE	T	G	C	Med	
					IEP	RR	RM	S/L	OT/PT/APE	T	G	C	Med	
					IEP	RR	RM	S/L	OT/PT/APE	T	G	C	Med	
					IEP	RR	RM	S/L	OT/PT/APE	T	G	C	Med	
					IEP	RR	RM	S/L	OT/PT/APE	T	G	C	Med	
					IEP	RR	RM	S/L	OT/PT/APE	T	G	C	Med	
					IEP	RR	RM	S/L	OT/PT/APE	T	G	C	Med	
					IEP	RR	RM	S/L	OT/PT/APE	T	G	C	Med	
					IEP	RR	RM	S/L	OT/PT/APE	T	G	C	Med	
					IEP	RR	RM	S/L	OT/PT/APE	T	G	C	Med	
					IEP	RR	RM	S/L	OT/PT/APE	T	G	C	Med	
					IEP	RR	RM	S/L	OT/PT/APE	T	G	C	Med	

Mary Garamella

FINAL PLACEMENT
Montpelier Elementary School

For September _____

Teacher _____ Grade _____

To be completed prior to _____

150

Student Name	Ret.	Read Level	Read Material (Series, etc.)	Math Level	Referrals — Circle Appropriate Areas								Last Year's Teacher
					IEP	RR	RM	S/L	OT/PT/APE	T	G	C	Med	
					IEP	RR	RM	S/L	OT/PT/APE	T	G	C	Med	
					IEP	RR	RM	S/L	OT/PT/APE	T	G	C	Med	
					IEP	RR	RM	S/L	OT/PT/APE	T	G	C	Med	
					IEP	RR	RM	S/L	OT/PT/APE	T	G	C	Med	
					IEP	RR	RM	S/L	OT/PT/APE	T	G	C	Med	
					IEP	RR	RM	S/L	OT/PT/APE	T	G	C	Med	
					IEP	RR	RM	S/L	OT/PT/APE	T	G	C	Med	
					IEP	RR	RM	S/L	OT/PT/APE	T	G	C	Med	
					IEP	RR	RM	S/L	OT/PT/APE	T	G	C	Med	
					IEP	RR	RM	S/L	OT/PT/APE	T	G	C	Med	
					IEP	RR	RM	S/L	OT/PT/APE	T	G	C	Med	
					IEP	RR	RM	S/L	OT/PT/APE	T	G	C	Med	
					IEP	RR	RM	S/L	OT/PT/APE	T	G	C	Med	
					IEP	RR	RM	S/L	OT/PT/APE	T	G	C	Med	

Mary Garamella

Montpelier Public School System
Montpelier, Vermont
Math Skills Continuum

Name _____

Date of Birth _____

This continuum lists skills incorporated in the math programs of the Montpelier Public School System. The skills will coordinate the curriculum in a system where teacher instruction integrates varied methods, materials, and activities

SCHOOL YEAR	MATH/CLASSROOM TEACHER	GRADE

REMEDIAL OR SPECIAL HELP

SCHOOL YEAR	MATH/CLASSROOM TEACHER	GRADE

DIRECTIONS FOR RECORDING MATH PROGRESS

/ • Introduction of competency in instructional setting   [/]

X • Initial mastery of competency at that grade level   [X]

Satisfactory performance is 90% – 100%

151

CONTENT

NUMERATION SKILL

	K	1	2	3	4	5	6

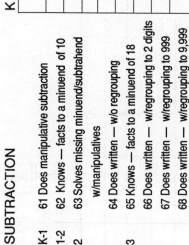

K-1
1 Counts forward to 10
2 Counts backwards to 10
3 Counts up to 10 objects
4 Names before/after to 10
5 Writes numbers to 10
6 Uses ordinal numbers to 10
7 Counts forward to 100
8 Reads numbers to 29

1-2
9a Counts forward by 10's
9b Counts forward by 5's

2
9c Counts forward by 2's
10 Counts backwards by 1's from100
11 Names before/after to 100
12 Reads numbers to 100
13 Writes numbers to 100
14 Does manipulative trading to 3 digits
15 Names numbers as odd or even
16 Uses symbols =, >, <

3
17 Names before/after to 1000
18 Reads numbers to 9,999
19 Writes numbers to 9,999

4
20 Reads numbers to 9,999,999
21 Writes numbers to 9,999,999

5
22 Writes number names to 100
23 Names before/after to 9,999,999

SETS/ATTRIBUTES

K-2
25 Sorts into given categories
26 Copies/continues a given pattern
27 Orders non-equivalent sets

FRACTIONS

3
28 Reads fractions to 10ths & pictures
29 Writes fractions to 10ths & pictures
30 Finds equivalent fractions w/manipulatives
31 Reads /writes any fraction

4-5
32 Reduces to lowest terms

SUBTRACTION

	K	1	2	3	4	5	6

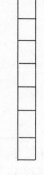

K-1
61 Does manipulative subtraction

1-2
62 Knows — facts to a minuend of 10

2
63 Solves missing minuend/subtrahend w/manipulatives
64 Does written — w/o regrouping
65 Knows — facts to a minuend of 18

3
66 Does written — w/regrouping to 2 digits
67 Does written — w/regrouping to 999
68 Does written — w/regrouping to 9,999

MULTIPLICATION

3-4
69 Knows X facts to a product of 100

4
70 Does X with 1 digit multiplier w/regrouping

5
71 Does X with 2 digit multiplier
71 Does X with 3 digit multiplier

DIVISION

3-4
73 Identifies —, —, X, —
74 Knows — facts to a dividend of 100
75 Does long division w/1digit divisor
76 Finds average for 2-5 numbers (sum< 1000)
77 Finds average for up to 10 numbers
78 Does long division w/2 digit divisors

ROUNDING

4-5
79 Rounds to nearest: 10,100, 1000

APPLICATIONS

K-2
80 Measures with a standard

3-5
81 Knows centi-, milli-, & kilo-/English units
82 Linear: measures to nearest cm/ English units
83 Liquid: measures to nearest 10 ml/ English units
84 Weight: measures to nearest 10 g/ English units

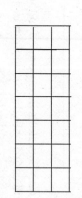

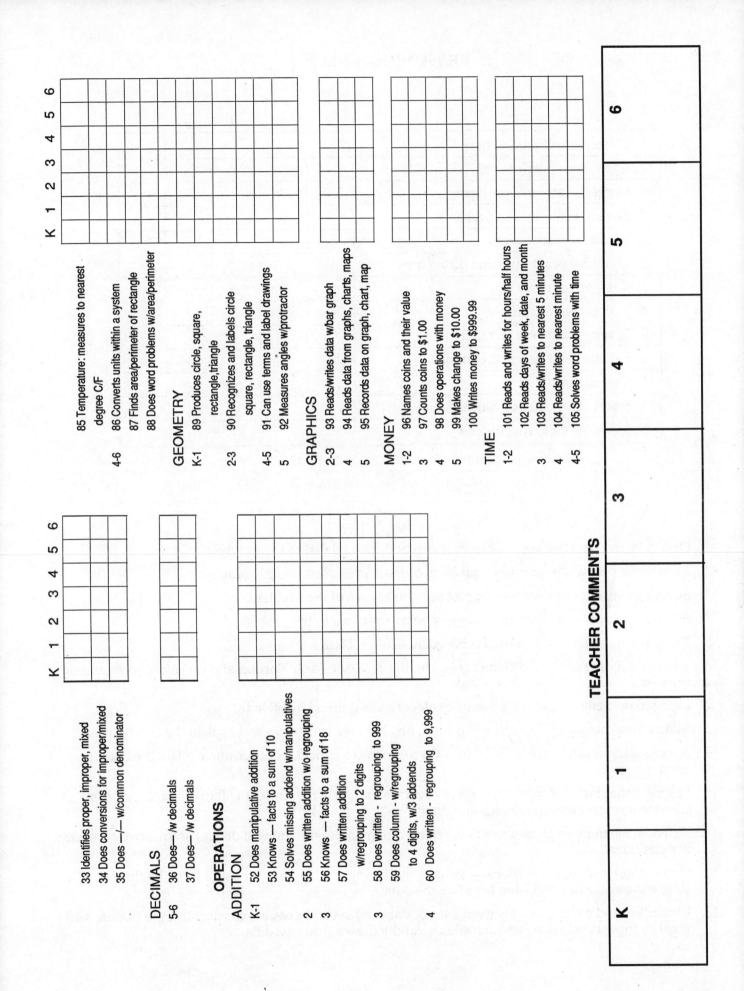

K 1 2 3 4 5 6

33 Identifies proper, improper, mixed
34 Does conversions for improper/mixed
35 Does —/— w/common denominator

DECIMALS

5-6
36 Does—/w decimals
37 Does—/w decimals

OPERATIONS

ADDITION

K-1   52 Does manipulative addition
53 Knows — facts to a sum of 10
54 Solves missing addend w/manipulatives
2   55 Does written addition w/o regrouping
3   56 Knows — facts to a sum of 18
57 Does written addition w/regrouping to 2 digits
3   58 Does written - regrouping to 999
59 Does column - w/regrouping to 4 digits, w/3 addends
4   60 Does written - regrouping to 9,999

85 Temperature: measures to nearest degree C/F
4-6   86 Converts units within a system
87 Finds area/perimeter of rectangle
88 Does word problems w/area/perimeter

GEOMETRY

K-1   89 Produces circle, square, rectangle,triangle
2-3   90 Recognizes and labels circle square, rectangle, triangle
4-5   91 Can use terms and label drawings
5   92 Measures angles w/protractor

GRAPHICS

2-3   93 Reads/writes data w/bar graph
4   94 Reads data from graphs, charts, maps
5   95 Records data on graph, chart, map

MONEY

1-2   96 Names coins and their value
3   97 Counts coins to $1.00
4   98 Does operations with money
5   99 Makes change to $10.00
100 Writes money to $999.99

TIME

1-2   101 Reads and writes for hours/half hours
102 Reads days of week, date, and month
3   103 Reads/writes to nearest 5 minutes
4   104 Reads/writes to nearest minute
4-5   105 Solves word problems with time

TEACHER COMMENTS

K	1	2	3	4	5	6

REASONING SKILLS

	K	1	2	3	4
1. Observes and reports data					
2. Identifies a problem					
3. Suggests causes of problem					
4. Suggests solutions to problem					
5. Predicts consequences					
6. Identifies similarities and differences					
7. Categorizes items					
8. Makes own categories					
9. Arranges items sequentially					
10. Distinguishes fact and opinion					
11. Defends positions					
12. States summaries or conclusions					
13. Identifies valid conclusions					

1. Observes and reports data — observe and report data related to the example.

2. Identifies a problem — identify a problem or issue presented in the example.

3. Suggests causes of problem — suggest possible causes of the problem.

4. Suggests solutions to problem — suggest some solutions to the problem.

5. Predicts consequences — predict consequences of problem solutions.

6. Identifies similarities and differences — identify at least two similarities and two differences among the items.

7. Categorizes items — put the items into categories as defined by others.

8. Makes own categories — put the items into his/her own categories and explain the criteria used.

9. Arranges items sequentially — arrange the items into a logical sequence and explain the criteria used.

10. Distinguishes fact and opinion — given several statements the student will distinguish between statements of fact and statements of opinion.

11. Defends positions — given a moral or ethical dilemma the student will defend at least two contrasting positions.

12. States summaries or conclusions — given a chart, graph, table, map, or list of facts the student will state a summary or conclusion based on the data.

13. Identifies valid conclusions — given a list of data and several possible conclusions, the student will identify those conclusions which could be validly drawn from the data.

MONTPELIER PUBLIC SCHOOL SYSTEM
MONTPELIER, VERMONT
READING SKILLS CONTINUUM

Name _____

Date of Birth _____

This continuum lists skills incorporated in the reading programs of the Montpelier Public School System. The skills will coordinate the curriculum in a system where teacher instruction integrates varied methods, materials, and activities.

SCHOOL YEAR	READING / CLASSROOM TEACHER	GRADE

REMEDIAL / SPECIAL

SCHOOL YEAR	READING / CLASSROOM TEACHER	GRADE

DIRECTIONS FOR RECORDING READING PROGRESS:

Place a slash in the space next to the skill introduced. ◺

When the child shows satisfactory performance on that skill, complete an ☒

Satisfactory performance is 90% – 100%

READING

	K	1	2	3	4

K-3
1. Recognizes name in print
2. Recognizes left/right progression
3. Blends sounds into words
4. Reads/follows printed directions
5. Recalls ideas – silent reading
6. Finds facts in story
7. Knows Dolch — Kucera/Francis words
8. Recalls specific details
9. Deciphers words in context
10. Uses punctuation to get meaning
11. Reads words — 3-letter clusters (blends)
12. Reads words — Silent letter(s)
13. Reads diphthongs
14. Reads manuscript/cursive
15. Recognizes main idea
16. Reads without vocalizing
17. Summarizes (orally)
18. Recognizes/uses synonyms/antonyms
19. Identifies:
    A. Character
    B. Plot
    C. Setting

4
of passage of reading

REASONING

K-3
20. Draws inferences and conclusions
21. Uses context clues to understand the meaning of unfamiliar words
22. Distinguishes fact/opinion
23. Uses facts to support story interpretation
24. Reads passage and sequences events

155

LITERATURE

K-3

25. Interprets feelings of characters
26. Recognizes parts of book
    - A. Index
    - B. Table of contents
27. Discusses different genre of literature:
    - A. Poetry
    - B. Fiction
    - C. Fables

EXPOSED TO AT LEAST TEN OF THE FOLLOWING:

28. Mother Goose
29. Hans C. Anderson
30. Grimm's Fairy Tales
31. Kipling's Just So Stories
32. Stone Soup
33. Little Engine That Could
34. Millions of Cats
35. Peter Rabbit
36. Winnie the Pooh
37. Where the Wild Things Are
38. Curious George
39. Aesop's Fables
40. Cinderella
41. Little Red Hen
42. Chicken Little
43. Cat In the Hat
44. Laura Ingalls Wilder
45. American Folk Tales
46. Poetry (Haiku)

4

47. Identifies/uses figurative language to enhance quality of literature
48. Discusses language which creates a different mood
49. Distinguishes:
    Fiction/nonfiction
    Biography/autobiography

	K	1	2	3	4

Literature continued

4

IS EXPOSED TO THE FOLLOWING:

50. Cricket in Times Square
51. Charlie and the Chocolate Factory
52. Mrs. Frisby and the Rats of Nimh
53. Visit from St. Nick
54. Poetry

	K	1	2	3	4

SPEAKING / LISTENING

K-3

55. Communicates freely orally
56. Speaks 4 word sentences
57. Rhymes words
58. Tells story using pictures in sequence
59. Follows oral directions (3 Step)
60. Listens to recall details
61. Dictates captions
62. Speaks grammatically correctly
63. Uses correct punctuation (inflection)
64. Uses correct subject/verb agreement
65. Gives 3-step oral directions
66. Uses telephone for own use
67. Uses telephone to get/give messages
68. Gives simple introduction(s)
69. Listens to get main idea

MEDIA

K-3

70. Uses card catalog

4

71. Locates print and non-print materials on an assigned basis
72. Reads newspaper(s)/magazine(s) to learn about current events

SPELLING SKILLS

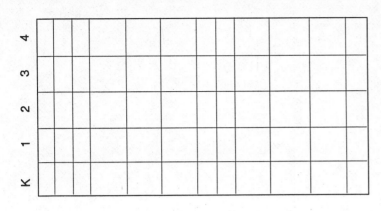

Columns: K | 1 | 2 | 3 | 4

K-3
86. Recognizes fine letter likenesses/differences
87. Names and recognizes letters
88. Spells simple CVC words
89. Knows sound/letter correspondence –
    Long/short vowels
90. Knows sound/letter correspondence –
    Consonants
91. Arranges words in alphabetical order
    (1-3 letters)
92. Uses consonant blends/digraphs in encoding
93. Recognizes compound words
94. Corrects spelling errors as part of
    the writing process

4
95. Arranges words in alphabetical order
    (1-4 letters)
96. Uses the dictionary for meanings/
    spellings of words
97. Recognizes and uses homonyms

GRAMMAR

Columns: K | 1 | 2 | 3 | 4

K-3
73. Uses capital letters at the beginning
    of sentences
74. Reads/understands prefixes
    un/be/re/dis/en-in
75. Reads/understands suffixes
    s/ed/ing/ly/er/y/es/est/
    ful/less/able/ness/s/or
76. Recognizes plural forms   s/es
77. Recognizes paragraphs

4
78. Aware of margins
79. Uses plural forms   ves/ies
80. Recognizes sentence types:
    Imperative
    Interrogative
    Declarative
    Exclamatory
81. Identifies words in sentences as:
    Nouns
    Verbs
    Adjectives

STUDY

K-3
82. Recognizes colors
83. Sustains him/herself at task(s)
84. Classifies words

4
85. Sustains him/herself at task(s)

157

Comments:
Teacher: _____ Grade: _____

Comments:
Teacher: _____ Grade: _____

Comments:
Teacher: _____ Grade: _____

Comments:
Teacher: _____ Grade: _____

WRITING

	K	1	2	3	4

K-3
98. Places name on assigned work
99. Writes full name
100. Recognizes/writes letters
101. Matches lower/upper case letters
102. Copies material
103. Writes 2-3 complete sentences
104. Summarizes (written)
105. Writes a short friendly letter
106. Uses the possessive form
107. Uses correct punctuation (. ! ?)
108. Uses steps of writing process appropriate to grade and level***

4
109. Revises/edits written work
110. Writes legibly in manuscript/cursive

WRITING PROCESS

Stimulus
Prewriting
Rough Draft
Rereading
Responding
Editing
Revising
Final copy
Evaluating

Math and Language Skills Continuum Cards

1. The classroom teacher is responsible for the recording of all of the information on each skills continuum card.

    A. All skills, including Chapter I and special education, that are introduced to a student during that grade.
    B. All skills, including Chapter I and special education, that are mastered by the student during that grade. (Supporting paper-pencil documentation or the date of teacher observation of the mastered skill is needed.)
    C. The teacher's name and skill recording in blue or pencil if this is the child's first year in the grade, and in red if the child is repeating.
    D. The specials who are working with a child each year (for IEP, need to list case manager only) need to write in blue or pencil, and in red for repeat year.
    E. Appropriate comments, please date. Comments must be factual and provable.
    F. Date of student entering (or date of change from one room to another).
    G. Be sure birthdate and date of entry is complete and accurate.
    H. All repeat information is to be done in red.

2. Some "best practices" include the following:

    A. List the textbooks or trade books (math, spelling, phonics, reading, handwriting, etc. with level and company) that are used for the skill instruction.
    B. Reference teaching methods and techniques (whole language, process writing, manipulative math) by grade level.
    C. Some teachers pass on incompleted workbooks to next year's teachers.
    D. Don't use "lovely little girl" or "lazy like his brother" type of comments.
    E. Add previous school or private kindergarten by date of entry, if known.
    F. List type of penmanship being introduced.
    G. Comments on use of computer are helpful.

3. Good idea to include in the student folder:

    A. Contact log of phone calls or conversations with parents.
    B. Copies of referrals to IST.
    C. Copies of recommendation for retention form.
    D. Teacher's copy of active IST, 504, Chapter I and IEP and/or behavior plans.

Mary Garamella

Learners

| Learning Disabled | Chap I | "Gray-Area" Children
Children with "Invisible" Disabilities | Non-labeled Learners | Gifted & Talented |

Children Enter School on a Broken Front

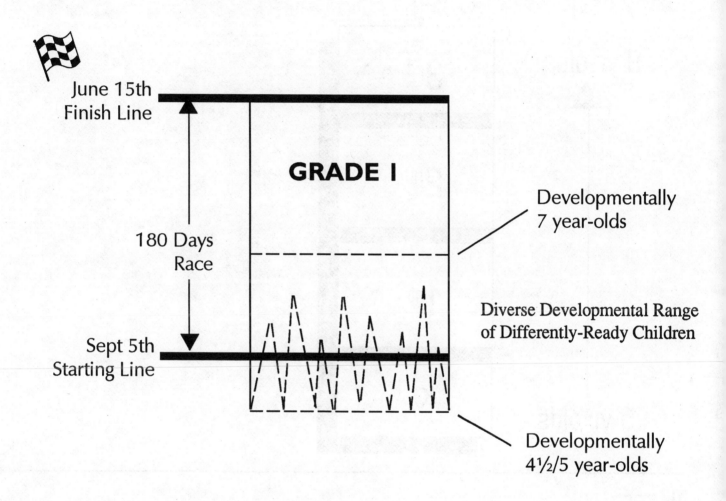

June 15th
Finish Line

GRADE I

Developmentally
7 year-olds

180 Days
Race

Diverse Developmental Range
of Differently-Ready Children

Sept 5th
Starting Line

Developmentally
4½/5 year-olds

Notes:

Traditional Graded
Primary Configuration

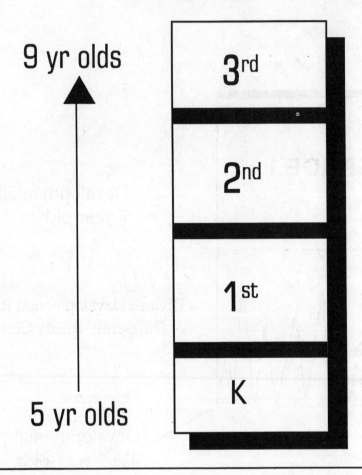

9 yr olds

3rd

2nd

1st

K

5 yr olds

Notes:

Looping With Kindergarten (½ day) and First Grade

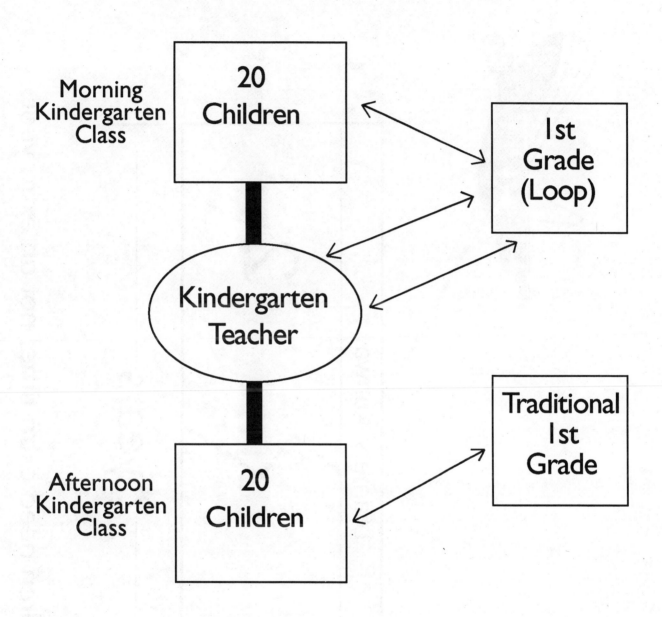

NOTES:

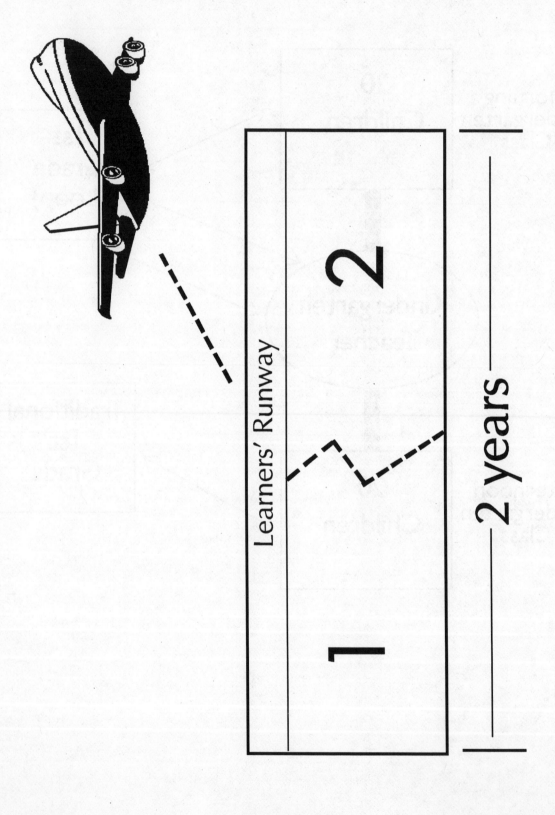

Learners' Runway

1

2

2 years

Some children need extra time, not an extra year.

Looping Configuration

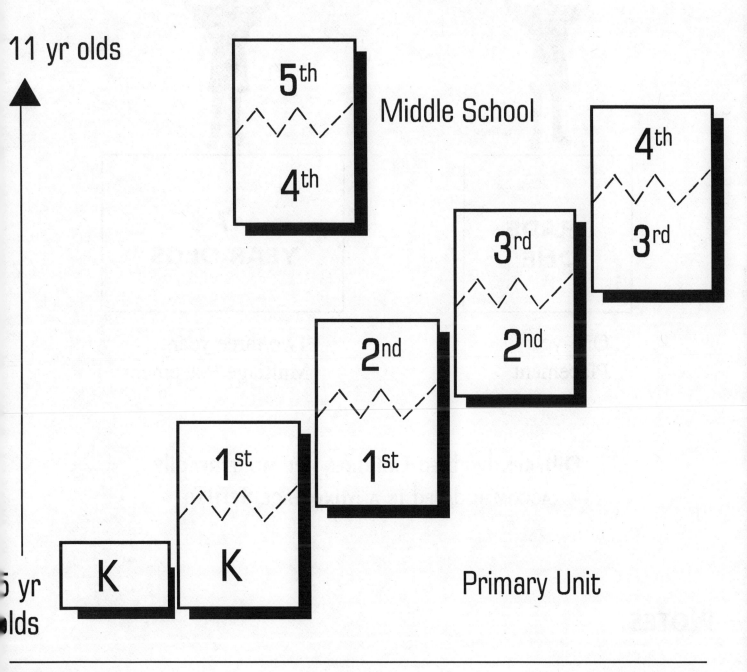

11 yr olds

Middle School

5 yr olds

Primary Unit

Notes:

Inclusion Education in the Multiage Classroom

GRADE ONE	6•7•8 YEAR-OLDS

One-year
Placement

Two/three year-
Multiage Placement

Differently-abled Children are more readily
accommodated in a Mixed-age Setting

NOTES:

Multigrade Configuration

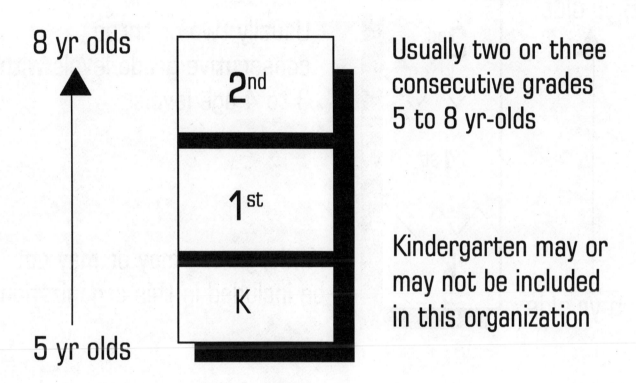

8 yr olds

5 yr olds

Usually two or three consecutive grades 5 to 8 yr-olds

Kindergarten may or may not be included in this organization

Notes:

Multiage Grouping Configuration

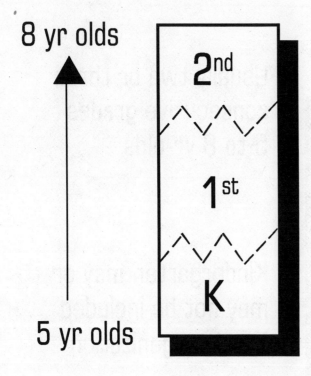

8 yr olds

2nd

1st

K

5 yr olds

Usually two or three consecutive grade levels with 3 to 4 age levels

Kindergarten may or may not be included in this organization

Notes:

Ungraded Primary Configuration

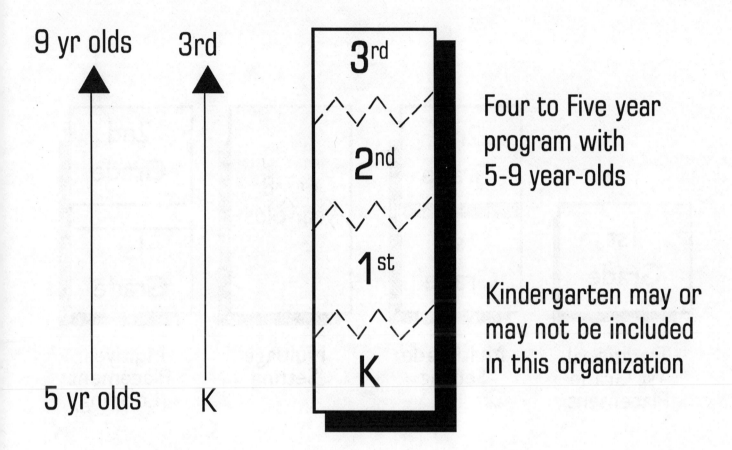

9 yr olds   3rd

3rd
2nd
1st
K

5 yr olds   K

Four to Five year program with 5-9 year-olds

Kindergarten may or may not be included in this organization

Notes:

Age/Grade Configuration

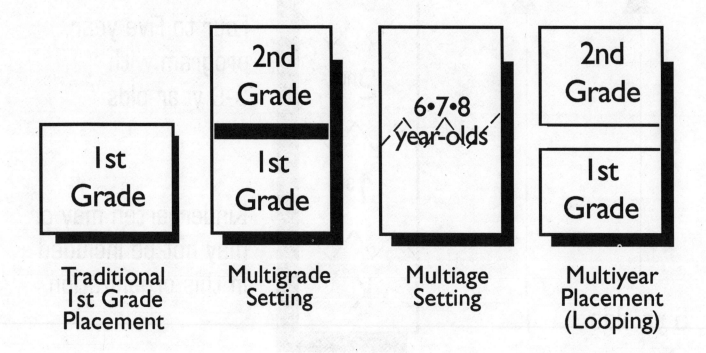

| Traditional 1st Grade Placement | Multigrade Setting | Multiage Setting | Multiyear Placement (Looping) |

Notes:

18 Levels VS. 6 Grades

Grade	Levels
6	18
	17
	16
5	15
	14
	13
4	12
	11
	10
3	9
	8
	7
2	6
	5
	4
1	3
	2
	1
K	

GRANT'S 1ST LAW of DIVERSITY
The greater the student developmental diversity, the more complex the curriculum and Instruction.

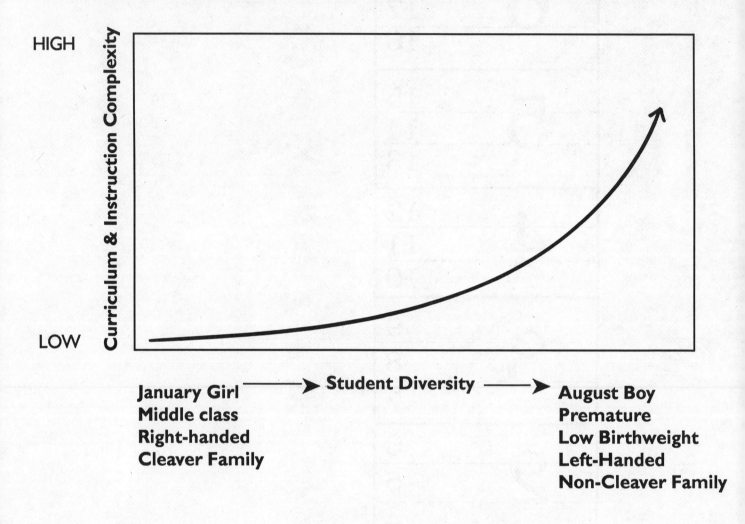

HIGH

Curriculum & Instruction Complexity

LOW

January Girl ——————➤ Student Diversity ——————➤ August Boy
Middle class   Premature
Right-handed   Low Birthweight
Cleaver Family   Left-Handed
                                                    Non-Cleaver Family

NOTE: A classroom teacher's workload increases in proportion to student diversity

Looping Requires a Two-Teacher Partnership

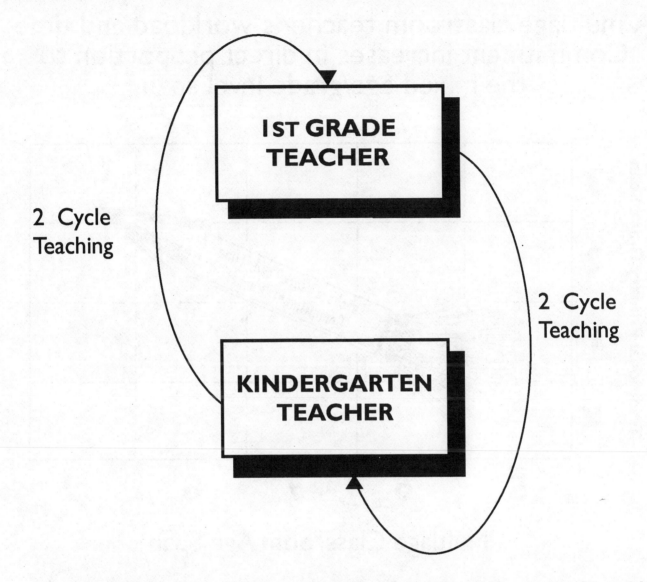

2 Cycle
Teaching

1ST GRADE TEACHER

2 Cycle
Teaching

KINDERGARTEN TEACHER

The kindergarten teacher is "promoted" to first grade with the class and keeps students for a second year.

The 1st grade teacher returns to kindergarten to pick up a new class and begins another two-year cycle.

Notes:

GRANT'S 2ND LAW of DIVERSITY
A multiage classroom teacher's workload and time Commitment increases in direct proportion to the mixed-age/grade level span

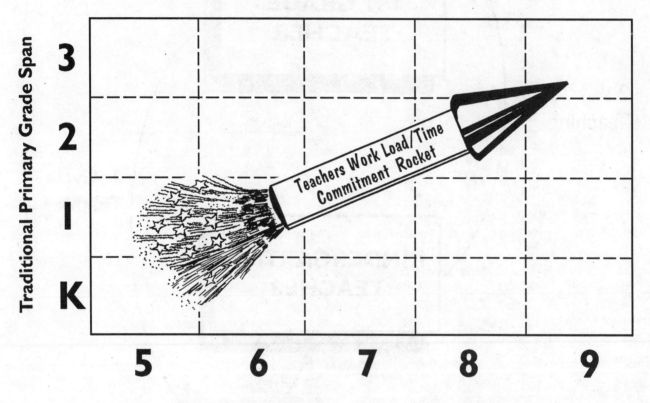

Traditional Primary Grade Span

3
2
I
K

Teachers Work Load/Time Commitment Rocket

5 6 7 8 9

Multiage Classroom Age Span

The Primary Multiage Classroom

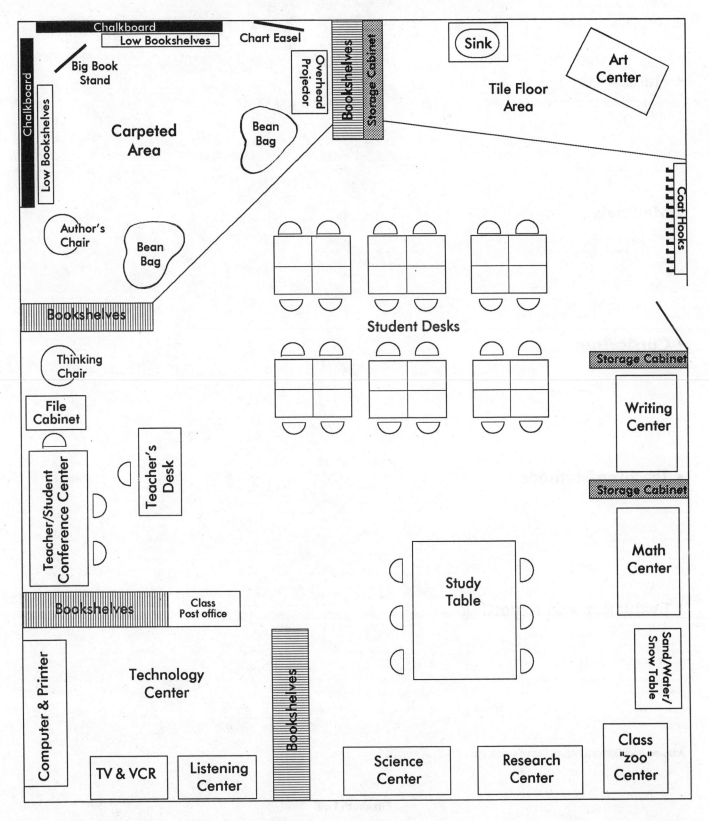

Multiage Programs That Work

- **Goals**

- **Framework**

- **Materials**

- **Curriculum**

- **Teaching Methods**

- **Evaluation and Reporting**

Adapted from Barbara Nelson Pavan's research

Elizabeth Lolli

Pros and Cons of Multiage

Advantages

Children
- Favors socialization
- Favors independence
- Favors interaction with peers

Being in a multiaged classroom has no negative effect on school achievement.

Teachers
- Serve as resource people
- Revitalized by challenge
- Refocus on child's whole development

Parents
- Variety of experiences for the child
- Acquisition of good work habits
- Sense of discipline
- Responsibility
- Independence gained
- Positive peer relationships

Cautions

Children
- Lack of time for teacher contact
- More time spent with youngest age
- Imbalanced ability group left in other classrooms if also have graded groupings

Teachers
- Extra work load
- Stress level increases
- Isolation from those with single-aged class
- Inappropriate curriculum and materials
- Lack of training

Parents
- Will curriculum be covered?
- Decision made because of budget
- Older child wasting time, slower child less support

Recommendations for Multiage Programs

1. Study philosophical and pedagogical reasons for multiage

2. Develop multiage curriculum and resources

3. Extensive training for teachers
   - Classroom organization
   - Small and large group instruction
   - Production of instructional materials
   - Testing/assessment strategies

4. Observation time in other multiage schools

Elizabeth Lolli

Multiage Grouping Needs

Individual Groups

conferencing with child to check progress
reteaching a skill to the child
listening to the child read
responding to child's writing
responding to child's project/learning center
observing child interacting with others

Small Groups

discussion groups
group conferencing to check progress
reteaching a skill to small group
reader's theater
dramatic play/drama
cooperative learning tasks
problem-solving groups
project groups
small group response to writing
small group response to individual shared reading/poetry
recommendations of books

Whole Groups

Mandated skills instruction
Introductory skills
Shared reading
Poetry time
Grammar skill instruction
Teacher model — writing time, oral reading, experiments

Multiage Classroom Strategies

- Project Areas / Learning Centers

- Classroom Physical Arrangement

- Classroom Atmosphere / Discipline

Strategies

Individual, Continuous Progress
Literature-based / Whole Language
Hands-on Mathematics
Hands-on Content Areas
Responding to Learning
Cooperative Learning
Peer Tutoring
Self-Evaluation
Peer Evaluation

Team Teaching Groups

Teachers working together to teach children.

Problem Solving — common topic or problem (can be community-based or simply content areas)

Needs Requirement — new instruction on concept, skill (these are identified by individual child's goals)

Reinforcement — more work on specific area, task (skill has been taught, not quite mastered yet)

Interest — those interested in a topic (in-depth study of different sections of topic)

Learning Style — common pattern of learning (utilizing the 7 intelligences and learning styles)

Elizabeth Lolli

Ten Steps to Multiage Programs

1. Understand what multiaging means. Begin with combined classes if necessary, but within one-two years <u>truly</u> start to multiage.

2. Discuss multiaging with administrators, parents, and other teachers.

3. Determine the age breakdown for each classroom unit.

4. Condense the curriculum into a one year realistic set of goals. Concentrate on mandated goals and objectives for the oldest child in the room at first.

5. Match eligible children into each age unit. Be conscious of social and emotional growth as well as cognitive growth.

6. Double check the heterogeneity of the classroom mixture. Each room must contain a mixture of ages, ability levels and social needs.

7. Avoid placing all discipline problems or lower level children in the same classroom.

8. Determine the teaching strategies which will best serve the mixture of students. These will change as class groupings change.

9. Design special projects areas or learning centers which can cover a wide range of ability levels. These are not paper-pencil tasks but truly problem-solving, hands-on experiences.

10. Determine three evaluation strategies that will provide authentic, diagnostic information for you and the parents. Be selective in trying everything that is new. You can only manage so much!

Elizabeth Lolli

Framework for Multiage Schools

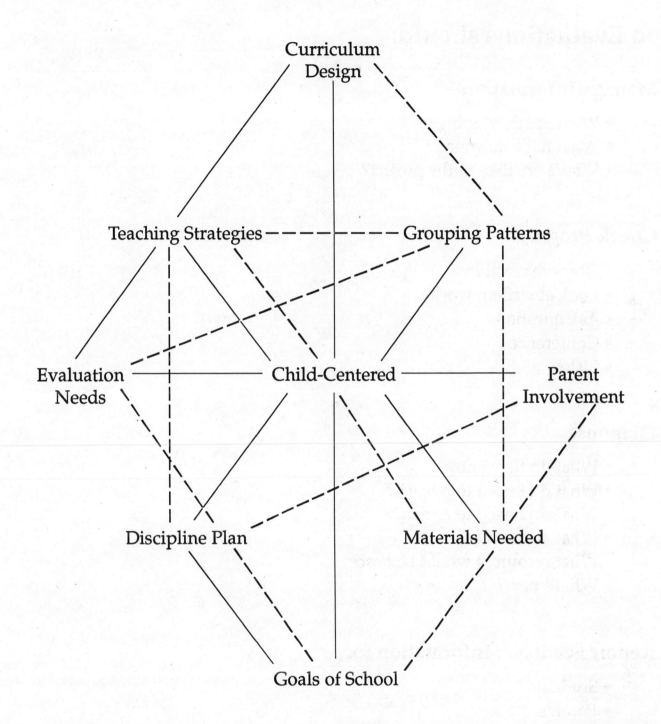

Developed by Elizabeth J. Lolli, Middletown, OH 1992

Elizabeth Lolli

Evaluating Student Progress

Good Evaluations should:

Manage Information

- What are they doing?
- What have they read?
- Where are they in the project?

Check Progress

- Observe reactions
- Look at written work
- Ask questions
- Conference
- Listen

Diagnose

- What do they know?
- What do I need to reteach?
- What do I need to enrich?
- What are their interests?
- What resources would be best?
- What's next?

Report Feedback Information to:

- Students
- Parents
- Administrators
- The community

Elizabeth Lolli

Making Sense of Assessment

Types of Authentic Assessment

- Portfolio
- Anecdotal Records
- Reading Logs
- Comprehension Matrix
- Discussion Record
- Performance Samples
- Outcome Checklist

Roles in Evaluation

- Teacher

- Student

- Parent

Elizabeth Lolli

Language Assessment Sheet

Name _____ **Valid Dates** _____

Indicators of Development
Key: + = consistently, * = sometimes, N = not yet

Speaking and Listening

Communicates clearly with others _____
Uses expanded vocabulary _____
Repeats nursery rhymes, songs, chants _____
Dictates stories, ideas, sentences _____
Listens to others _____
Talks about reading and writing _____

Reading

Interested in reading materials _____
Joins in shared reading activities _____
Understands story line (plot) _____
Retells story in sequence _____
Pretend or memory reads _____
Recognizes some sight words _____
Derives meaning from text _____
Has knowledge about letters _____
Uses environmental print _____

Writing

Interested in writing (print) _____
Pretend writes (scribble) _____
Spends time writing _____
Uses invented spelling _____
    random letters _____
    representation letters _____
    phonetic spelling _____
        conventional spelling/high frequency words _____
Uses writing to communicate _____
Uses literary structures _____

Social

Shares with others _____
Works cooperatively with others _____
Respects authority/peers _____
Remains on task _____
Listens and shares ideas with others _____

Developed by Elizabeth Lolli

Elizabeth Lolli

Parent Goal Sheet

Please fill out the goal sheet, using the information you have about your child's needs.

Academic

1. What are your child's strongest academic areas?

2. What are your child's interests in the strongest academic area? Is there something in this area that your child really likes or excels in?

3. What would you like to see your child learn about the strongest academic area?

4. What does your child need additional work on, academically?

5. Is there a topic that your child dislikes in the area(s) he/she needs additional work in? If so, what topic?

6. What should be your child's three main academic goals for the first nine weeks?

7. What should be the three long-term goals for your child's academic progress for the school year?

8. Please make any other comments necessary about your child's academic abilities.

Social

1. What are your child's strongest social skills?

2. What would you like to see your child learn about social skills?

3. What does your child need additional work on, socially?

4. What should be your child's three main social goals for the first nine weeks?

5. What should be the three long-term goals for your child's social progress for the school year?

6. Please make any other comments necessary about your child's social skills.

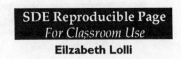

Physical

1. What are your child's strongest physical abilities?

2. What are your child's interests in the strongest area?   Is there something in this area that your child really likes or excels in?

3. What would you like to see your child learn about the strongest physical area?

4. What does your child need additional work on, physically?

5. Is there a topic that your child dislikes in the area(s) he/she needs additional work in? If so, what topic?

6. What should be your child's three main physical goals for the first nine weeks?

7. What should be the three long-term goals for your child's physical progress for the school year?·

8. Please make any other comments necessary about your child's physical abilities.

Emotional

1. Is there anything that makes your child very happy or excited? If so, what?

2. Is there anything that makes your child sad? If so, what?

3. Does your child have a fear of anything which would relate to school? If so, what?

4. What should be the three emotional goals for your child for the school year?

5. Please make any additional comments you feel appropriate.

Developed by Elizabeth Lolli, Central Academy/Nongraded.

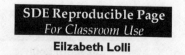

Central Academy Individual Education Plan

Academic Goals	Assessment Instruments	Effective Dates	Date Tested	Mastery Level
Math				
Reading				
English/Grammar				

Involving Parents

Central Academy Parent Connection
Volume 1 — November 2, 1992

During the coming thematic unit, Celebrations, the children will be studying about the celebrations around the world, transportation, and cultural traditions. This unit will last from November 9 – December 18.

The language arts skills which will be focused on include:

Early Primary:
  Final consonants
  Short vowels
  Digraphs (magic "h")
  Contractions
  Topic
  Details
  Appropriate literary terms

Late Primary:
  Inferential main idea/details
  Entry words/guide words (dictionary)
  Adjectives
  Verbs
  Literal main idea/details
  Appropriate literary terms

Some at home activities which you can do with your child to encourage the language skill building process are listed. Please do not feel you must do these every night or for longer than 20 minutes per night. They are simple but effective ideas for parent/child study time.

1. Pick a favorite book. Read or have your child read it to you. Ask your child to pick out various elements in the book like contractions, words with long vowel sounds, or tell you the main idea. Allow the child to ask you the same type of questions from the same or a different book. Do not be discouraged if your child doesn't yet understand the skill, although you may want to remember it for your next goal conference.

2. Visit a library and look up material from other countries. Possibly contact friends or relatives who may be from other countries and interview them.

3. Help your child invent a new mode of transportation for the next century. Have your child draw, write about or describe the new vehicle.

4. Talk about one family tradition that you have. Help your child try to find out where and when the tradition started. Have your child share this information with other extended family members.

5. Help your child write/draw/tell a story about a new tradition your family would like to start. Help your child tell the details about the new tradition.

6. Read, read, read with your child.

7. Talk about books, experiences, feelings, and playtime with your child.

Elizabeth Lolli

Central Academy Nongraded
Together Everyone Achieves More
(T.E.A.M.)

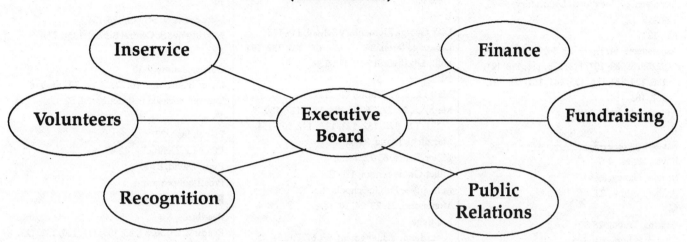

All parents participate on at least one of the committees to accomplish the year-long goals.

Daily Schedule

8:00 **Attendance, lunch count**

8:15 **Exercise video**

8:30 **Language arts**

11:25 **Lunch/recess**

12:15 **Math**

1:00 **Content projects**

1:45 **Specials/teachers plan**

2:30 **Oral reading**

2:45 **Dismissal**

Elizabeth Lolli

INDEX

CRYSTAL SPRINGS BOOKS!

Professional Books For
Elementary
Educators

NEW

The Complete Lesson Plan Book

- Flexible, Multi-purpose Planner
- Integrated Curriculum Ideas
- Assessment Suggestions
- Theme-based Book Lists
- Special Events Activities
- **Handy Pocket Folders**

available April 1993

3176 (K-3) $9.95

1993 – 94

100% Refundable Guarantee
1-800-321-0401

To Our Friends and Customers,

Our goal at Crystal Springs Books is to provide you with the best books and material available to elementary school educators. We have designed our current offering to reflect the exciting changes taking place in classrooms throughout the country. Specifically, we've included selections which provide scores of ready-to-use classroom ideas. Also, you will find many wonderful professional books to guide and support you as you develop a child-centered environment where all students can learn and grow together.

If you need any further information about the products in this catalog, please call us toll-free at **1-800-321-0401**. And remember, though we feel all our products are among the best you can find, you must be the final judge. We will gladly refund any purchase if you are not completely satisfied.

Wendy, Betsy, Lorraine
Rob, Ryan, Putnam

Sincerely,

Lorraine Walker

Lorraine Walker
Crystal Springs Books Manager

P.S. If you're ever in the Monadnock Region of southern New Hampshire, stop in and visit our warehouse store in Peterborough. Call us at **1-800-321-0401** for directions.

Return Policy

We guarantee **100% satisfaction** on any books or materials we sell. Returned items will be accepted within **30** days as long as they are in saleable condition.

Ordering Information

Individuals:
Orders must be prepaid using check or credit card.

Prompt Shipping:
All in stock orders to the 48 contiguous states are shipped **UPS** within 48 hours. A street address is required for delivery.

3 Easy Ways to Place Your Order

Choose one of the following:

1.) Call **1-800-321-0401** with credit card or purchase order number.

2.) Mail your order to:

Crystal Springs Books
PO Box 577
Peterborough, NH 03458

3.) FAX orders to 603-924-6688.

Schools:
Orders may be prepaid or purchase orders are accepted.

Shipping, Handling, and Insurance Charge:

Up to $24.99	$3.50
$25 – 49.99	$5.00
$50 – 79.99	$8.00
$80 – 500.00	10% of order

FREE shipping for orders over $500

Ten Ways to Become a Better Reader

by Cindy Merrilees and Pamela Haack

Ten Ways to Become a Better Reader is especially valuable for parents and teachers who are searching for classroom-proven, practical advice on making the transition from traditional reading groups to whole-group reading.

Although the title says there are 10 ways to become a better reader, there is really only one — read! This book includes ideas and activities that encouraged Merrilees and Haack's students to do just that. 48 pp.   1221   **$7.95**

Write On Target

by Cindy Merrilees and Pamela Haack

Write On Target offers a wealth of easily implemented ideas to help generate student interest in writing and meet the needs of a wide range of learners.

Experienced classroom teachers, Cindy and Pam give suggestions for writing individual student books, whole-group big books, journals, and creative writing booklets. They also explain how they solved the most frequently encountered problems of students writing every day. 63 pp.   1120   **$8.95**

Story Stretchers, More Story Stretchers, *and* Story Stretchers for the Primary Grades

by Shirley C. Raines and Robert J. Canady

Each book offers 450 ways to expand the impact and interest of 90 popular children's picture books. The activities are arranged in chapters with suggestions for integrating them into childhood curriculum units.

Raines and Canady offer a wealth of ideas for extending the book experiences through math, art, circle time, science, creative dramatics, snack time, music and movement activities — and more.

All three books are a wonderful resource for teachers, parents, and children's librarians.

Story Stretchers 251 pp.
   1119   **$14.95**
More Story Stretchers 254 pp.
   1245   **$14.95**
*Story Stretchers for the
   Primary Grades* 256 pp.
   3078   **$14.95**

Beginning In Whole Language: A Practical Guide

by Kristin Schlosser and Vicki Phillips

A compendium chock full of reproducible materials, activities, and ideas for putting whole language to work: board games, poetry cubes, big books, journal writing, and more. Illustrated with actual classroom photos. (K-2) 112 pp.   3140   **$12.95**

Why Whole Language

by Jay Buros

Based on Jay Buros' extensive experience as a teacher and consultant, this book explains the whole language approach through a detailed examination of classroom techniques. *Why Whole Language* provides information to help you set up a whole language classroom, find appropriate materials, integrate the curriculum through themes, and develop parental support. 119 pp.
P022   **$8.95**

Celebrate with Books

by Imogene Forte and Joy MacKenzie

What better way to celebrate special times than with a good book? This collection of seasonal and holiday thematic literature units will provide you with loads of fun and easy-to-do projects and activities to celebrate well-chosen pieces of literature all year long. It's the perfect complement to today's literature-driven curriculum. (1-4) 143 pp.   3160   **$12.95**

Put a Book in their Hands

by Mary Lee Blansett

Use these weekly thematic units to open up a whole new world for your beginning readers and writers. Jam-packed with skills-based games and activities, this exciting approach to teaching beginning reading skills will enliven and reinforce your entire language program. (K-1) 127 pp.
3305   **$10.95**

Read! Write! Publish!

by Barbara Fairfax and Adela Garcia

Simple instructions and diagrams show you and your students how to make 20 different books. Motivating writing activities and literature suggestions accompany each book idea. The language arts take on new meaning as budding authors write for "publication." (1-5) 70 pp.
3306   **$7.95**

Alternatives to Worksheets

by Karen Bauer and Rosa Drew

At last, a book of meaningful child-centered activities for teachers who want alternatives to worksheets. Directions are simple and the format is teacher-friendly. Contains 40 activities with hundreds of variations for seatwork. (K-4) 96 pp.   3103   **$8.95**

Transitions: From Literature to Literacy
by Regie Routman

Transitions provides support, encouragement, and ideas to teachers who are looking for alternatives to a reading program emphasizing skill-oriented basal texts and worksheets.

Drawing from her own experience, Routman describes an existing literature-based, whole language program that has worked well for students and teachers and offers suggestions of how any elementary classroom can benefit from the transition from standardized texts to literature. She presents material designed to demonstrate the alternatives available, to stimulate thinking, and to give teachers, parents, and administrators the knowledge and procedures that are necessary to make a change. Heinemann 352 pp. 1132 **$18.95**

Invitations: Changing as Teachers and Learners
by Regie Routman

Invitations is an invaluable, practical, easy-to-read text that has been written to support and encourage K-12 educators as they translate whole language theory into practice. This remarkably complete and well-organized resource provides specific strategies for the daily management and educational issues teachers think about and struggle with in their efforts to make teaching more relevant for their students and themselves. Heinemann (K-12) 644 pp. 3023 **$25.00**

150 Surefire Ways to Keep Them Reading All Year
by Ava Drutman and Diane Houston

Dozens of book-related classroom activities: games, contests, display and storage ideas, author birthdays, school-wide read-alouds, lots more. (K-6) 112 pp. 3076 **$12.95**

The New Read-Aloud Handbook
by Jim Trelease

Jim Trelease shows you how to raise a reader and bring your family closer at the same time. He explains: • how to begin reading aloud — and which books to choose; • how reading aloud awakens children's imaginations, improves their language skills, and opens new worlds of enjoyment; • how to coax children away from the television; • how time shared reading together is valuable to parents and children; • how individuals across America have raised reading scores and united communities. 290 pp. 1097 **$10.95**

Reading, Writing and Caring
by O. Cochrane, D. Cochrane, S. Scalena and E. Buchanan

Educational theory and research can lead to new classroom strategies, but if these new strategies don't work in a real classroom then they don't pass the final test.

The ideas and strategies outlined in this book have all been successfully used by classroom teachers. Children from various backgrounds have found success and enjoyment of learning through the use of this whole language approach. 216 pp. 1102 **$15.95**

Hey! Listen to This: Stories to Read Aloud
edited by Jim Trelease

Trelease brings together forty-eight read-aloud stories that parents and teachers can share with children ages 5–9. From folktales (*Uncle Remus, The Pied Piper of Hamelin,* and *The Indian Cinderella*) to classic favorites by such wonderful children's authors as Roald Dahl (*James and the Giant Peach*), E. B. White (*Charlotte's Web*), Beverly Cleary (*Ramona the Pest*), C. S. Lewis (*The Lion, the Witch and the Wardrobe*), and L. Frank Baum (*Ozma of Oz*). In addition, Trelease has written a special introduction to each story and makes suggestions for further reading. (K-3) 414 pp. 3296 **$11.00**

Read Aloud Anthology

98 stories for all grades and all occasions: holidays, seasons, special people, other cultures, and countries. Includes 50 quick ideas for reading motivation, story starters, and other strategies. (1-6) 192 pp. 3145 **$12.95**

Meet the Authors and Illustrators: 60 Creators of Favorite Children's Books Talk about their Work
by Deborah Kovacs and James Preller

Anno, Eric Carle, E.B. White, Chris Van Allsburg, Bruce Degen, and dozens of other favorite children's authors and illustrators provide easy-to-read profiles, with bibliographies, extension activities, index of authors, and illustrators by birthdate. (K-6) 142 pp. 3074 **$19.95**

Teaching with Caldecott Books: Activities that Cross the Curriculum
by Christine B. Moen

Use such Caldecott winners as *On Market Street, Strega Nona, Where the Wild Things Are, Frog and Toad Are Friends, Jumanji, The Snowy Day,* and nine more to promote language acquisition. Includes model lessons plus critical thinking questions, teaching tips, and extension activities. (K-3) 179 pp. 3304 **$14.95**

Literature-Based Seasonal and Holiday Activities
by Mary Beth Spann

28 favorite children's books (*Sarah Morton's Day; Angelina's Christmas; Arthur's Valentine; Our Martin Luther King Book*) are the springboards for games, arts and crafts projects, writing ideas, recipes, and other creative activities. Includes reproducible game boards. (K-3) 112 pp. 3075 **$12.95**

Linking Literature & Writing
by Shirley Cook & Kathy Carl

This whole language resource contains stimulating activities to use with selected children's books. Organized by month to provide activities for the whole year, this title "links" 174 favorite children's books to writing. (1-4) 240 pp. 4001 **$14.95**

Incorporating Literature into the Basal Reading Program
by Judith Cochran

Finally, a commonsense approach that does not "throw the baby out with the bath water." This jumbo handbook is so well organized and researched you can't go wrong. It's all here, from daily lesson plans to adapting basal program worksheets. This important work will certainly become the nucleus of reading programs everywhere! (K-6) 160 pp. 4004 **$14.95**

Into the Think Tank with Literature
by Jo Ann Pelphrey

Teach your beginning readers to expand their thinking skills. Lesson plan outlines present a story or rhyme with activities that take into account the varied needs of K-3 readers. Follow-up activities range from hands-on projects to role playing and student interaction. Let literature take your class into a think tank. (K-3) 160 pp. 4000 **$14.95**

Linking Literature & Comprehension
by Shirley Cook

This power-packed resource provides stimulating activities in conjunction with 125 carefully selected children's books. These comprehension activities are arranged in a monthly thematic format to supplement your year-round reading program. (K-4) 240 pp. 4002 **$14.95**

Teaching Through Themes
by Gare Thompson

Hands-on guide to choosing themes, selecting the literature, and building the themes into a year-round literature program, plus specific teaching and assessment strategies. Includes 6 model themes with bibliographies. (1-6) 176 pp. 3251 **$15.95**

Insights to Literature
by Judith Cochran

Here are two complete reading programs designed to accompany widely acclaimed books. Each piece of literature is presented through an individual unit and teacher's guide. Reproducible units contain comprehension questions and activities for each book chapter along with journal writing activities. The teachers' guides contain pre/post reading questions and activities that touch on all areas of the curriculum. Everything is correlated to Bloom's Taxonomy with a simple-to-use symbol indicating the thinking skills level. The Primary Grades edition features 3 wordless books, 21 picture books, and 5 novels. The Middle Grades version is designed to accompany 10 popular books. Don't miss these exciting and complete resources. (Primary) 240 pp. 4005 **$14.95**   (Mid. Grades) 240 pp. 4006 **$14.95**

If You're Trying to Teach Kids How to Write, You've Gotta Have this Book!
by Marjorie Frank

This is the handbook at the top of every required resource list. Why? The title says it all! This is a favorite how-to book for understanding and working with the whole writing process, an at-your-fingertips source of ideas for starting specific activities, and a ready-when-you're-in-need manual for solving writing problems. If you've ever said, "How do I get kids to write on their own?" "I have this kid who just won't!" "I just don't have time," or "I always run out of ideas by October," then this book is for you! (K-6) 232 pp. 4007 **$12.95**

Story Journal
by Shirley Cook

Shirley Cook is from the team that brought you the very popular LINKING LITERATURE & WRITING resource. By request, she has produced this new middle grades format just for you! Seventeen wonderful books are the theme for daily journal writing activities. Each activity introduces new vocabulary words and provides thought-provoking writing stimulators for every book. At the end of each unit, you will find extended activities to integrate literature with the curriculum and to exercise creative thinking. (4-8) 240 pp. 3165 **$14.95**

Assessment and Evaluation in Whole Language Programs

Edited by Bill Harp

Examines the basic principles of whole language assessment and evaluation practices. This book includes strategies for assessment in primary, intermediate, special education, bilingual, and multicultural settings.

"A scholarly, yet practical work that not only examines the growing research base that supports whole language, but offers realistic suggestions for tackling the many thorny issues involved in the assessment and evaluation of students." 232 pp. 2075 **$16.25**

Portfolio Assessment and Evaluation

by Janine Batzle

This book contains useful and practical information about assessment strategies and answers the questions teachers have about portfolio assessment. • How do I assess students' progress without standardized tests? • What is a portfolio? • How do I set up and use portfolios in the classroom? • What goes in a portfolio? • Who is involved in assessment? • Where and how should assessment take place? (K-6) 125 pp. 4014 **$15.00**

The Early Detection of Reading Difficulties, Third Edition

by Marie M. Clay

Part One of *The Early Detection of Reading Difficulties* provides for the systematic observation of young children's responses to classroom reading instruction. Part Two contains a set of Reading Recovery procedures for use in an early intervention program with young children having difficulty with beginning reading. Heinemann. 144 pp. 1025 **$17.95**

Sand *and* Stones — "Concepts About Print" Tests

by Marie M. Clay

Diagnostic tools which can be used with the new entrant or non-reader because the child is asked to help the examiner by pointing to certain features as the examiner reads the book. *The Early Detection of Reading Difficulties* presents the theoretical background, administration details, and scoring interpretation of the tests. Heinemann.
Sand (20 pp.) 1107 **$3.50**
Stones (20 pp.) 1117 **$3.50**

Evaluation in the Literature-Based Classroom: Whole Language Checklists

Reproducible, hole-punched assessment sheets for individual, group, and class evaluation for grades K-3 and 4-6. Includes instructions, plus rationales. (K-6) 38 pp. 3288 **$7.95**

Evaluation: Whole Language, Whole Child

by Jane Baskwill and Paulette Whitman

Manageable alternatives to traditional testing procedures, alternatives that are simple and clear as practiced by experienced whole language teachers. (K-6) 44 pp. 3111 **$7.95**

Evaluation: A Team Effort

by Linda Picciotto

Specific how-to's for teacher, parent, and student involvement in the evaluation process. Includes sample student work, suggested reporting, and recording techniques. (K-3) 64 pp. 4015 **$9.95**

Cooperative Learning

Cooperative Learning: Getting Started

by Susan Ellis & Susan Whalen

Hands-on guide to this key learning strategy. Includes solutions to possible problems, outlines of six different classroom models, and other specific how-to's. (K-6) 72 pp. 4016 **$9.95**

Cooperative Learning Lessons for Little Ones

by Lorna Curran

This is the only comprehensive book on cooperative learning lessons and activities for primary grades. The teacher's manual has 36 lessons which focus on language development and social skills. Adaptions of structures for young children make cooperative learning possible for primary students who have not yet mastered the reading and writing skills. The lessons are based on children's literature. Blackline masters are included. (K-2) 153 pp. 3114 **$15.00**

Cooperative Learning

by Spencer Kagan

Included are step-by-step instructions for 100 structures and hundreds of activities to get started. The book provides comprehensive information on the development of social skills, conflict resolution, classroom set-up and management, scoring and recognition, lesson planning, cooperative sports, and cooperative learning research. (all grades) 376 pp. 3113 **$25.00**

The Cooperative Learning Guide & Planning Pak for Primary Grades

by Imogene Forte & Joy MacKenzie

Keep interest high and learning fun. This resource comes complete with primary thematic units and projects for the entire year. Included in a bonus section are quick-and-easy cooperative activities and planning, recordkeeping, and study guide worksheets. (1-4) 144 pp. 4017 **$12.95**

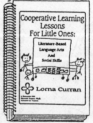

Creative Resources for the Early Childhood Classroom
by Judy Herr and Yvonne Libby

An entire year of activities for the preschool classroom in one volume. Organized on a theme basis, 57 themes and their activities include gardens, construction tools, zoo animals, hats, and much more. Each unit includes a flow chart, theme goals, concepts for the children to learn, vocabulary words, how to integrate the themes into learning centers, and resource books. Also includes a thorough discussion on how to plan a curriculum using a thematic approach. 567 pp. plus appendix. 3117 **$31.95**

Get Ready, Set, Grow!
by Eileen Morris and Stephanie Crilly

This comprehensive, completely tested calendar-book provides 44 weeks worth of learning activities — plus summer-fun ideas! All activities are carefully sequenced and organized into special thematic units that include:
• indoor/outdoor play
• art activities
• essential learning skills
• rhythm and music
• snacks and recipes
• storytime
• and more!
108 pp. 3374 **$11.95**

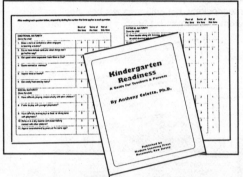

Kindergarten Readiness Checklists & Guide
by Anthony Coletta, Ph.D.

Now there's an effective way to gather the parent input you need when determining grade placement and designing an appropriate curriculum. Dr. Coletta's checklists cover a range of developmental factors that can affect a child's performance in kindergarten and are designed so that parents can complete them quickly and easily. The helpful guide provides valuable background information on kindergarten readiness, a framework for evaluating checklist and assessment results, and new information on the readiness goal.
Guide (32 pp.) 3209 **$4.95**
Checklists (pkg. of 25) 3210 **$14.95**

Joyful Learning:
A Whole Language Kindergarten
by Bobbi Fisher

Bobbi Fisher discusses whole language theory and offers practical, applicable advice on such topics as shared reading, the reading and writing process, math manipulatives, dramatic play, assessment, and communication with parents. A valuable resource for curriculum planners and administrators. Heinemann. 243 pp. 3025 **$18.50**

KinderUnits
by Esther Howard and Dianne Faulk

A complete resource of thematic units designed specifically for young learners. *KinderUnits* promotes the development of skills such as visual discrimination, sorting, classifying, and counting, while including content in the areas of art, health, language arts, math, music, science, and social studies. Complete with snack suggestions, field trips, and party ideas. 128 pp. 3158 **$11.95**

Positively Kindergarten: A Classroom-proven, Theme-based, Developmental Guide for the Kindergarten Teacher
by Beth Lamb, Ph.D. and Phyllis Logsdon, Ph.D.

Positively Kindergarten offers information for understanding the developmental philosophy and stages of children; organizing the classroom and the school day; planning and using theme units; and working with peers, parents, and administrators. 146 pp. P038 **$14.95**

The Whole Language Kindergarten
by Shirley C. Raines and Robert J. Canady

This practical volume includes an abundance of whole language activities within the classical content areas of reading, writing, science, art, music, and mathematics. It offers clear suggestions on how to interest children in books and print; how to structure group-work to emphasize whole language philosophy; and how parents can reevaluate their roles to better understand and effect classroom change. In addition, each chapter contains examples of kindergartens where programs have been implemented and describes how the changes were organized, as well as how the children reacted. 272 pp. 3095 **$20.50**

How to Make Pop-Ups *and* How to Make Super Pop-Ups
both by Joan Irvine

Anyone can make pop-ups. Find a piece of paper, a pair of scissors, some crayons, and a little glue. In minutes make greeting cards that talk, rockets that fly, or a zoo full of animals.

Both books feature: • easy-to-follow directions; • step-by-step instructions; • illustrations for each pop-up creation; • projects for all levels and abilities; • ideas for birthday cards, invitations, holiday decorations, gifts — and more! Great ideas to use for making books for the classroom.

Pop-Ups 93 pp. 1043 **$6.95**
Super Pop-Ups 96 pp. 3297 **$6.95**

A Book of One's Own
by Paul Johnson

A comprehensive guide to book art. By developing skills such as writing, story construction, design, illustration, binding methods, and paper technology, the author shows how book making can enhance many different areas of the curriculum. Heinemann. 119 pp. 3107 **$17.50**

Book Cooks:
Literature-Based Classroom Cooking
Stir up a batch of eager readers. 35 recipes for your favorite books, easy preparation, tips on managing classroom cooking, and integrated learning activities for student cooks.

Book Cooks — (K-3) 80 pp. 3166 **$9.98**
Book Cooks — (4-6) 80 pp. 3276 **$9.98**

Is Your Storytale Dragging?
by Jean Stangl

Read original stories such as "Nibble, Nibble," "Pam's Magic Trick," and "The Unexpected, Disappearing Guest." Simple props enliven these fold-and-cut paper stories, stringboard stories, and flip chart stories! (PreK-3) 80 pp. 2062 **$8.95**

Literature-Based Art Activities
Fun-to-make art projects inspired by 45 favorite children's books. Common classroom art materials are used to create these original projects. Each project includes a list of related literature titles and integrated learning activities. What a way to build a lifelong love of literature!

Grades K-3, 104 pp. 3079 **$9.98**
Grades 4-6, 104 pp. 3128 **$9.98**

Teacher's Holiday Helper
by Lynn Brisson

Fresh and easy to use, you'll find hats, ornaments, greeting cards, booklets, certificates, and worksheets ready to reproduce and make. Save time, save money. (K-6) 96 pp. 3279 **$9.95**

Teacher's Bag of Tricks
by Patty Nelson

Here's a "bag of tricks" no elementary teacher should be without! It's filled with 101 instant lessons, activities, puzzles, and more, for language arts, math, science, art, and general classroom enrichment. (K-6) 80 pp. 3248 **$8.95**

Math

Integrating Beginning Math & Literature
by Carol A. Rommel

Now you can integrate children's literature and mathematics throughout the entire school year with fun-filled, high-interest activities. Thirty-one favorite books are used to involve children in active exploration of beginning math concepts in a "whole learning" environment. (K-3) 180 pp.   4008   **$8.95**

600 Manipulatives and Activities for Early Math
by Diane Peragine

More than 600 cut-out-and-use multi-purpose manipulatives and lessons for reinforcing such concepts as big/bigger/biggest; shapes; the numerals zero-ten; adding and subtracting; classifying; categorizing. (K-2) 176 pp.   3302   **$19.95**

Making Multiplication Easy: Strategies for Mastering the Tables through 10
by Meish Goldish

Dozens of games, puzzles, songs, and reproducibles that replace rote methods of teaching. Fun, creative strategies work with children of all abilities. Includes take-home ideas, review activities, answer key. (2-4) 64 pp.   3077   **$7.95**

Teaching Thinking and Problem Solving in Math
by Char Forsten

How to utilize cooperative learning, graphing, logic, working backwards, estimating, making a table, drawing a picture, and other proven strategies to build problem-solving skills. Includes cross-curricular applications. Geared to the new math standards. (2-6) 96 pp.   3094   **$10.95**

Math Medley
by Sylvia Gay & Janet Hoelker

Fresh out of ways to teach your young students beginning math concepts? Everyday household items are utilized as manipulatives for the 210 hands-on math activities contained in this book. Allow your students to begin to understand mathematical concepts spontaneously and with enjoyment! (Pre K-1) 64 pp.   4009   **$7.95**

Do-It-Yourself Math Stories
by Allyne Brumbaugh

Add students' names and their choice of numbers and you have 20 personalized math adventure stories that involve addition, subtraction, multiplication, division, and problem solving. Developed to meet today's new math guidelines. (2-5) 96 pp.   3143   **$10.95**

A Collection of Math Lessons from Grades 1 through 3
by Marilyn Burns and Bonnie Tank

A Collection of Math Lessons from Grades 3 through 6
by Marilyn Burns

A Collection of Math Lessons presents practical, classroom-tested ideas for teaching mathematics through problem solving. Using classroom vignettes, Marilyn Burns presents exciting and practical lessons for promoting thinking and reasoning, implementing cooperative learning groups, using concrete materials, and integrating writing into math instruction. Each book includes helpful illustrations and many samples of children's work.
(1-3) 193 pp.   2071   **$14.95**
(3-6) 176 pp.   2072   **$14.95**

Science

Integrating Science & Literature
by Judith Cochran

Every literature selection in this resource becomes a springboard for scientific exploration. Each unit includes a teacher's guide, a science activities page, student activity pages, and a thematic activities page, all with clear, easy instructions. All activities are keyed to Bloom's Taxonomy and are linked to other areas of the curriculum. (K-4) 144 pp.   4010   **$12.95**

Hug A Tree: And Other Things to Do Outdoors with Young Children
by Robert E. Rockwell, Elizabeth A. Sherwood, and Robert A. Williams

Each of the learning experiences in *Hug A Tree* has a suggested age level, a clear description of what will be done, and suggestions for follow-up learning. Special emphasis is placed on using natural environments for learning lan-guage, spatial and mathematical relationships, and much more. (Pre K-2) 108 pp.   2061   **$9.95**

Bugs to Bunnies: Hands-On Animal Science Activities for Young Children
by Kenn Goin, Eleanor Ripp, and Kathleen Nastasi Solomon

This complete resource features hundreds of hands-on activities to teach young children, ages 4-7, the science of animals and help answer their most frequently asked questions. The book includes over 200 activity ideas in eight units on "all about animals," insects, spiders, amphibians, reptiles, fish, birds, and mammals.

Each unit is filled with stories, easy-to-use activity ideas for large and small groups, and reproducible worksheets. (Pre K-2) 192 pp.   2057   **$14.95**

202 Science Investigations
by Marjorie Frank

These fun investigations cover life, physical, earth, and space science. Perfect for individual or group activity and complete with "no-fail" directions. Also includes glossary of science words and symbols. (K-6) 240 pp.   4011   **$14.95**

Add Some Music

Kathie Cloonan has used favorite children's and holiday songs to produce two series. Integrating music into a whole language classroom gives children reading success they can sing about. Her books contain ideas and patterns for making big books, mini books and class books to accompany the songs on her cassettes.

Sing Me a Story, Read Me a Song:
Book 1	1012	$9.95
Book 2	1242	$9.95
Cassette	1166	$11.95

Whole Language Holidays:
Book 1	3223	$9.95
Book 2	3224	$9.95
Cassette	1263	$11.95

Art

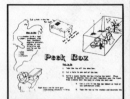

Rainbow

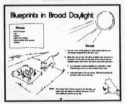

Puddles

I Can Make a Rainbow
by Marjorie Frank
 Hundreds of delightfully-illustrated rainbow-colored pages contain step-by-step instructions for unique art experiences with most every art medium! Highly recommended. (K-6) 300 pp.   3361 **$16.95**

Puddles & Wings & Grapevine Swings
by Imogene Forte & Marjorie Frank
 A perfect companion to . . . RAINBOW. 304 brightly-colored pages are filled with activities, games, & art projects using easy-to-find, natural materials. Includes crafts for all seasons; things to grow; things to do with sticks, stones, sand & mud; weather & ecology experiments; recipes for fun & food . . . and more! Suitable for indoors or out! (K-6) 304 pp.   3360 **$16.95**

Pick up a Poem Series

Arnold Lobel

Share the magic of poetry with whimsical, wonderful selections by poets like Jack Prelutsky, Judith Viorst, and Eve Merriam, enhanced by the illustrations of Eric Carle, Tomie dePaola, Marc Brown, and others. Each volume contains ten beautiful full-color poetry posters, reproducible poems, and a wealth of extension activities. (1-6) 11" x 17" **$11.98 each**

3180	The Four Seasons
3181	Animal Fair
3182	All about You and Me
3183	Fabulous Favorites
3184	Holidays and Special Days
3185	Ridiculous Rhymes

Michael Flanders   *Eric Carle*

8

Poetry Place Anthology

More than 600 poems to celebrate the seasons and scores of holidays...to inspire art projects, bulletin boards, and creative dramatics...to give a lift to every day of the year. (K-6) 192 pp.
3091 **$12.95**

Pass the Poems Please
by Jane Baskwill

Dinosaurs and teddy bears, exploring and pretending, stargazing and camping out; all the adventures of a young child's world are gently presented in this collection of poems for pre-school and early grades. But look carefully — exciting activities are hidden away in the illustrations: Share this book with small friends and wait for them to say, "read it again."
32 pp.   1092   **$6.50**

If You're Not Here, Please Raise Your Hand: Poems About School
by Kalli Dakos

This delightful book celebrates the world of elementary school in thirty-eight poems that capture the excitement, challenge, heartbreak, and wonder of classroom life.
60 pp.   3045   **$12.95**

Let Me Be . . . THE BOSS
Poems for Kids to Perform
by Brod Bagert

Brod Bagert offers teachers an array of practical techniques to spark a child's natural love of poetry. He calls it the Performance Method, a system which recognizes that poetry is an oral art that comes alive when it is performed. The Performance Method is easy to learn, fun to do, and powerfully effective. 54 pp.
3237   **$14.95**

The Butterfly Jar
by Jeff Moss

Moss, one of the original creators and head writer for *Sesame Street*, will introduce the reader to wise, wacky, and memorable characters. Inside *The Butterfly Jar*, you will find Lonesome Joan, who won't let anyone teach her anything, Eugene, the boy whose socks don't match, and Johnny, who foolishly sticks jellybeans up his nose. 115 pp.
3109   **$15.00**

Alligator Pie
by Dennis Lee

Since it appeared in 1974, *Alligator Pie* has won the hearts of children throughout Canada, and the chant of "Alligator pie, alligator pie/If I don't get some I think I'm gonna die" has become a timeless children's anthem. Full of memorable verses and light-hearted illustrations. 64 pp.   2068   **$6.50**

The Ice Cream Store
by Dennis Lee

In Lee's imaginative collection, readers take a wonderful trip aboard a rocketship, meet skinny marinka dinka, dig a hole to Australia, and listen to a trombone-playing walrus. Warmly illustrated, it's a kid and crowd pleasing collection. 58 pp.   3205   **$14.95**

Street Rhymes Around the World
edited by Jane Yolen

This is a magnificent collection of games, chants and songs from around the world that children will enjoy reading and discussing. Jane Yolen has brought a wide variety of world cultures to children through the universal language of play. (ages 4-10) 40 pp.   3081   **$16.95**
Order by 8/15/93 for special price of **$12.75**

Upside Down and Inside Out
by Bobbi Katz

Imagine a world where kids made all the rules and the day is upside down. Imagine a delightful collection of poems that allows us to experience the world as a bit absurd. This is one of those special books that comes along every once in a while. (ages 4-8) 32 pp.   3089   **$14.95**
Order by 8/15/93 for special price of **$11.25**

Spelling

Spel . . . Is a Four-Letter Word
by J. Richard Gentry

Often spelling is taught in a way offensive to children. This creates a set of false dichotomies that prejudice children against spelling. This practical book demonstrates how children can learn to spell. *Spel . . . Is a Four-Letter Word* is devoted to helping teachers and parents teach spelling as part of the reading-writing process. 56 pp.   1113   **$7.95**

Teaching Kids to Spell
by J. Richard Gentry and Jean Wallace Gillet

This comprehensive new work offers the best treatment available for setting the foundations of spelling through the early use of invented spelling. For teachers, school administrators, and parents who want to understand the complex process of spelling, *Teaching Kids to Spell* will be a valuable resource. Heinemann. 128 pp.   3250   **$12.50**

Words I Use When I Write, Grades 1-2 and More Words I Use When I Write, Grades 3-4
by Alana Trisler and Patrice Howe Cardiel

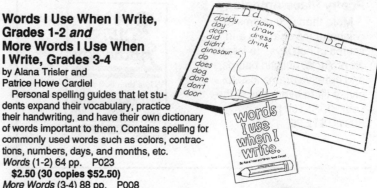

Personal spelling guides that let students expand their vocabulary, practice their handwriting, and have their own dictionary of words important to them. Contains spelling for commonly used words such as colors, contractions, numbers, days, and months, etc.
Words (1-2) 64 pp.   P023
  $2.50 (30 copies $52.50)
More Words (3-4) 88 pp.   P008
  $2.75 (30 copies $60.00)

Common Ground: Whole Language and Phonics Working Together
by Priscilla L. Vail

A guide for educators who want to provide students with the phonics instruction and skills they need within the context of a whole language learning approach. *Common Ground* provides an overview of appropriate reading and instructional methods. (K-4) 86 pp.   P040   **$8.95**

Spelling for Whole Language Classrooms
by Ethel Buchanan

An experienced classroom teacher explains how increased spelling proficiency is a developmental process. Buchanan outlines the stages of spelling development and shows how to develop grade level expectations, evaluate spelling growth, and create a spelling environment.

The content is really a whole language spelling curriculum presented within the framework of a theory of spelling development. 156 pp.   3039   **$18.95**

Learning Phonics and Spelling in a Whole Language Classroom

A book that assists teachers in keeping phonics and spelling in perspective and in developing strategies (word sorts, cluster analysis, homophone pairs, silent letter search, cumulative charts, word webs) for teaching these basics within the context of a language-rich classroom. (K-3) 128 pp.   3236   **$15.95**

Jim Grant Materials

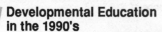

I Hate School: Some Commonsense Answers for Parents Who Wonder Why

I Hate School has helped thousands of teachers and parents become ardent supporters of developmental placement. The book focuses on the dilemma of children placed in the wrong grade. It includes signs and signals that identify the overplaced child from kindergarten through college. 124 pp.   P007   **$9.95**

Developmental Education in the 1990's

Working with thousands of educators across the country, Jim Grant understands the kinds of questions educators are facing. His book helps clarify developmental issues by answering 93 of the questions most frequently asked by teachers and parents. 144 pp.   P015   **$10.95**

Worth Repeating: Giving Children a Second Chance at School Success

Worth Repeating squarely confronts the controversial topic of grade retention for young students. Jim examines this critical issue without jargon and challenges those academic voices that study the statistics and forget the child. 205 pp.   P024   **$9.95**

Jim Grant's Book of Parent Pages

Jim developed these helpful handouts so that teachers could communicate more easily with parents. Important messages are presented in an inviting format — 16 8" x 11½" pages that fold into attractively illustrated notes for individualized addressing. Topics include: childhood stress checklist, school and divorce, accepting the readiness idea, love and limits, and seven secrets to school success.   P012   **$24.95**

Every Parent's Owners' Manuals
by Jim Grant and Margot Azen

Owners' Manuals is a series of concise, humorous booklets (written as take-offs on car manuals) that outline predictable developmental behaviors of three, four, five, six, and seven-year-old models at home and in school.

Each manual presents information about the particular model's parts, language control panel, and operation and maintenance for home and school use. 16 pp. (each manual) P011 (specify model year)   **$.75**

10

The Nongraded Elementary School
by John Goodlad & Robert Anderson

The best known work of Goodlad and Anderson, it is the single most quoted book on the topic of nongraded schools. First published in 1959, it forecasted the changes to come. 248 pp.   3303   **$19.95**

Nongradedness: Helping It To Happen
by Robert Anderson & Barbara Pavan

The most current, in-depth book by two of the nation's most knowledgeable educators on nongradedness. Along with up-to-date research, this book covers structural mechanisms, learning modes, assessment and much more. A great book for getting started. 240 pp.   3226   **$24.00**

Multiage Classrooms: The Ungrading of America's Schools
compiled by The Society For Developmental Education

Designed to help educators understand the whys and hows of setting up multiage programs. Includes research findings, articles, and the collective wisdom of many who have "been there" in addressing questions all multiage educators face. Also contains an extensive bibliography and practical, proven ideas for involving parents and assessing student progress. Due May 1993.   3216   **$24.95**

The Nongraded Primary: Making Schools Fit Children

The increasing need for concise, current information on the nongraded primary was the driving force behind this booklet. Published by the American Association of School Administrators. 27 pp.   3219   **$3.50**

How to Untrack Your School
by Paul George

George will help you in achieving one of the main goals of a continuous progress program . . . untracking students. Learn how rigid ability grouping (tracking) creates inequities, erodes students' self-esteem, and produces 7 other negative consequences. 42 pp.   3214   **$9.95**

Making the Transition From Graded to Nongraded Primary Education *and* Nongraded Education: Mixed Age, Integrated and Developmentally Appropriate Education for Primary Children
both by Joan Gaustad

This pair of books will assist staff members in understanding the fundamental need to change from a graded to a nongraded primary.
Making, 41 pp.   3215   **$5.95**
Nongraded, 38 pp.   3218   **$5.95**

The Multi-Grade Classroom: Myth and Reality
by Margaret Gayfer, Ed.

This book clearly shows the advantages as well as the difficulties for children, parents and teachers in a multigraded organization. It is one of the few books that shows both sides of this topic. 57 pp.   3217   **$11.95**

Teaching Combined Graded Classes: Real Problems and Promising Practices

Down to earth presentation of the ups and downs of combined grade classes. A straight forward, easy-to-read publication that will help you avoid the pitfalls of organizing a mixed-grade classroom. 58 pp.   3220   **$7.95**

Ready to Learn: A Mandate for the Nation
by Ernest Boyer

The most up-to-date description of today's student population. This book is The Carnegie Foundation's documentation for changing to a developmental approach to education. 193 pp.   3177   **$8.95**

Developmentally Appropriate Practice in Early Childhood Programs Serving Children From Birth Through Age 8
by S. Bredekamp, Ed.

This definitive work is our profession's consensus of what are appropriate and inappropriate teaching practices for infants through eight-year-olds. 92 pp.   3284   **$6.95**

Also available:

3190	The Case for Mixed-Age Grouping in Early Education, L. Katz, D. Evangelou, & J. Hartman, 60 pp.	**$9.00**
4016	Cooperative Learning: Getting Started (see page 4)	**$9.95**
P015	Developmental Education in the 1990's (see page 10)	**$10.95**
3201	How to Change to a Nongraded School, Madeline Hunter, 82 pp.	**$9.95**

P007	I Hate School! (see page 10)	**$9.95**
3300	Into Teachers' Hands (see back cover)	**$24.95**
P038	Positively Kindergarten (see page 5)	**$14.95**
3221	Ungraded Primary Programs: Steps Toward Developmentally Appropriate Instruction, Joint Study by KY Ed. Assoc. and AEL, 102 pp.	**$6.95**

Prod. #	Title	Author	Price
3150	Abiyoyo	P. Seegers	$15.95
3173	Abuela	A. Dorros	$14.00
1002	Alexander & the Terrible...	J. Viorst	$3.95
2000	Amelia Bedelia & the Baby	P. Parish	$3/50
2001	Amelia Bedelia & the Surprise	P. Parish	$3.50
3104	Amelia Bedelia Goes Camping	P. Parish	$3.50
3327	Amelia Bedelia Helps Out	P. Parish	$3.50
3328	Amelia Bedelia's Family Album	P. Parish	$3.50
1090	Animals, Animals	E. Carle	$18.95
3188	Argyle	B. Wallace	$13.95
3105	Ask Mr. Bear	M. Flack	$3.95
3167	Aunt Flossie's Hats	E. F. Howard	$14.95
1252	Baseball Bats for Christmas	M. A. Kusugak	$5.95
3129	Berlioz The Bear	J. Brett	$14.95
3174	Best Christmas Pageant Ever	B. Robinson	$3.95
2067	Big & Little	R. Kraus	$12.95
3175	Big Tree, The	B. Hiscock	$13.95
3161	Biggest Bear, The	L. Ward	$5.95

Prod. #	Title	Author	Price
3106	Biggest Pumpkin Ever, The	S. Knoll	$2.50
1005	Blue-Eyed Daisy, A	C. Rylant	$2.50
2003	Box Car Children #1	G. Warner	$3.50
1007	Bridge to Terabithia	K. Paterson	$2.95
3130	Brother Eagle, Sister Sky	S. Jeffers	$15.00
2004	Brown Bear, Brown Bear	B. Martin Jr.	$14.95
3064	Carl Goes Shopping	A. Day	$11.95
3065	Carl's Afternoon in the Park	A. Day	$11.95
3066	Carl's Christmas	A. Day	$11.95
1009	Castle in the Attic	E. Winthrop	$2.95
1010	Cay, The	T. Taylor	$3.50
3053	Charlie Anderson	B. Abercrombie	$12.95
2006	Chicken Book	G. Williams	$3.99
2007	Chicken Soup with Rice	M. Sendak	$2.95
3146	Chicken Sunday	P. Polacco	$14.95
3277	Chrysanthemum	K. Henkes	$13.95
2081	City Mouse, Country Mouse	B. Bettelheim	$2.50
2008	Clifford at the Circus	N. Bridwell	$2.25
2009	Clifford the Big Red Dog	N. Bridwell	$2.25
2010	Clifford the Big Red Dog (bk & cass)	N. Bridwell	$5.95
2011	Clifford the Small Red Puppy	N. Bridwell	$2.25
1013	Cloudy with a Chance of Meatballs	J. Barrett	$3.95
3278	Come Back, Amelia Bedelia	P. Parish	$3.50
2012	Cool Kid Like Me	H. Wilhelm	$12.95
1014	Cracker Jackson	B. Byars	$3.95
3100	Curious George	H.A. Rey	$4.95
3102	Curious George Gets a Medal	H. A. Rey	$4.95

Prod. #	Title	Author	Price
3331	Curious George Learns the Alphabet	H.A. Rey	$4.95
3332	Curious George Rides A Bike	H.A. Rey	$3.95
3333	Dark, Dark Tale, A	R. Brown	$4.99
3043	Dark, Dark Tale, A (Giant)	R. Brown	$17.95
1019	Day Jimmy's Boa, The	T. H. Noble	$3.95
3031	Day Jimmy's Boa, The (Giant Book)	T. H. Noble	$17.95
1230	Day the Goose Got Loose, The	R. Lindbergh	$12.95
3283	Dear Mr. Blueberry	S. James	$12.95
1022	Dicey's Song	C. Voigt	$3.50
3285	Don't Forget to Write	M. Selway	$12.95
3067	Earth Hounds as Explained by...	J. Willis	$12.95
3123	Earth Mobiles	J. Willis	$14.00
3124	Earth Tigerlets	J. Willis	$13.95
3068	Earthlets as Explained by...	J. Willis	$13.95
3050	Education of Little Tree, The	F. Carter	$10.95
3287	Elizabeth & Larry	M. Sadler	$4.95
3195	Elizabeth, Larry & Ed	M. Sadler	$14.00
3163	Encounter, The	J. Yolen	$14.95
1026	Enormous Egg, The	O. Butterworth	$3.25
3139	Fables	A. Lobel	$5.95
3162	First Forest, The	J. Gile	$13.95
1260	First Grade Can Wait	L. Aseltine	$11.95
1031	First Grade Takes a Test	M. Cohen	$2.95
1224	Fish Eyes	L. Ehlert	$14.95
3051	Fly Away Home	E. Bunting	$13.95
3121	Fourth Little Pig, The	T. Celsi	$5.50
2014	Freckle Juice	J. Blume	$2.95
2015	Frog & Toad Are Friends	A. Lobel	$3.50
2016	Frog & Toad Together	A. Lobel	$3.50
3293	Frog Prince Continued	J. Scieszka	$14.95
2017	Germs Make Me Sick	M. Berger	$4.50
3069	Good Dog, Carl	A. Day	$11.95
3294	Good Work Amelia Bedelia	P. Parish	$3.50
1228	Goodnight Moon	M. W. Brown	$3.95
3199	Goodnight Owl	P. Hutchins	$3.95
3164	Grandfather's Day	I. Tomey	$12.95
3138	Grandfather Twilight	B. Berger	$5.95
3035	Great Gray Owl (Giant Book)	O. Cochrane	$15.95
3036	Great Gray Owl (Mini Book)	O. Cochrane	$3.45
3028	Growing Vegetable Soup (Giant Book)	L. Ehlert	$19.95
1039	Hatchet	G. Paulsen	$3.95
1041	How a Book Is Made	Aliki	$5.95
3026	How Much is a Million	D. M. Schwartz	$3.95
1042	How to Eat Fried Worms	T. Rockwell	$2.95
2021	Huge Harold	B. Peet	$4.95
1049	I Have to Go	R. Munsch	$4.95
2022	I Just Forgot	M. Mayer	$1.95
3299	I Need a Lunchbox	J. Caines	$14.00
1050	I'll Always Love You	H. Wilhelm	$3.99
3047	If You Give a Moose a Muffin	L. J. Numeroff	$12.95
2023	If You Give a Mouse a Cookie	L. J. Numeroff	$10.95
1053	Indian in the Cupboard	L. R. Banks	$3.25
2024	Ira Sleeps Over	B. Waber	$4.95
3206	Iron Giant	T. Hughs	$4.95
1056	It Looked Like Spilt Milk	C. Shaw	$3.95
3126	Jamberry	B. Degen	$3.95
1058	James & the Giant Peach	R. Dahl	$3.95
3308	Jim and the Beanstalk	R. Briggs	$5.95
3052	Jolly Christmas Postman, The	J. & A. Ahlberg	$16.95
1231	Jolly Postman, The	J. & A. Ahlberg	$15.95
2026	Just for You	M. Mayer	$1.95
2027	Just Grandma & Me	M. Mayer	$1.95
1222	Just Grandpa & Me	M. Mayer	$1.95
3148	Just Plain Fancy	P. Polacco	$14.95
3307	Knots on a Counting Rope	B. Martin Jr. & J. Archambault	$14.95
2066	Laura Charlotte	C. Galbraith	$14.95
3154	Legend of Bluebonnet	T. dePaola	$5.95
3312	Legend of Sleepy Hollow, The	W. Irving	$15.95
3037	Legend of the Goose & the Owl (Giant Book)	O. Cochrane	$15.95

12

Prod. #	Title	Author	Price
3038	Legend of the Goose & the Owl (Mini Book)	O. Cochrane	$3.45
1244	Legend of the Indian Paintbrush	T. dePaola	$5.95
1065	Leo the Late Bloomer	R. Kraus	$5.95
2029	Light in the Attic, A	S. Silverstein	$14.95
3054	Linnea in Monet's Garten	C. Bjork & L. Anderson	$11.95
3314	Little Old Lady Who Wasn't Afraid	L. Williams	$4.95
3316	Little Polar Bear	H. de Beer	$13.95
3317	Little Polar Bear Finds a Friend	H. de Beer	$13.95
1071	Love You Forever	R. Munsch	$4.95
1238	Lyddie	K. Paterson	$3.99
3320	Madeline	L. Bemelmans	$4.50
3321	Madeline & the Bad Hat	L. Bemelmans	$3.95
2088	Make Way for Ducklings	R. McCloskey	$3.95
3137	Miss Nelson Has a Field Day	J. Marshall	$4.95
2060	Miss Nelson Is Back	J. Marshall	$3.95
1074	Miss Nelson Is Missing	J. Marshall	$3.95
1094	Mitten, The	J. Brett	$14.95
2033	More Bunny Trouble	H. Wilhelm	$3.95
2034	More Fun with Dick & Jane	M. Gallant	$6.95
1076	Mostly Michael	R. K. Smith	$2.95
2083	Mouse Soup	A. Lobel	$3.50
2082	Mouse Tales	A. Lobel	$3.50
3147	Mrs. Katz and Tush	P. Polacco	$15.00
1077	My Brother Sam Is Dead	J.L. & C. Collier	$2.75
3135	My Five Senses (Giant Bk.)	Aliki	$19.95
3136	My Great Aunt Arizona	G. Houston	$15.00
3040	My Little Pigs	D. Bouchard	$6.95
3359	My Little Red Car	C. Demarest	$14.95
1078	My Mama Says	J. Viorst	$3.95
3335	My Teacher is an Alien	B. Coville	$2.99
3336	Mysterious Tadpole	S. Kellogg	$3.95
1080	Nana Upstairs and Nana Downstairs	T. Paola	$3.95
1223	Napping House, The	A. Wood	$13.95
1234	Napping House, The (Giant Book)	A. Wood	$19.95
1081	Nighty Nightmare	J. Howe	$2.95
1240	Nobody's Perfect	N. Simon	$10.95
1083	Now One Foot, Now the Other	T. de Paola	$5.95
1256	Oh the Places You Go	Dr. Seuss	$12.95
2059	Old McDonald	Ill. P. Adams	$5.95
1085	On My Honor	M. D. Bauer	$2.75
1086	One-Eyed Cat	P. Fox	$3.50
1243	Owl Moon	J. Yolen	$14.95
3159	Pain & the Great One, The	J. Blume	$3.95
1089	Paper Bag Princess	R. Munsch	$4.95
1093	Piggybook	A. Browne	$5.95
1235	Pinkerton Behave (Giant Book)	S. Kellogg	$17.95
3056	Polar Bear, Polar Bear	B. Martin, Jr & E. Carle	$13.95
3171	Polar Express, The	C. Van Allsburg	$17.95
2078	Popcorn Book	T. dePaola	$5.95
3168	Principal from the Black Lagoon	M. Thaler	$2.50
3147	Rebus Treasury	Highlights for Children	$9.95
3149	Rechenka's Eggs	P. Polacco	$14.95
1103	Return of the Indian	L. R. Banks	$3.25
1105	Rosie & Michael	J. Viorst	$3.95
1106	Sadako & 1000 Paper Cranes	E. Coerr	$2.75
1108	Sarah, Plain & Tall	P. MacLachlan	$2.50
1226	Shoes from Grandpa	M. Fox	$13.95
3044	Show and Tell	R. Munsch & M. Martchenko	$4.95
2039	Sideways Stories from Wayside School	L. Sachar	$2.95
1109	Sign of the Beaver	E. G. Speare	$3.25
3172	Signmaker's Assistant, The	T. Arnold	$14.00
3157	Sleeping Ugly	J. Yolen	$6.95
3151	Song & Dance Man	K. Ackerman	$4.95
1115	Starring First Grade	M. Cohen	$2.95
3187	Stinky Cheese Man, The	J. Sciestzka & L. Smith	$16.00
1116	Stone Fox	J. R. Gardiner	$3.50
3059	Stopping by Woods on a Snowy Evening	Illus. S. Jeffers	$12.95
3033	Story of Ferdinand	M. Leaf	$3.95
1121	Summer of the Monkeys	W. Rawls	$3.25
2041	Superfudge	J. Blume	$3.50

Prod. #	Title	Author	Price
2043	Teacher from the Black Lagoon	M. Thaler	$2.50
3170	Terrible Eek, The	P. Compton	$14.95
1125	There Was an Old Lady	P. Adams	$5.95
2044	There's a Boy in the Girls' Bathroom	L. Sachar	$2.95
2084	There's a Nightmare in my Closet	M. Mayer	$3.95
1236	There's a Nightmare in my Closet (Giant)	M. Mayer	$16.95
1126	This Is the House that Jack Built	P. Adams	$5.95
1127	This Old Man	P. Adams	$5.95
3253	This Quiet Lady	C. Zolotow	$14.00
1128	Thomas' Snowsuit	R. Munsch	$4.95
1129	Today Was a Terrible Day	P. R. Giff	$3.95
3168	Train to Lulu's	E. F. Howard	$14.95
3329	Tree of Cranes	A. Say	$16.95
3330	Trouble with Trolls	J. Brett	$14.95
2045	True Story of the Three Little Pigs	Scieszka	$14.95
1133	Tuck Everlasting	N. Babbitt	$3.50
2087	Very Busy Spider, The	E. Carle	$16.95
2046	Very Hungry Caterpillar, The	E. Carle	$15.95
2047	Very Quiet Cricket, The	E. Carle	$18.95
3342	Wagon Wheels	B. Brenner	$3.50
2050	Wayside School Is Falling Down	L. Sachar	$3.50
3343	We're Going on a Bear Hunt	M. Rosen	$15.95
3062	What Cows Do When No One Is Looking	B. Thompson	$6.00
1141	When Will I Read?	M. Cohen	$2.95
1144	Where the Red Fern Grows	W. Rawls	$3.50
2051	Where the Sidewalk Ends	S. Silverstein	$14.95
2085	Where the Wild Things Are	M. Sendak	$4.95
3344	Wild Christmas Reindeer	J. Brett	$14.95
3345	White Snow, Bright Snow	A. Tresselt	$3.95
2052	Whingdingdilly	B. Peet	$4.95
3346	Whoo-oo Is It?	M. McDonald	$14.95

PLEASE CALL US IF YOU ARE LOOKING FOR A TITLE NOT LISTED HERE.

Best Seller
Managing the Whole Language Classroom, K-6
by Beverly Eisele

This complete teaching resource guide is packed with ideas for organizing the classroom, scheduling the day, communicating with parents and integrating the curriculum. Easy-to-implement ideas, resources and forms will help you effectively manage your whole language classroom. 136 pp. 3001 **$15.00**

Managing Your Child-Centered Classroom

A full range of supportive techniques and teaching aids for the child-centered classroom. This helpful guide provides an extensive compilation of photocopy masters designed to help you make learning centers, thematic units, and other whole language activities. You'll save time and will inspire your students to read and write. (1-4) 121 pp. 3131 **$18.95**

The Early Childhood Teacher's Every-Day-All-Year-Long Book
by Imogene Forte

Everything you need to make lesson plans, schedule activities, set up learning centers, develop units, prepare arts & crafts projects, create exciting bulletin boards, and teach basic skills is right here at your fingertips! (PreK-1) 304 pp. 4013 **$16.95**

Learning to Teach . . . Not Just for Beginners

A real working resource book, packed with proven, effective strategies for managing a classroom, first-day tips, classroom organization and management ideas. Also covered: the multi-ability classroom, shoring up self-esteem, and other practical strategies for mentor teachers, veterans, and beginners alike. (K-6) 304 pp. 3311 **$19.95**

Top Notch Teacher Tips 1: All Across the Curriculum

Hundreds of quick activities and tips created by actual classroom teachers and compiled from the "Teacher's Express" column in INSTRUCTOR Magazine. Organized by chapters on reading, language arts, math, social studies, science. (K-6) 128 pp. 3152 **$12.95**

Top Notch Teacher Tips 2: Seasons and Holidays

A fresh, idea-packed compilation of hundreds of seasonal and holiday activities and teaching tips from the "Teacher's Express" column in INSTRUCTOR Magazine. Bulletin boards, crafts, games, and helpful management tips. (K-6) 128 pp. 3326 **$12.95**

The Complete Lesson Plan Book

This multi-purpose planner was designed with flexibility in mind. The oversized pages can be organized according to days of the week and/or subject areas. Also included are whole language-based ideas integrating math, science, and social studies. Plus assessment suggestions, theme-based book lists, ideas for celebrating special events, and **handy pocket pouch folders.** (K-3) *Available in April 1993* 3176 **$9.95**

Into Teachers' Hands
A Whole Language Sourcebook

Each October, the Society For Developmental Education publishes its new sourcebook which includes up-to-date information, articles, presenter handouts, and resources on developmental education and integrated language arts.

Includes whole language resources, professional bibliography, and sections on multiage and accommodating the needs of differently-abled students in the classroom. (PreK-6) 347 pp. 3300 **$24.95**

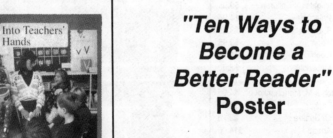

"Ten Ways to Become a Better Reader" Poster

Bold, primary colors. 34" x 21". 3093 **$3.95**

Crystal Springs Books
Northgate, P.O. Box 577, Peterborough, NH 03458

To order:

3 Easy Ways to Order! Call us toll free
1-800-321-0401
(603) 924-9380

OR

 Mail this form to the address above

OR

 Fax this form to us at (603) 924-6688. Available 24 hours.

Ship to: Name _____   Grade/Title _____

Mailing Address _____
(Street address, please! UPS will not deliver to a P.O. Box)

City _____   State _____ Zip _____

Telephone (_____) _____

100% Refundable Guarantee

Payment By:

☐ Check Enclosed

☐ MasterCard (16 digits)   ☐ Visa (13 or 16 digits)   ☐ Discover (16 digits)

[ ][ ][ ][ ][ ][ ][ ][ ][ ][ ][ ][ ][ ][ ][ ][ ]
Card Number

[ ][ ] — [ ][ ]   _____
Expiration Date   Cardholder Signature

☐ Purchase Order # _____

School Name _____

Billing Address _____

City _____ State _____ Zip _____

Billing Office Phone (_____) _____

Item No.	Description	Qty.	Price	Amount

(Prices subject to change without notice)

Subtotal	
Shipping & Handling	
TOTAL	

Shipping, Handling, and Insurance:

Up to $24.99 .... $3.50
$25.00 to $49.99 .... $5.00
$50.00 to $79.99 .... $8.00
$80.00 to $500.00 .... add 10% of order

FREE shipping and handling for orders over $500.

fold along this line

PLACE
STAMP
HERE

_____

_____

_____

Crystal Springs Books
PO Box 577
Route 202 Northgate
Peterborough, NH 03458-0577

MULTIAGE

----

fold along this line